Canadian Political Structure and Public Administration

THIRD EDITION

Geoffrey Booth
Colleen O'Brien

2008
Emond Montgomery Publications Limited
Toronto, Canada

Emond Montgomery Publications Limited
60 Shaftesbury Avenue
Toronto ON M4T 1A3
http://www.emp.ca/college

Printed in Canada.

We acknowledge the financial support of the Government of Canada through the Book Publishing Industry Development Program (BPIDP) for our publishing activities.

Acquisitions and developmental editor: Tammy Scherer
Marketing coordinator: Kulsum Merchant
Supervising editor: Jim Lyons, WordsWorth Communications
Copy editor: David Handelsman, WordsWorth Communications
Typesetter: Nancy Ennis, WordsWorth Communications
Proofreader: Jamie Bush
Indexer: Paula Pike, WordsWorth Communications
Cover designer: John Vegter

Library and Archives Canada Cataloguing in Publication

Booth, Geoffrey J., 1962-
    Canadian political structure and public administration / Geoffrey Booth, Colleen O'Brien. — 3rd ed.

Includes index.
ISBN 978-1-55239-257-7

    1. Canada—Politics and government. I. O'Brien, Colleen, 1970– II. Title.
JL75.B66 2008   320.471   C2007-905971-6

For our parents

Contents

Preface

If, as the old saying goes, "A week in politics is a lifetime," then we've come several generations since the publication of the second edition of *Canadian Political Structure and Public Administration* in the summer of 2004. So much has changed, and yet we see many similar themes manifesting themselves in new events: freedom versus security, civilian oversight and police accountability, the meaning of justice and fairness in a diverse society—the list seems unending.

The third edition builds upon its predecessor, by connecting new examples to these academic discussions. Care has been taken to update and refresh formal political content, as well as the text's "Get Real!" sections, which take theoretical ideas and apply them to contemporary domestic and international events. These sections have, in most cases, been totally revamped or updated. This edition also benefits from the addition of co-author Colleen O'Brien, whose keen political insight and ability to perform regular "reality checks" made the writing and editing phases not only bearable, but enjoyable as well. In addition, both authors wish to acknowledge the impeccable research and critical reading skills of Maureen Riche, without whose prompt and professional assistance neither author would have achieved success. Special thanks also to Aaron Gouin for his assistance and well-considered advice regarding the field of corrections in the larger Canadian political context and to Stephen Schattin for his heroic rescue of a critically injured computer and its contents.

Finally, let us not forget that inspiration comes from others we love and respect—Julianne Ecclestone, Ava and Ryan O'Brien Haaheim, Maureen Riche, and our beloved brothers and sisters—long may they harmonize.

Geoffrey Booth and Colleen O'Brien
October 2007

PART I

Introduction to Politics and Public Administration

CHAPTER 1

Introductory Concepts

CHAPTER OBJECTIVES

After completing this chapter, you should be able to:

- Describe basic tenets of political theory such as power, compliance, and the rule of law.

- Define politics and the various ways that it affects Canadian citizens.

- Explain the evolution of government as a social institution and how we as citizens determine the extent of a government's authority and legitimacy.

- Describe the relationship between politics and public administration from a practical, as well as a theoretical, standpoint.

- Understand, in general, the purpose and content of this text.

- Describe Canadian participation in elections, and consider reasons in favour of and against introducing a system of mandatory voting.

WHAT IS POLITICS?

To many of us, the terms "politics" and "public administration" are both mysterious and intimidating. This discomfort is reinforced daily by media reports of dishonesty, corruption, and ineptitude, which seem to pop up at regular intervals. It may surprise you that anyone pays attention to what goes on in government, let alone becomes involved in public life. However, thousands of people continue to play a part in governing this country, and without them we would in fact have no country. The system of government we live with today reveals much about our history and our values as Canadians. And, despite the seemingly endless barrage of criticism hurled at it, Canada's government remains one of the best models of problem solving through political compromise and dialogue in the world today.

How did we earn such an enviable global reputation? What are the essential components of Canadian political structure, and how do they interact with one another? What is the historical context for this intricate and ever-changing dance among political partners? And finally, how does all of this express itself in the realms of law enforcement and public safety? These are but a few of the many topics we will cover in the chapters that follow. To begin, we should define some terms necessary for a clear understanding of politics and public administration in Canada.

Politics is about relationships. Indeed, folksinger Pete Seeger once noted that putting two human beings together in a room was all that was required. Because we have competing opinions and ideas about what is desirable, our relationships with one another imply power. In other words, the capacity to make others comply with your wishes means that you have power over them. The study of politics concerns itself with the distribution of power and how it is to be used in a particular social context. This study ranges from individual interaction right up to the international level, where nation states coexist and compete with one another. Where and whenever we come into contact with others, there is politics.

politics
the social system that decides who has power and how it is to be used in governing the society's affairs

At its root, **politics** is fundamentally about power and who decides how this power is to be used. We can think of power as the capacity of one person or group to impose decisions on another person or group. In other words, politics is about getting your own way. Likewise, "compliance" refers to the obedience that an individual or group demonstrates in response to the wishes of those who have power.

There are many ways to achieve power. Using influence, persuasion, brute force, charisma, negotiation, or compromise are only some of them. Perhaps without knowing it, you have already experienced examples of this in your own life. Growing up, you may have had to share a television with other members of your family. How did you decide who got to watch what program at what time of day? What if something you wanted to watch was in someone else's time slot? What about programs that exceeded your time allotment? Did your age, attitude, or status have any influence on whether you got to watch what you wanted? What role did your parents play in determining what was acceptable viewing for your family? All of these questions help to illustrate the power relations between you and members of your family. Now consider what it would be like to come to a decision about virtually anything in a country of more than 32 million people. This happens every day as government officials engage in the shared task of keeping Canada running. We elect politicians at the federal, provincial, and municipal levels of government to represent our individual and collective interests and bring them to the attention of the state.

WHAT IS POWER?

Before proceeding, it is useful to establish some fundamental elements of political theory, so that as we move to examine Canada's political structure, you will be able to make useful connections between politics as an academic discipline and politics as it is practised in reality. In political theory, power is often subdivided into three main categories: force, persuasion, and legitimate authority. Force, or coercion as it is sometimes called, refers to the threat or actual use of violence (death, injury) or social sanctions (imprisonment, fines), in order to enforce compliance. Persuasion refers to debate, discussion, compromise, and any other non-violent means of achieving one's will. While these first two concepts embody external submission on the part of an individual, legitimate authority refers to an internal recognition by an individual that others have the power to impose their will by virtue of their position, or the institution they represent. In other words, we respect their decision because we respect the source of their power and agree to obey its representatives.

Governments use all three types of power to impose decisions upon citizens, but it is legitimate authority that justifies political power in a modern democratic country such as Canada. We agree to abide by the laws of our country as they are passed down from our political establishment because those who create them (politicians) are ultimately answerable to us through the electoral process. In other words, political accountability ensures that political power is used in a fair, reasoned, and justifiable manner.

WHAT IS GOVERNMENT?

"Why can't we all just get along?" This might be considered a standard observation of a newcomer to the study of politics. After all, if politics is about power, then let's just agree not to bother one another and everything should be fine, right? This formula for social harmony appears enticing (particularly to those of us old enough to remember the 1960s); however, it presupposes an almost intuitive sensitivity and saint-like deference. People will eventually disagree about something, and some mutually acceptable process is needed to resolve these disputes. We achieve this to varying degrees through the exercise of government. A brief story may help to clarify some of these concepts for you.

Life in Hobbes Hall

It's your first day at college and boy, are you happy. You were lucky enough to land a room in Hobbes Hall, the new campus residence. Funds for its creation were donated by a group of political science instructors, in recognition of Thomas Hobbes, a 17th-century British political philosopher.[1] The opportunity to stay at Hobbes Hall appealed to you because there is only one rule: "There are no rules." Because the place is new, the donors have decided to allow students total freedom to, in effect, create a society as they might wish it to be. All summer long you anticipated the possibilities of living away from your parents, free of obligations and responsibilities to anyone but yourself. The first couple of weeks at Hobbes Hall are great, if a little noisy. Everyone you meet is happy, and it appears as if the semester will be a positive experience. Soon, however, differences in lifestyle begin to create rifts in the residential population. Some people play loud music at all hours; others leave dirty dishes in the communal kitchen sink for days on end; and still others have friends over who show no concern at the litter they leave behind. This is a never-ending source of irritation for you, but others on your floor don't seem to mind. "Take it easy," they tell you, reminding you that there are neither rules nor enforcement protocols and that the minor annoyances are not worth getting upset over. By November the residence has taken on the look of a trash heap. Nobody has assumed any social obligation to keep common areas clean. It seems everyone has resorted to looking after only what is directly under their control, and some have not even bothered to do this. One weekend, several rooms are broken into and valuables stolen. This causes a furor among residents and some blame neighbours for the incidents. A couple of weeks later, it happens again. This time, accusations result in some pushing and shoving. It is clear to you that things are getting out of hand. Leaving the situation as it is is bound to have disastrous consequences, as students trade recriminations and threaten one another with revenge for alleged acts and suspected wrongdoings. Order and security presuppose collective responsibility, but this in turn necessitates rules, thus limiting individual freedom. You discuss this with other concerned students and collectively, you draw up an agenda to discuss the situation. Your first challenge is to convince everyone living at the residence that these issues must be addressed. In other words, everyone affected by these decisions must recognize and respect their validity and agree to abide by the principles they represent. They must accept that these rules are objective and are applied fairly to all. There are some other fundamental issues to be addressed:

1. What is an acceptable balance between individual freedom and the "collective good"?

2. Who will draft the rules and oversee the interests of Hobbes Hall?

3. How will the rules be enforced?

4. How will disputes be mediated in a manner that both parties will find acceptable?

5. What if a complaint is made against a residence action, rule, or decision?

Although fictitious, this scenario illustrates the absolute necessity of government in human affairs. Because we are social by nature, we need to organize ourselves in a way that protects us all from external and internal threats, yet allows us to preserve and nourish our individual differences. The questions posed above address some of the fundamental challenges that face a modern democratic society such as Canada. They also touch upon the importance of public respect and acceptance of government's authority over its citizens. For example, you cannot simply draft your own rules for Hobbes Hall and expect others to abide by them. You lack any legitimate authority to do so. Being selected by your peers to represent their interests through a residence election may grant this power to you. However, you maintain this position only so long as you maintain their respect and support. The power we grant our politicians, although much broader in scope, is no different. They must be prepared to justify their decisions during their term in office, and make every effort to demonstrate to the public that they are acting in the best interests of constituents.

Now that you are familiar with the need for government as a concept, it will be easier to understand how and why it functions the way it does in a country such as Canada, and more importantly, how it relates to justice and law enforcement. All countries rely on power to survive. One of the basic tests of state recognition is that it controls a fixed population and geographic territory. As indicated earlier, the power required to acquire such prerequisites can be coercive, persuasive, and/or granted by citizens through legitimate authority. While non-democratic countries tend to resort to the more brutal elements of power, democracies rely upon authority for their continued legitimacy. This requires democratic forms of government to be accountable to citizens. Further, this must be evident at all stages in the political process; otherwise, citizens may lose faith in the legitimacy of the system and thus imperil its credibility. Because this text is concerned with Canadian political institutions, it will focus primarily upon how we as Canadians facilitate and manage political power at the federal, provincial, and municipal levels of government, while preserving public respect for it.

Answering the question "What is government?" is not easy. **Government** is a formal system within which political power is exercised. Still, this doesn't capture the incredible complexity of government, both as a concept and as a practice. Government is present in so many aspects of our lives that many of its activities go unnoticed.

Government has a long history dating back as far as the beginnings of human civilization itself, and many people have written about its form and function. As stated earlier, **authority** refers to government's ability to make decisions that are binding on its citizens. As long as the general population accepts that some groups or individuals in society have power to issue and enforce these commands, they will obey them. If citizens respect where the decisions come from, they will accept them, whether they agree with these decisions or not. **Legitimacy** refers to the moral obligation citizens feel to obey the laws and pronouncements issued by those in authority.

Taken together, these concepts explain why we as Canadians abide by the laws our governments make for us. Even if we think that a law is misguided or misses the point, we still recognize that our politicians have the right to pass laws for the greater good of society. If each Canadian decided instead to disobey laws whenever he or she chose, the system of law and its enforcement would simply break down. Imagine the implications this scenario could have in the area of transportation. The absence of a general acceptance of rules, enforced by police and other authorities, would quickly lead to misunderstandings over road use, disputes arising from accidents, arbitrary speed limits, and ultimately unsafe conditions for everyone. As members of a society that recognizes the wisdom of authority and legitimacy in its political system, we assume that our governments will act for the greater good of society, even if this means that our personal freedom is limited by these decisions.

In a democracy, the concepts of authority and legitimacy are tied directly to what is known as the **rule of law**. The rule of law ensures that all citizens, regardless of social rank, are subject to the laws, courts, and other legal institutions of the nation. For example, a prime minister who is found guilty of a crime cannot pass a law to make his or her infraction legitimate. The rule of law also demands that *all* government actions be legal—that is, they must be approved and accepted by a justice system that is free from state interference. This guards against the possibility that government officials might resort to illegal actions to accomplish a task. This is also why police forces take such care to ensure that officers respect the law in the course of carrying out their duties. Violating the rights of an accused or collecting evidence illegally damages the credibility of an investigation, almost always results in charges being dropped, and may result in legal action being taken by the defendant. The rule of law ensures fair and equitable treatment by a government, and as we will see later, it forms an integral part of Canada's system of justice and public safety.

How Law Enforcement Fits In

Policing is an integral part of Canada's public justice system and is therefore one link responsible for preserving the rule of law. If people lose faith in their government, there is a danger that they will also lose faith in the rule of law. This is why as a society we go to such lengths not only to "do justice"—ensure the rights of accused individuals, make sure that police follow proper legal procedures, and so on—but also to demonstrate to all Canadians that justice is seen to be done.

government
a formal system within which political power is exercised

authority
government's ability to make decisions that are binding on its citizens

legitimacy
the moral obligation citizens feel to obey the laws and pronouncements issued by those in authority

rule of law
the concept that all citizens, regardless of social rank, are subject to the laws, courts, and other legal institutions of the nation

How and Why We Accept the Rule of Law

The process of demonstrating that justice is seen to be done belongs in large part to the media, which cover both the successes and the failures of the justice system in this regard. For example, it is common practice for the media to publish the details of a court case. This practice is consistent with the public's right to know the workings of the justice system. In some rare situations, however, this right is suspended in order to ensure an accused person's right to a fair trial. Public trust in the legal system can never be taken for granted in any society. We must be reminded through the words and deeds of public officials that every effort is being made to ensure that justice is done so that when problems occur they can be remedied efficiently and effectively.

An important reason Canadians live within the framework of laws, regulations, and political decisions is that they can hold their political representatives accountable through the process of elections. Elections are a way to ensure continued citizen support for the authority and legitimacy of their governments, and they force elected politicians to be accountable for what they have done (or not done) during their term as elected representatives. As we will see in later chapters, Canadian political tradition, the process of choosing candidates, party affiliation, and other socioeconomic issues play a large part in determining how the public's judgment plays itself out in the political scene.

THE ART OF GOVERNMENT: POLITICS AND PUBLIC ADMINISTRATION

The aim of this textbook is to give you a practical overview of Canada's political structure and the bureaucracy through which much of its operation is carried out. Politics and public administration, although sharing a common purpose of furthering the public good, often go about doing so in different ways. The nature of this relationship, as we will see, can be complementary or competitive, resulting in new approaches to government policy.

For the purposes of this text, the term "politics" will be used to refer to the work of politicians at the federal, provincial, and municipal levels of government who are elected by the people they represent. We treat the subject of politics separately from that of public administration because, although one can argue that all aspects of government involve both political and administrative elements, it is politicians who must ultimately answer to us for what their particular level of government has done from one election to the next.

Public administration is more challenging to define because, as we will discover later in this text, it can be understood to include every non-elected person who is employed by government. Often referred to as the **civil service** or **public service**, this branch of Canadian political structure hypothetically includes anyone employed in a publicly funded activity, such as policing, firefighting, and teaching. However, convention normally limits public administration to people who are directly tied to the administrative function of a particular level of government, such as policy implementation and evaluation. The public service takes the policy decisions of elected politicians and turns them into concrete action. For example, suppose a

public administration
the branch of the political structure, consisting of public employees, that turns the policy decisions of elected politicians into action

civil service
people who are directly tied to the administrative function of a particular level of government

public service
the civil service

local municipality's councillors hear concerns from constituents about the need for a sidewalk to help children travel safely to and from a school in an area with heavy traffic. The political will of the council is dictated to the municipality's public works department, which in turn sends out a crew to construct the sidewalk.

This simple example skips many of the intermediary steps involved in accomplishing such a task (see chapter 4 for details), but it illustrates what might be called the "classic" model of communication between politicians and public servants. As we will see in later chapters, a complex system of communication exists among these branches of Canadian political structure, and this system often blurs the line between those responsible for creating policy and those who are ultimately held responsible for implementing it.

WHY STUDY POLITICAL STRUCTURE AND PUBLIC ADMINISTRATION?

You should now have some idea as to why students interested in the fields of justice and public safety should understand Canadian political structure and public administration. As an agent of law enforcement, it is essential that you understand your legal rights and obligations. This knowledge extends beyond the rules and regulations of your employer to encompass where and how the legitimate authority of the state is delegated to public agencies, such as police forces, whose sworn duty it is to uphold laws passed by the state and to maintain respect for the rule of law. In this sense, you represent the public good and therefore have a responsibility to know how government works—that is, the origin and implementation of public policy through government legislation. This knowledge enables you to understand and appreciate more fully your role in the overall administration of justice and to understand the roles of other key players in developing, interpreting, and administering law.

This text, and the course it represents, also provides you with an understanding of your rights and responsibilities as a Canadian citizen. This too should help to better acquaint you with the structure and day-to-day practice of government at the federal, provincial, and municipal levels and with their relationship to justice and public safety. Your familiarity with Canadian political structure and public administration will give you an advantage as you prepare to meet the challenges and changes currently facing law enforcement in Canada.

STRUCTURE OF THIS BOOK

Following is a brief overview of some of the topics you will encounter as you read through the sections of this book. Keep in mind that while each chapter attempts to focus on a particular area of interest, all of the topics are interrelated because issues and decisions in one sector of government and public administration often have an impact on other sectors.

Chapter 2 presents a brief history of the events that led to Confederation in 1867 and how Canada's political structure was established at that time. The chapter explains the origin of the three levels of government in the context of the Canadian constitution, and provides some historical background that will help you better understand the political issues that face Canadians today.

Chapter 3 focuses on the constitution from its inception as the *British North America Act* through its patriation in 1982, including attempts at constitutional reform. Attention is given to the *Canadian Charter of Rights and Freedoms*[2] and its impact on Canadians' individual and collective rights, as well as to its effects on law enforcement and the role of the courts in the political and constitutional process.

Chapter 4 begins with an explanation of representative and responsible government, and then explores the electoral process and the role of candidates. It goes on to examine the structure and roles of the three levels of government—federal, provincial, and municipal—and defines their executive, legislative, and judicial functions. The process of making laws at each level of government is also explained. The chapter introduces the interrelationships among the three levels of government, a topic that will be explored in more detail in later chapters. Chapter 4 also introduces First Nations in the Canadian political structure, presenting a brief history of the relationship between First Nations and non-Native government.

Chapter 5 describes the evolution of government services in Canada in general and law enforcement in particular. The chapter then encourages you to look at the "big picture" by using what you learned in the previous chapters to discuss some current issues in Canadian politics as they relate to policing and the justice system. Particular attention is paid to influences on the political process at all levels of government and how these have direct and indirect effects on law enforcement. Chapter 5 concludes with a discussion of police responses to changing social realities.

With this political context in place, the focus shifts to an emphasis on public administration. Chapters 6 and 7 explore the meaning of public administration with a view to helping you recognize its relevance and relation to the political process. In particular, you will discover how political and public administration entities rely on each other for mutual benefit and, ultimately, survival. It will become evident that tension also characterizes this relationship as political and administrative forces attempt to achieve specific goals. These chapters also briefly summarize theories of bureaucracy to see how these have influenced the evolution of a modern public service in Canada. You will then have an opportunity to explore the similarities and differences between private and public administration. Particular attention is given to recent trends toward government privatization of public facilities, such as prisons.

Chapter 8 focuses on the "glue" that binds politics and administration—public policy. Using examples, the chapter illustrates the many complex—and often unpredictable—stages that take place while policy is being created, implemented, and evaluated. The chapter ends by examining how creating public policy can be a difficult balancing act, especially when policy makers strive to protect the Charter rights of all Canadians while, at the same time, attempting to keep government spending (and thus taxes) at a satisfactory minimum.

Chapters 9 and 10 complete our exploration of the complex world of public administration by examining the structure and organization of the civil service in Canada today, with particular emphasis on those components that play a role in the system of justice and law enforcement. These chapters describe the many ministries, agencies, and Crown corporations that constitute the public service. You will discover how public policy is transformed into administrative law and become aware of the differences between this type of legislation and others, such as constitutional law. As well, you will see how politicians and public servants work together to meet the challenges that arise in government. By analyzing examples, such as the role of Ontario's Special Investigations Unit (SIU) in overseeing police activity, you will also discover that disagreement and conflict are an ongoing part of the relationship between government and the public service.

Chapter 11 focuses on your part as a constituent in our government system. The chapter presents some of the benefits of getting involved in politics, especially at the municipal level, as well as some suggestions on how to do so. As you prepare for a career in law enforcement, it is our hope that at this point you will understand and feel confident about your role in Canadian society, both as a representative of law enforcement and as a private citizen.

Get Real!
APPLYING WHAT YOU HAVE LEARNED: SHOULD VOTING BE MADE MANDATORY?

Most of this chapter has been dedicated to impressing upon readers the nature and necessity of politics. You are no doubt already aware that it affects all of us in significant ways. And yet, many Canadians—especially young people—don't bother to vote in elections. Overall voter participation has been declining for over 20 years.[3] In fact, only 52.6 percent of eligible voters participated in the 2007 Ontario election,[4] while between 60 and 65 percent of voters participated in each of the last two federal elections, in 2004 and 2006 (see figure 1.1).[5] This could be because an increasing number of us feel like our individual contribution means very little in the overall outcome of elections. We might dislike the slate of candidates, none of whom seems to represent our interests. Or, we may be participating indirectly by supporting interest groups (local environmental organizations, for example) that lobby politicians on our behalf. Finally, we may simply be turned off by the barrage of negative images hurled at us by the media on a daily basis.

This trend of decreasing voter turnout should be of particular concern for justice professionals, because of its close relation to the public's continued faith in the legitimacy of government and the rule of law. As one research study puts it, "The more citizens become non-participants in key political events such as elections, the greater the likelihood that appeals to shared values and common purpose will fall on deaf ears."[6] Loss of respect for the authority of public institutions and the decisions and laws they make can lead to a similar disrespect for those who enforce them, namely, police services, the courts, and other justice agencies.

This concern has led some people to call for mandatory voting in our electoral system. Democratic countries such as Australia and Belgium have instituted mandatory voting laws that fine non-voters for failing to carry out this duty. As a consequence, voter turnout regularly surpasses 90 percent in these jurisdictions. In 2004, mandatory voting in Canada was proposed as a Senate bill (Bill S-22), but did not proceed past second reading due to strong opposition. Supporters contend that mandatory voting produces better democracy by encouraging a wide range of opinions and interests across society, particularly those that might otherwise go unheard. Detractors point to a fundamental principle of democratic freedom, which is that citizens should be free to *choose* whether they wish to exercise their right to vote. Being forced to vote, they argue, may in fact produce even more apathy and resentment toward the political process, since politicians won't have to coax support from citizens, nor will the latter see the act as meaningful. There is no doubt that democracy depends on our participation for its continued survival. However, the means to achieve it may in the end be as controversial as the issue itself.[7]

FIGURE 1.1   Voter Participation in Federal Elections, 1953–2006

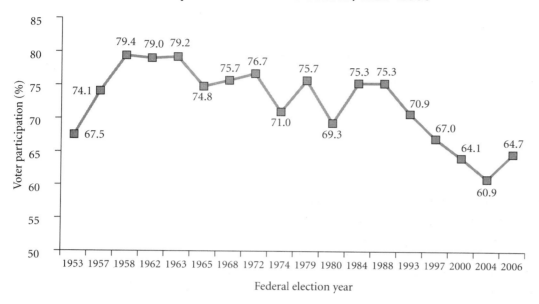

Source: Elections Canada, Voter Turnout at Federal Elections and Referendums, 1867–2006 (2007), www.elections.ca. Calculations and adaption rest with the authors.

SUMMARY

We can understand politics both as an abstract concept and as a concrete practice. At its root, politics is about power and who gets to decide how it is used. Power is the ability of one person or group to impose decisions on another person or group. The degree to which the latter person or group obeys the former determines the degree of compliance. Power can be exercised through external means such as coercion and persuasion, or through citizen respect for legitimate authority. In concrete terms, politics, government, and public administration are different, but interrelated, components of the Canadian political structure. Politics is about power and who decides how it is to be used in the management of a country's affairs. Government is a system of organizing a society so that disputes can be resolved or prevented. Public administration, as the term is used in this book, refers to the process of administering the functions of government as well as to the people who perform those functions (often called the civil service).

The concepts of authority and legitimacy, which are closely linked to the rule of law, help to explain why Canadians are willing to allow governments and their representatives to make laws and policy decisions and are willing to abide by those laws and decisions.

The remainder of this book will discuss these topics and the interrelationships among them in more detail, with a view to placing the role of law enforcement in a larger political context.

KEY TERMS

authority

civil service

government

legitimacy

politics

public administration

public service

rule of law

NOTES

1. This story reflects many of the so-called truths illustrated by Hobbes in *Leviathan*. Written in 1651, this seminal work of political theory demonstrated the absolute necessity of sovereign government by describing a world in which there were no rules at all. The inevitable result, according to Hobbes, would be a "war of every man against every man" because people would have no legitimate authority through which to resolve conflicts, nor would they trust one another to be fair and impartial. Thus, the dictums contained within *Leviathan* underscore the importance of public respect for the rule of law, and the agents of public law enforcement who uphold it. See Thomas Hobbes, *Leviathan*, C.B. Macpherson (intro. and ed.) (London: Penguin, 1985), book I, ch. XIII and ch. XVII.

2. *Canadian Charter of Rights and Freedoms, part I of the Constitution Act, 1982*, RSC 1985, app. II, no. 44.

3. For trends by federal elections, see Lynda Hurst, "Now, It's Your Turn," *Toronto Star* (January 23, 2006), A1.

4. According to figures released by Elections Ontario the day after the October 10 election, only 4.4 million of 8.8 million eligible citizens cast a vote. See CBC News, "Ontario Voter Turnout a Record Low" (October 11, 2007), available online at www.cbc.ca.

5. See the Elections Canada website at www.elections.ca. Click on the link "Past Elections" then "Voter Turnout at Federal Elections and Referendums, 1867-2006."

6. Centre for Research and Information on Canada, quoted in Lynda Hurst, "Are Young Voters Down for the Count?" *Toronto Star* (September 14, 2003), A14.

7. For further reading and additional sources, see articles by Andrew Coyne and Clifford Orwin, reprinted in Mark Charlton and Paul Barker (eds.), *Crosscurrents: Contemporary Political Issues*, 4th ed. (Toronto: Thomson Nelson, 2002), 282-289.

EXERCISES

Multiple Choice

1. The rule of law ensures that

    a. all citizens are subject to the laws of the nation

    b. even top-ranking politicians cannot override the law

    c. government treats all citizens fairly and equitably

    d. all government actions are legal

    e. all of the above

2. "Politics" can be defined as

    a. the loss of authority

    b. power, decision making, and who has control

    c. budgets and tax cuts

    d. the conflict between two formal political parties

3. In modern democracies such as Canada, public support of government rests on the concept(s) of

    a. legitimate authority

    b. zero-tolerance law enforcement

    c. supremacy of unelected authority, such as the police

    d. benevolent dictatorship

4. High-profile court cases such as the 1995 *Bernardo* trial require substantial amounts of time and money to prosecute because of

    a. the rule of law

    b. statements made by government ministers

    c. special exemptions under the constitution

    d. the public's demand for justice

5. The fundamental role of public administration is to

    a. formulate public policy

    b. make laws for Canadians

    c. govern Canadian society

    d. make decisions that are binding on citizens

    e. turn policy decisions of politicians into concrete action

True or False?

_____ 1. Government has existed for as long as human civilization.

_____ 2. In political terms, "compliance" refers to the obedience of a person or group to the wishes of a person or group with power.

_____ 3. Police services are the only government agencies responsible for preserving public faith in the rule of law.

_____ 4. One of the fundamental challenges of politics is balancing individual freedom with the public good.

_____ 5. In Canada, the prime minister has the right to pass a law to avoid being charged with a crime he or she has committed.

Short Answer

1. Define politics and explain the various ways that it affects Canadian citizens.

2. How do we as citizens determine the extent of a government's authority and legitimacy?

3. What is the relationship between politics and public administration from a practical, as well as a theoretical, standpoint?

PART II

Political Structure

CHAPTER 2

Unity Through Diversity: Canada Becomes a Nation

CHAPTER OBJECTIVES

After completing this chapter, you should be able to:

- Understand the historical development of Canada and its federalist system of government.
- Explain the British and Canadian roots of Canada's original constitution.
- Identify the origins of the three levels of government in Canada.
- Describe the division of powers between the federal and provincial governments.
- Critically analyze federal–provincial issues and how they affect each level of government.

INTRODUCTION

Understanding Canadian politics requires understanding Canadian history. This chapter briefly summarizes some of the major events and factors that have contributed to the current shape and character of our country and its justice system.

The British North American and British officials who laid the political foundations for what became the nation of Canada might have some difficulty recognizing this country today. Canada has undergone many changes, particularly over the last 150 years, changes that have had a profound impact on the way Canadians understand themselves and their country.

PRE-CONFEDERATION

Canada became a country on July 1, 1867, marking the culmination of centuries of social, political, and economic development. Although estimates vary widely, the general consensus among scientists is that the first humans arrived on the continent approximately 60,000 years ago.[1] They gradually migrated along the Pacific Coast and then into the interior as glaciers receded. Eventually, they populated all regions of North and South America. Aboriginal societies were many and diverse by the time Europeans first made contact with this part of the world. These societies had a collective population estimated at 100 million, 10 million of whom lived north of Mexico.[2] European contact with Aboriginal peoples can be traced to the year 1000; however, it was not until the French began a colony along the St. Lawrence River in the early 1600s that Europeans began to settle permanently in northern North America.

KNOW YOUR HISTORY, KNOW YOUR POLITICS

Origins of Canada and Its System of Justice

When we think of Canada as it is today, many of us take for granted that we have always been a nation composed of 10 provinces stretching from the Atlantic to the Pacific oceans and 3 northern territories. It is easy to forget that today's Canada has undergone many changes. In terms of its politics, geography, and social structure, our country has a shared Native/non-Native heritage dating back some 400 years. Jacques Cartier's tentative voyages during the 1530s and Samuel de Champlain's establishment of Quebec in 1608 are generally considered the benchmarks for European settlement in Canada. In what became known as New France, settlement grew along the St. Lawrence River valley, while French explorers and traders eventually made their way through the Great Lakes region and down the Mississippi River to the Gulf of Mexico. Many Aboriginal groups participated in this trade alliance. However, as the Dutch, and then the British, increasingly challenged the French for dominance in this area, pressure mounted on Aboriginal peoples living in the area to take sides in the dispute and to surrender land for settlement.

Although a basic system of justice existed in New France in its early development, it was not until King Louis XIV elevated the colony to a royal province of France in 1663 that a formal bureaucracy took shape. In accordance with this designation, New France was headed by a governor, who wielded ultimate power over the entire colony. Directly below him was the intendant, who was responsible for justice, public order, and financial matters. As such, the intendant managed the colony's military and administrative budget, headed its police, and oversaw municipal fortifications. He also came to preside over the Sovereign Council (Superior Council after 1703), which made laws and supervised the lower courts. Court cases and other administrative details were the responsibility of the attorney general. Together, these officials administered legislation passed by the Council. Petty disputes were often decided by the seigneur (landowner) of the community, or the local priest.[3]

Frontier conditions created unique problems for justice officials in New France. Laws could be enacted, but enforcement was often difficult, since settlement was scattered and officials were few in number. As one historian has observed, inhabitants "obeyed when it was convenient, and ignored the law when it suited them." However, this did improve over time, as the colony grew.[4]

The Atlantic colonies of Nova Scotia, New Brunswick, Prince Edward Island, and Newfoundland developed justice systems in keeping with English criminal and civil customs. However, a lack of qualified people and the necessary government institutions resulted in a somewhat uneven evolution. Thus, each settlement adopted the necessary infrastructure to fulfill justice-related obligations according to local needs. For example, Halifax already boasted a jail by 1758, only nine years after the city was established. Conversely, in spite of being one of Britain's oldest colonial outposts, Newfoundland had no proper legal system at all until 1729 and was not granted a legislature until 1824.[5] The fact that the legal system relied heavily on citizen volunteers further discouraged an embrace of fundamental principles of justice. As one author has noted, "Policing was carried out by volunteer and usually reluctant citizens. Magistrates were appointed from the ranks of the general population, had little or no knowledge of the law or judicial procedures, and some could barely read or write. They were the subjects of constant complaints and ridicule."[6]

With the cession of New France to the British in 1763, English criminal and civil law was applied in all of British North America. Political realities soon forced the British to acknowledge the widespread acceptance of the *French Civil Code,* which had been brought from France in the 1660s and had been in effect until the conquest. Officially recognized in the *Quebec Act of 1774,* this system of laws remained in effect until 1857, when major reforms were undertaken, culminating in the *Civil Code of Lower Canada,* proclaimed in 1866. It was updated again in 1994 and is now known as the *Quebec Civil Code.* Thus, while all other jurisdictions in Canada apply English common law to civil matters, Quebec's long tradition of using the *Civil Code* continues.[7] Although distinct from English common law, the *Civil Code* proved no more successful than its counterpart in terms of application. For many similar reasons, "justice in Lower Canada was, at best, dispensed very unevenly and in a most inequitable manner."[8] However, matters gradually improved, as officials and citizens came to appreciate the importance of professional qualifications in the justice system.

The *Constitution Act of 1791* divided Quebec into Upper and Lower Canada (later Ontario and Quebec, respectively). The Upper Canadian legislature adopted the principles of British law in 1792, as the basis for its system of justice. In spite of pressure from some legal professionals to substitute English with American precedents in arguing civil cases, senior court officials insisted on the preservation of the former, in deference to what they thought to be "superior" British legal decisions and traditions. Locally, a justice of the peace and district sheriff administered the law. The former presided over courts sessions held four times yearly in each area. The Courts of Quarter Session merged with the civil district courts in 1795, laying the foundation of local justice until 1841. As in the British legal system, more serious crimes were heard in the assize courts.

As had been the case in New France a century earlier, justice as it was practised in the British North American colonies often fell short of the standards to which it aspired. As one historian put it: "in a day when police forces were non-existent, investigation methods were primitive, and crimes went unreported, many offenders must have escaped detection."[9]

As the 19th century progressed and Enlightenment attitudes took hold, more attention was paid to justice issues in each of the colonies. Through acceptance of ideas such as equality and freedom, the public came increasingly to appreciate the importance of establishing and maintaining a fair and equitable legal system, complete with courts and professional legal officials. Thus, on the eve of **Confederation**, Canada embraced two legal systems, each of which had distinct origins and had adapted to a particular set of circumstances.

Confederation
the union of former British colonies that resulted in the formation of Canada on July 1, 1867

CONSIDERING CONFEDERATION

On a more general level, the British North American colonies confronted several political, social, and economic challenges during the middle decades of the 19th century.

Earlier attempts at political union had failed. However, by the 1860s, a number of factors coaxed four of the colonies—Canada West, Canada East, New Brunswick, and Nova Scotia—into considering the creation of one central government while retaining their respective rights to govern themselves.

The populations of the British North American colonies in the 1860s were, for the most part, small and rural. They were also largely isolated from one another by geography, the sheer size of the land they occupied, and a limited transportation system. The four founding members of Confederation had little in common. Canada West, the largest colony, had a population mainly made up of English, Scottish, and Irish immigrants. Canada East's French-speaking population was mainly native-born with a shared history going back to the 1600s; the Catholic Church had a strong influence in this colony, where local governments reflected the local church parishes. The much smaller populations of the Atlantic colonies were also mainly native-born and English-speaking.[10]

A proposed political union of the British North American colonies in 1841 failed to resolve many of the political problems that had led to rebellions in 1837 and 1838 in Upper Canada and Lower Canada. The reasons for these rebellions had been building for years and were the result of class tensions, ethnic tensions in Lower Canada between francophones and anglophones, and frustration over the lack of democratic representation in the colonial governments, which were dominated by members of a wealthy elite. In 1841 Britain had united Upper and Lower Canada into the Province of Canada, giving each—now called Canada West and Canada East—equal political representation in a United Assembly.

Although Lower Canada's population had historically been larger than that of Upper Canada, this was not the case by the 1860s. Due to large waves of immigration, Upper Canada grew very quickly after the War of 1812, quadrupling from 100,000 to 400,000 inhabitants between the years 1815 and 1840. By 1851, the population of Canada West (formerly Upper Canada) surpassed that of Canada East (formerly Lower Canada) for the first time.[11] At Confederation there were approximately 1.5 million people living in Ontario, and about 1 million in Quebec. Canada at this time had a total population of 3.5 million.[12]

The new assembly of 1840 passed laws for both colonies, but its members continued to reflect the interests of their respective territories, reproducing the split between French and English Canadians. Thus the government remained deadlocked. Another form of government was sought, and by the early 1860s, calls to unite the British North American colonies began to be heard. The Atlantic colonies sought a Maritime federation as well to strengthen their economies.

The Desire for Union

A factor that contributed to interest in a new union was the growing desire to build an intercolonial railway to connect all of British North America. The railway would facilitate trade and help bring more settlers into the region. At the time, most transportation was by water. Canals helped to connect the many lakes and rivers to otherwise landlocked areas, but they were of little use in the winter. Railways were a logical alternative. The only problem was their cost—building and maintaining them was extremely expensive, a fact that put railways out of the reach of any one colony. Working together, however, such a venture was feasible.

Confederation also promised trade advantages. Until 1849 the colonies had enjoyed preferential treatment in their trade with Britain. Colonial exports were guaranteed a share of the British market, even if these goods could be obtained more cheaply elsewhere. Britain abandoned this policy after 1849, however, opting for free trade—an economic system based on buying goods at the lowest possible price. The British North American colonies now had to compete among themselves and with bigger, established American competitors who benefited from a much larger population base. It made economic sense for the colonies to unite to create a strong market capable of competing in trade.

Finally, concerns about defence made Confederation seem like a good idea. Since the American Revolution of 1776, the British North American colonies had repeatedly been targets of attack from the Americans. Border invasions during the American Revolution and the War of 1812, in which the United States aimed to seize the colonies, as well as minor incursions during the 1830s, had made the British North Americans distrust the Americans. The time seemed right to band together in the interest of self-preservation.

CONFEDERATION

In September 1864, representatives of three of the Atlantic colonies—New Brunswick, Nova Scotia, and Prince Edward Island—met in Charlottetown to discuss the possibility of a maritime union. Representatives from the Province of Canada joined the Charlottetown Conference to try to persuade the Atlantic colonies of the benefits of a larger union. The Atlantic delegates weren't convinced, but agreed to meet with the Canada West and Canada East representatives in Quebec in October to discuss the idea further.

Debates over Confederation and the form of government of the new union continued at the Quebec Conference and in the colonies. Newfoundland took part in these negotiations, as did Prince Edward Island, but these two colonies eventually decided against joining the new union.

On July 1, 1867, the Dominion of Canada, under Prime Minister John A. Macdonald, was born out of four former colonies when the British Parliament passed the *British North America Act* (BNA Act).[13] Canada's form of government was unique in the world: our country was part of the British Commonwealth; its head of state was the British monarch; and its constitution—embodied in the BNA Act—was a British statute. Today, Canada is an independent nation, but the decisions made at Confederation continue to affect Canadian government and politics.

The New Government

Canada was born out of a compromise among its four founding provinces. Because of the strong local traditions and allegiances that existed at the time of this political union, the would-be provinces of the new country were reluctant to transfer all of their political power to the newly formed national government. What resulted was a **federal system** whereby political powers were split between a strong central, or federal, government and the governments of the original four provinces. Each level of government was granted certain powers over specific areas, as stated in the BNA Act. Although the federal government was allotted most of the political power, the later growth in importance of areas of provincial jurisdiction, such as health and education, increasingly challenged the position of the federal government to decide many political matters.

federal system
Canada's government structure, which divides political power between the federal government and the provincial governments, with greater power resting in the federal government

A country as geographically vast and culturally diverse as Canada needed a system of government based on equality in a context of diversity. The federal system means that political power is shared between the federal government based in Ottawa and the provincial governments. It is doubtful that Canada would or could have been created in any other way. Today, the federal government serves all Canadians, including the 10 provinces and 3 territories, while each provincial government serves only the people living within that province (the territories, although they have more independence today than in the past, are still financially dependent on the federal government and do not have the same constitutional powers as the provinces).

Confederation was seen by its supporters as a solution for many of the difficulties discussed earlier. It was thought that a union would brace the scattered provinces against possible US aggression and make it easier to defend their navigational rights on the St. Lawrence River and their fishing rights at sea. Confederation was further designed to foster a national economy in which there would be improved transportation facilities, including winter access to the sea. It was hoped that the resources and industries of the provinces would complement one another, thus increasing the prosperity and self-sufficiency of the whole. The Fathers of Confederation also looked toward the future, when the united country would help to speed up the development and settlement of the Canadian northwest and ultimately include a Pacific province.

There was significant pressure for political union, but also equally strong counterpressures calling for local cultures, traditions, and interests to be preserved. These counterpressures were particularly strong in French-speaking Canada and the Maritimes. Although a compromise on a federal system was worked out and embodied in the BNA Act, the actual terms of the Act were not universally supported by all the people who were affected, including First Nations, who were placed under the control of the federal government. This helps to explain the continuing struggle to this day for Aboriginal recognition and right of self-determination, which will be discussed in later chapters of this book.

POST-CONFEDERATION

Wooing the West Coast: British Columbia

The most densely populated area of pre-European North America, the Northwest coast of the continent, was first visited by the Spanish in about 1590. Russian fishing fleets frequented the coastline in search of sea otter and other wildlife; however, Britain soon became dominant in the area. In 1849, Britain asked the Hudson's Bay Company to establish and look after a settlement on Vancouver Island. Victoria became its capital in 1849. The new colony of British Columbia was established in 1858, to protect British sovereignty against the thousands of Americans who flocked north to the Fraser River Gold Rush. The two colonies—Vancouver Island and British Columbia—merged in 1866, but decided not to accept an offer to join Confederation. However, following the American purchase of Alaska in 1867, many people in the colony feared that it might be annexed by the United States. With Britain seeking to reduce its colonial possessions, the only realistic solution was to join the new country of Canada. The federal government of John A. Macdonald promised to assume the colony's debts and dangled the prospect of a rail link that would ultimately connect Canada from the Atlantic to the Pacific. Macdonald's offer did the trick and British Columbia joined Confederation in 1870. The 25,000 Aboriginal peoples that represented more than 75 percent of British Columbia's population were never consulted.

The Way Out West: Rupert's Land

Named in honour of a cousin of Britain's King Charles II, this vast area of land included parts of modern-day Quebec, northern Ontario, all of Manitoba, and parts of Saskatchewan, Alberta, and the Arctic. Rupert's Land had been granted to the newly formed Hudson's Bay Company in 1670 as a means of establishing an English presence in the North American fur trade, dominated at that time by New France. Following Confederation, the federal government moved quickly to acquire the land, and thanks to British pressure, purchased it in 1869 for $1.5 million, quite a bargain, considering that the United States had paid Russia $7.2 million for Alaska just two years earlier. The province of Manitoba was created in 1870, following skillful negotiations between Métis leader Louis Riel and the federal government. The province's initially limited geographic area was eventually extended north to include the southern part of the District of Keewatin in 1912.

The completion of the Canadian Pacific Railway in 1885 opened up areas of settlement farther west, resulting in the eventual creation of the provinces of Saskatchewan and Alberta, in 1905. The Yukon Gold Rush of 1896 prompted the federal government to create a separate district, called Yukon Territory, to protect and reinforce Canadian jurisdiction in an area flooded by 40,000 people in just four years.[14]

Maritime Holdouts: Prince Edward Island and Newfoundland

Representatives of both Prince Edward Island and Newfoundland attended pre-Confederation conferences. The initial meeting had even taken place in Charlottetown in September 1864. Prince Edward Island already had more than 100 years of British colonial history behind it by the 1860s. Proud of local tradition, many Islanders did not like the terms of Confederation, and some even preferred annexation to the United States. In any event, overwhelming debt incurred through an over-ambitious railway project forced Prince Edward Island to approach the federal government in 1873 for financial assistance. Rather than see their taxes increase dramatically, Islanders decided to join the Dominion in 1873.

Initially, Newfoundland seemed much more amenable to the prospect of Confederation. But its strong tradition and historical affinity for a British, rather than Canadian, connection, made joining the mainland a hard sell. Confederation with Canada became the main issue in the colony's 1869 election. With 19 of 27 seats in the House of Assembly taken by anti-confederate supporters, the issue fell off the political agenda. Eventually, however, economic depression and British pressure would bring Newfoundland into Confederation, albeit 82 years later, in 1949.[15]

THE CONSTITUTION

British Roots

constitution
a document that outlines the basic principles of government of a country and the fundamental rights and freedoms enjoyed by its citizens

As mentioned above, the BNA Act was the piece of British legislation that united the four founding provinces of the new country and gave Canada its **constitution**—a document that outlines the basic principles of government of a country and the fundamental rights and freedoms enjoyed by its citizens. The Act also allowed for future provinces to join the federation.

Both the written and the implied parts of the Act bore the unmistakable imprint of Britain, although the federal structure was an important exception. Formally, the Act provided that the British monarch (whose representative in Canada is the governor general) was to be the chief executive officer and head of the new country. There was also to be a **bicameral legislature**—two Houses of Parliament—consisting of the House of Commons and the Senate (explained in more detail in chapter 4), which correspond to the British House of Commons and House of Lords. Each House was to have an equal voice in Canadian legislation, except that, as in the British Parliament, financial measures were to be initiated in the House of Commons. This practice still exists—no government financial bills may initiate in the Senate. Canada also inherited from Britain

bicameral legislature
a government structure that consists of two Houses of Parliament; in Canada, the House of Commons and the Senate

- the political party system;

- the principle under which executive authority resides in the prime minister and Cabinet and only nominally in the Queen and governor general (which will be discussed in more detail in chapter 4);

- the principle of responsible government (also discussed in chapter 4), which was hard won by the provinces at Confederation, requiring that the executive must at all times be responsible to and retain the support of a majority of the popularly elected House of Commons; and

- the theory of the supremacy of Parliament and of the provincial legislatures, within their respective powers, as determined ultimately by the courts.

Canadian Contributions

In addition to those parts of the constitution inherited from British tradition, a large number of conventions and practices of constitutional significance have gradually been developed and established within Canada.

An outstanding exception to the general rule of British influence on the Canadian constitution was Canada's departure from the unitary state. The United Kingdom, then as now, was a unitary state in which the local authorities were established and governed by legislation passed by the British Parliament. At first, in the pre-Confederation conferences, the representatives of what was to become Ontario favoured the creation of a **legislative union**, as the unitary state was then usually called, with power concentrated entirely in the central Parliament and government. It became clear, however, that the French-speaking and Maritime colonies would not agree to surrender complete legislative jurisdiction to any central authority, and that a federal system that gave the provinces the right to make and administer laws relating to mainly local matters was the only practical solution.

legislative union
a structure of government in which power is concentrated in a central Parliament

Division of Powers

The strong regional differences that led each province to insist on retaining certain powers and responsibilities resulted in the **division of powers** between the federal and provincial governments. The powers and responsibilities—or **jurisdiction**—of each level of government are set out in sections 91-93 of the BNA Act. Section 91 lists the powers of the federal government, while sections 92-93 list those of the provinces. Section 95 gives the federal and provincial governments shared powers over immigration and agriculture. Table 2.1 summarizes the division of powers.

Section 92(8) gives the provinces the power to form municipalities and municipal governments. Section 93 gives the provinces control over education, subject to certain clauses designed to safeguard the rights of Roman Catholic and Protestant minorities. Finally, although section 95 gives Parliament and the provincial legislatures shared power over agriculture and immigration, in case of conflict the federal government prevails.

Although there is much dispute today as to which level of government is most politically powerful, the terms of the BNA Act suggest that Canada's federal government was intended to be a strong authority. This is certainly true today, given the power of the federal government to raise revenues through various forms of taxation and to determine how to return this money to the various provinces under strict conditions.

division of powers
jurisdiction over major policy areas, as divided between the federal and the provincial governments

jurisdiction
sphere of influence or power

TABLE 2.1   Division of Powers

Federal Government

Section 91

- Maintenance of peace, order, and good government
- Public debt and property
- Trade and commerce
- Taxes
- Borrowing money on the public credit
- Postal service
- Census and statistics
- Militia, military, and naval service, and defence
- Setting of salaries of officers of the Government of Canada
- Beacons, buoys, lighthouses, and Sable Island
- Navigation and shipping
- Marine hospitals
- Sea coast and inland fisheries
- Ferries between a province and another country and between provinces
- Money
- Banking
- Weights and measures
- Bills of exchange and promissory notes
- Interest
- Patents
- Copyrights
- Aboriginal peoples and their lands
- Immigration
- Marriage and divorce
- Criminal law
- Penitentiaries

Provincial Governments

Section 92

- Amendment of constitution of province, with the exception of office of lieutenant governor
- Direct taxation for provincial purposes
- Borrowing of money on provincial credit
- Provincial government officers
- Public lands belonging to the province
- Reformatories
- Hospitals, asylums, and charities, other than marine hospitals
- Municipal institutions
- Shop, saloon, tavern, auctioneer, and other licences
- Local works other than shipping lines, railways, canals, and telegraphs that connect provinces or extend beyond provincial borders and any works that, although they operate within a province, are declared by the federal government to be for the general advantage of Canada or of two or more provinces
- Incorporation of companies operating only within a province
- Marriage ceremonies
- Property and civil rights
- Provincial justice system
- Imposition of fines, penalties, or imprisonment in enforcing provincial laws
- Any matters of a local or private nature

Section 93
- Education

Federal and Provincial Governments

Section 95
- Agriculture and immigration are shared responsibilities

Who Speaks for Canada? The Debate over Federal or Provincial Power

As you can see from table 2.1, the BNA Act assigns a variety of justice-related powers to the federal and provincial levels of government in Canada. For example, the federal government is responsible for criminal law, penitentiaries, and any matters having to do with the promotion of "peace, order, and good government." The provinces have been assigned jurisdiction over property and civil rights, liquor licences, and provincial justice systems. At Confederation, the intention was to make as clear as possible the distinction between the two levels of government. Almost from the outset, however, provinces began to challenge the dominance of the federal government in many areas. This defiance, although somewhat muted, re-emerged in a much more public way after World War II and the Quiet Revolution in Quebec. As Canada was transformed from a rural-agricultural to an urban-industrial society, it became apparent that some provincial areas of jurisdiction—health, education, and social assistance, to name just three—were becoming the most important to Canadian citizens. Provinces have argued increasingly for more flexibility and funding to cope with greater public demand for services.

The federal government, on the other hand, has argued since Confederation that only it can make decisions in the best interests of all Canadians. Allowing provinces too much political power threatens national standards and possibly even the rights of citizens now guaranteed under the *Canadian Charter of Rights and Freedoms*. It might also weaken Canada's voice in international affairs, since potentially 10 voices—not just one—would speak for Canada. Thus, coming to any kind of articulate consensus could prove impossible.[16]

Get Real!

RELATING JUSTICE TO FEDERAL–PROVINCIAL RELATIONS

Under Canada's constitution, the federal government has authority over the creation and subsequent changes to criminal law. Provinces are responsible for implementing the law, through their provincially administered justice systems. This separation of powers can sometimes lead to conflict, rather than cooperation. One such disagreement erupted over the Canadian gun registry. Introduced into Parliament by Prime Minister Jean Chrétien in 1995, Bill C-68 established harsher penalties for crimes involving the use of guns, created the federal *Firearms Act*, and required that gun owners be licensed and registered.[17] Many people living in central Canada and urban areas supported the registry, hoping that the program might curb violent crime in the cities. However, many Canadians living in the Western provinces and rural areas felt that the registry would do nothing to reduce crime, and would penalize gun owners by further increasing the bureaucracy of owning a firearm for those who used guns for legitimate reasons (such as control of coyotes and other wildlife that prey on farm animals and the euthanization of injured livestock). Opponents also pointed to the program's immense cost overrun, reported to have reached $2 billion, in contrast to its original estimate of $119 million.[18] As the debate continued, some provinces threatened not to prosecute citizens who failed to comply with the law, and officials in Ontario and Alberta argued that the registry imposed regulations that might exceed the federal government's constitutional jurisdiction.

In 2006, the newly elected federal Conservative government tabled a bill to scrap the registry and redirect the program funds to increase police staffing in Canadian communities. Provincial support for the move remains split along west–central and rural–urban divides. This emphasis on stronger policing is part of the Conservative government's law-and-order agenda, and its commitment to get tough on crime. Among other initiatives, Prime Minister Stephen Harper's proposed "tackling crime" program would increase minimum sentences for crimes involving firearms, and eliminate conditional sentences such as house arrest for serious offences. The suite of bills also includes reverse-onus legislation, which, not unlike "three strikes" legislation in the United States, would ensure longer sentences for individuals convicted of three serious offences. Again, individual provinces are raising concerns. For example, Saskatchewan's then NDP government said the new federal crime legislation could result in an increase in the number of Aboriginals in Canadian jails. (Aboriginals currently account for one in five admissions in the Canadian corrections system.) A prominent Newfoundland and Labrador criminal lawyer claimed the legislation was a political reaction to increased gun crimes in Toronto, and was not relevant in other regions where the violent crime rate is actually on the decline.[19] Many Canadian provinces, in fact, favour a very different approach to crime: restorative justice. Correctional Service Canada describes restorative justice as

> a non-adversarial, non-retributive approach to justice that emphasizes healing in victims, meaningful accountability of offenders, and the involvement of citizens in creating healthier, safer communities.[20]

Restorative justice projects, such as victim–offender mediation and peacekeeping circles, are currently under way in every province and territory in Canada.

What are the implications of such differences in approach between the federal and provincial governments? Do such policies necessarily work against one another, or can they work together to achieve the common goal of reducing crime? Do such debates weaken or strengthen Canada as a country? Would a stronger federal government be able to solve such disagreements? These questions form part of the ongoing dialogue between the provincial and federal levels of government.

SUMMARY

Canada is a federation, a government structure that divides political powers between the federal and provincial governments. Confederation grew out of the desire of former British North American colonies to solve the problems posed by a small, scattered population characterized by geographic, cultural, and economic diversity. Our government structure represents an attempt to balance divergent interests for the overall public good. To this day, the challenges associated with such a balancing act—such as the demands of regional interests, bilingualism, Quebec's francophone culture, and Aboriginals' desire for self-government, to name only a few—continue to be the subjects of political debate. The separation of powers between the federal and provincial governments can sometimes lead to conflict, as evidenced in federal–provincial disagreements over the gun registry and differences in approaches to justice.

KEY TERMS

bicameral legislature

Confederation

constitution

division of powers

federal system

jurisdiction

legislative union

NOTES

1. Conservative estimates place this migration as recently as 10,000 years ago, while more liberal approximations date the movement as far back as 100,000 years. The estimates vary widely, depending upon which evidence is cited. Confirmed archaeological finds in British Columbia, Alberta, and Nova Scotia prove that human settlement existed at least 10,000 years ago, but general consensus that a land bridge between Asia and Alaska existed up to 70,000 years ago has pushed estimates back. See R. Douglas Francis et al., *Origins: Canadian History to Confederation*, 4th ed. (Toronto: Thomson Nelson, 2002), 1-5. See also Olive Dickason, *Canada's First Nations: A History of Founding Peoples from Earliest Times*, 3rd ed. (Toronto: Oxford University Press, 2002), 4-11.

2. Francis et al., supra note 1, at 7-8.

3. Seigneurs had limited judicial authority over the habitants living on their lands, but they seldom exercised it. Priests enjoyed no such official powers, relying on moral influence to settle matters. See D. Owen Carrigan, *Crime and Punishment in Canada: A History* (Toronto: McClelland & Stewart, 1991), 299.

4. The overall crime rate in New France fell slightly, from 1 in 139 population in the 17th century to 1 in 150 in the 18th century. See Carrigan, supra note 3, at 21-22.

5. The delay was due in part to the transient nature of the fishery and British reluctance to ensure the administrative costs of a permanent settlement on the island. See Keith Matthews, *Lectures on the History of Newfoundland, 1500–1830* (St. John's, NL: Breakwater Books, 1988), 131-150.

6. Carrigan, supra note 3, at 307.

7. For a brief overview of the evolution of both English common law and the *Civil Code*, and the implications of each for Canadian law, see Philip Sworden, *An Introduction to Canadian Law*, 2nd ed. (Toronto: Emond Montgomery, 2006), 1-24.

8. During the years 1802–1825, people were hanged for crimes ranging in severity from shoplifting to murder. See Carrigan, supra note 3, at 301.

9. For more information on crime in British North America, see D. Owen Carrigan, supra note 3, at 15-50.

10. Margaret Conrad, Alvin Finkel, and Cornelius Jaenen, *History of the Canadian Peoples, Vol. 1: Beginnings to 1867* (Toronto: Copp Clark Pitman, 1993), 487.

11. Francis et al., supra note 1, at 245, 256, and 353.

12. Statistics taken from Francis et al., supra note 1, at 1-4.

13. *British North America Act, 1867*, 30-31 Vict., c. 3 (UK). Later renamed the *Constitution Act, 1867*. This will be discussed in detail in chapter 3.

14. For more information, see Alvin Finkel and Margaret Conrad, *History of the Canadian Peoples, Vol. 2: 1867 to the Present*, 2nd ed. (Toronto: Copp Clark Pitman, 1998), 59.

15. Summarized from R.D. Francis et al., *Destinies: Canadian History Since Confederation*, 4th ed. (Toronto: Thomson Nelson, 2000), 42-43.

16. For further analysis, see John Geddes, "Does Ottawa Matter?" *Maclean's* (September 2, 2001), 34-37. See also C. Richard Tindal, *A Citizen's Guide to Government*, 2nd ed. (Toronto: McGraw-Hill Ryerson, 2000), 237-271.

17. The *Firearms Act* in its entirety is available on the Department of Justice Canada website at http://laws.justice.gc.ca/en/showtdm/cs/F-11.6.

18. See CBC News, "Gun Registry Cost Soars to $2 Billion" (February 13, 2004), available online at www.cbc.ca. According to documents obtained by the CBC through the *Access to Information Act*, the gun registry has $2 billion dedicated to its implementation and maintenance. This amount is well in excess of the official government estimate put forth by the auditor general in 2002.

19. For reaction to the proposed get-tough-on-crime legislation from several Canadian news sources, see www.prisonjustice.ca/starkravenarticles/tory_govnt_proposals_0406.html.

20. See Correctional Service Canada, "Restorative Justice," available online at www.csc-scc.gc.ca/text/programs_e.shtml.

EXERCISES

Multiple Choice

1. The original members of Confederation were

   a. Canada West, Canada East, New Brunswick, and Newfoundland

   b. Canada West, Canada East, New Brunswick, and Nova Scotia

   c. Canada West, New Brunswick, Nova Scotia, and Prince Edward Island

   d. Canada East, Newfoundland, New Brunswick, and Nova Scotia

   e. Rupert's Land, Canada West, Canada East, and New Brunswick

2. Confederation promised

   a. economic advantages

   b. transportation advantages

   c. defence advantages

   d. trade advantages

   e. all of the above

3. The Canadian constitution, embodied in the BNA Act, borrowed from Britain

   a. a legislature composed of two Houses of Parliament

   b. the political party system

   c. the principle of responsible government

   d. b and c

   e. a, b, and c

4. A major departure of Canada from the British system of government was its structure as a

   a. unitary state

   b. legislative union

   c. constitutional monarchy

   d. federation

   e. all of the above

5. The powers of municipal, or local, governments are based in

   a. the constitution

   b. provincial powers to form and maintain local governments

   c. federal powers to form and maintain local governments

   d. all of the above

   e. none of the above

True or False?

_____ 1. Rupert's Land was purchased for $1.5 million.

_____ 2. A federal system of government gives all the power to the federal government.

_____ 3. The BNA Act was the first statute passed by the Canadian government.

_____ 4. The new nation of Canada was a legislative union, a government structure borrowed from Britain.

_____ 5. The federal government is responsible for maintaining peace, order, and good government.

Short Answer

1. Define "federation."

2. What factors contributed to Canada's formation?

3. What did Confederation's supporters hope to achieve with this union?

4. List some aspects of the Canadian political system that have their roots in Britain.

5. Which aspect of Canada's political system was a major departure from Britain's?

6. If you could rewrite our constitution, how would you divide federal and provincial authority in the areas of justice and law enforcement? Explain.

CHAPTER 3

The Constitution and the Canadian Charter of Rights and Freedoms

CHAPTER OBJECTIVES

After completing this chapter, you should be able to:

- Describe the history of the *Constitution Act, 1982*, including attempts to amend it.
- Explain the impact of the *Canadian Charter of Rights and Freedoms* on individual and collective rights of people in Canada.
- Describe the role of the Canadian judicial system in the political and constitutional process.
- Critically analyze how the *Canadian Charter of Rights and Freedoms* can be accommodated in a post-9/11 world.

INTRODUCTION

This chapter explains how our current constitution came to be, what that means for our political system, and why constitutional reform continues to be an objective of our federal and provincial governments. The chapter also discusses the significance of the *Canadian Charter of Rights and Freedoms* to Canadians in general and to our judicial system.

THE PATH TO PATRIATION

As chapter 2 explained, the constitution of Canada has its source in the *British North America Act of 1867*, the British statute that united the former British North American colonies to form the Dominion of Canada.

Because the Act was a British statute, Britain had the power to reject Canadian laws, pass laws that affected Canada, and interpret and amend (change) Canadian laws. Thus, when Britain declared war on Germany in 1914, Canada was automatically involved in World War I as well. The Canadian constitution could be amended only by Britain, so every time Canada's federal government wanted to amend the Act, it had to ask the British Parliament to pass legislation to do so. As well, Britain's Judicial Committee of the Privy Council served as Canada's last court of appeal. For example, when the federal government and Ontario could not agree on how to draw the Ontario–Manitoba border, soon after the latter's creation, the matter was argued before the British Empire's supreme legal authority, which ultimately ruled in Ontario's favour.[1] Even though the Supreme Court of Canada was created in 1875, disputes between Ottawa and the provinces continued to be referred to the Judicial Committee until 1949 when the Supreme Court of Canada finally assumed this responsibility.

World War I, or the Great War as it was then called, exposed many inner tensions, particularly between those who viewed the conflict as a foreign one having little or nothing to do with Canada and others who saw it as an opportunity to prove Canada's loyalty to the British Empire. Anti-war sentiment tended to be strongest in French-speaking areas of the country such as Quebec, while support for the war existed to varying degrees in other regions, particularly Ontario. The imposition of conscription in 1917 caused riots in the streets of Quebec City, and although few conscripted troops ended up serving overseas, the bitterness of the experience was but one more sign to French Canada that when push came to shove, its voice did not count.

As a nation, Canada came into its own following the war. Out of a country of just over 8 million people, 625,000 had served, 60,000 of whom died. Stunning victories, such as the Battle of Vimy Ridge, proved to the world that Canada was truly a member of the international community. In 1919, in recognition of Canadian achievements, Canada signed the Treaty of Versailles independent of Britain, an event that would have seemed impossible in 1914. In legal terms, however, Canada remained tied to the British Empire.

During the 1920s, further steps were taken to acquire a sense of nationhood. In 1923, Canada signed the Halibut Treaty with the United States, marking the first time an international agreement affecting it had not been signed by British officials. At the Imperial Conference of 1926, the dominions and Britain agreed to recognize one another as equal partners united in the British Commonwealth. By the end of the 1920s, Canada established its own diplomatic relations with Washington, Paris, and Tokyo. In addition, London appointed a high commissioner to conduct government-to-government relations with Ottawa, a task that had hitherto been assigned to the Crown's representative, the governor general.

Canada's growing sense of nationhood caused many Canadians to view the existing constitutional arrangement as both embarrassing and obsolete. Britain, for its part, was happy to comply with a Canadian request for change.

Canada gained more legislative independence from Britain with the passing of the *Statute of Westminster*[2] in 1931. With this statute, Britain aimed to simplify relations with Canada and other members of the British Commonwealth. The statute formally gave Canada authority over its domestic and external affairs and limited the British Parliament to legislating for Canada only when requested to do so by the Canadian government. However, because the federal and provincial governments couldn't agree on a constitutional **amending formula**—a process for changing the BNA Act—Britain retained its authority over Canadian constitutional amendments.

Over the ensuing years, various Canadian federal governments tried to reach agreement on an amending formula with the provinces for the **patriation** of the constitution—that is, to finally bring the constitution under the control of Canada. This became increasingly complex because the federal government and the provinces could not agree on an amending formula that would permit changes to the constitution. The provinces, led initially by Quebec, sought greater control over economic and social policy. They wanted to reverse the trend toward centralization at the federal level of government, which had been particularly strong as a result of the Great Depression and the two world wars. The Quiet Revolution in Quebec, which ushered in significant political, social, and economic reforms after the provincial election of 1960, re-awakened a sense that Quebec once more should assert its special place in Canada as one of the two founding partners in Confederation. The transformation reshaped Quebec society in several ways. Quebeckers

> acquired a new confidence in themselves that encouraged them to challenge the inequalities they faced as French-speaking Canadians. They strongly criticized a Canada in which the bureaucracy spoke only English, in which French enjoyed no official recognition in nine provinces, and in which the economy functioned—even within Quebec—largely in English. Here indeed were the makings of a new nationalism.[3]

This new, more confrontational era in federal–provincial relations rekindled debates about how Canada should operate—as a highly centralized state, or as a loose confederation of autonomous provinces. Prime Minister Lester B. Pearson summed up the challenge in a speech in late 1964:

> National unity does not imply subordination in any way of provincial rights or the alienation of provincial authority. It does require a government at the centre strong enough to serve Canada as a whole; and its full realization demands a strong Canadian identity with the national spirit and pride that will sustain and strengthen it.[4]

As other provinces began to demand more autonomy within Confederation, both levels of government attempted to resolve how this could be accomplished "in house"—that is, within a Canadian constitutional framework that could provide a means of making amendments without having to submit these changes to the British Parliament for approval. Both parties came close in 1964, with the Fulton-Favreau formula, a proposal named after Davie Fulton and Guy Favreau, the two federal justice ministers who had conceived it. Under this plan, unanimous consent would be required to approve any constitutional change of national importance.

Continuing disagreement over the formula prevented its acceptance, but in 1971, another possible solution emerged. The federal government proposed a formula giving Ontario and Quebec a veto. The provinces agreed to meet in Victoria

amending formula
a legal process for changing a constitution

patriation
the process of removing the Canadian constitution from British control and bringing it under Canadian control

in June, to discuss what had become known as the Victoria Charter. Just prior to the conference, however, Quebec premier Robert Bourassa demanded that the provinces be given substantial control over social programs. As a result, no agreement was reached.

As the decade progressed, the provinces increasingly demanded more powers, which would entail constitutional reform (recall from chapter 2 that the BNA Act divided powers between the federal and provincial governments, with the federal government retaining the greatest power). Quebec, for example, continued to demand control over social programs and economic policies. The election in Quebec of the separatist Parti Québécois in 1976, led by René Lévesque, gave greater urgency to these demands.

At the end of the decade, the constitutional debate re-emerged, as Prime Minister Pierre Trudeau, seeing no federal–provincial compromise, announced that the federal government would unilaterally patriate the constitution. Only Ontario and New Brunswick came onside. In September, the Supreme Court ruled that, while the federal government could act unilaterally, it defied the convention of provincial consultation. Meanwhile, the dissenting premiers met in Vancouver to come up with a counterproposal. This group brought its "Vancouver Charter" to Ottawa in November 1981, in hopes of derailing the federal initiative. However, at a secret meeting held after midnight on November 5, some provincial representatives worked out a compromise that contained elements of the Vancouver Charter and would include a Charter of Rights and Freedoms, something upon which Trudeau had insisted. All of the premiers, save one, were awakened and summoned to the meeting. Quebec premier René Lévesque was not invited. The next day, nine provinces and the federal government announced that a deal had been reached. The chain of events became known in Quebec as the "Night of the Long Knives," since it appeared that many of that province's concerns had been sacrificed in order to achieve an agreement. Thus, Quebec did not sign the resulting constitutional document. (Although Quebec is still not a signatory to the constitution, the province benefits from and operates within the constitution of Canada.) Regardless, on April 17, 1982, Queen Elizabeth II gave royal assent to the new *Constitution Act, 1982*, officially making our constitution a wholly Canadian document, with its own amending formula.

BRINGING THE CONSTITUTION HOME

It took another British statute, the *Canada Act* of 1982,[5] to patriate the Canadian constitution. The *Canada Act* confirmed that British legislation would no longer apply to Canada. Canada's new *Constitution Act, 1982*[6] combines the old *British North America Act* (which was renamed the *Constitution Act, 1867*), the amending formula, and the *Canadian Charter of Rights and Freedoms*.[7]

The constitution contains five different amending formulas, depending on the circumstance and the part of the country affected (see the box on pages 39 and 40).

Amendments to the constitution itself require the approval of Parliament and two-thirds (7 of 10) of the provinces that, combined, contain at least 50 percent of Canada's total population. Amendments that affect representation in the House of

CONSTITUTION ACT, 1982

Part V
Procedure for Amending Constitution of Canada

General procedure for amending Constitution of Canada

38. (1) An amendment to the Constitution of Canada may be made by proclamation issued by the Governor General under the Great Seal of Canada where so authorized by

(a) resolutions of the Senate and House of Commons; and

(b) resolutions of the legislative assemblies of at least two-thirds of the provinces that have, in the aggregate, according to the then latest general census, at least fifty per cent of the population of all the provinces.

Majority of members

(2) An amendment made under subsection (1) that derogates from the legislative powers, the proprietary rights or any other rights or privileges of the legislature or government of a province shall require a resolution supported by a majority of the members of each of the Senate, the House of Commons and the legislative assemblies required under subsection (1).

Expression of dissent

(3) An amendment referred to in subsection (2) shall not have effect in a province the legislative assembly of which has expressed its dissent thereto by resolution supported by a majority of its members prior to the issue of the proclamation to which the amendment relates unless that legislative assembly, subsequently, by resolution supported by a majority of its members, revokes its dissent and authorizes the amendment.

Revocation of dissent

(4) A resolution of dissent made for the purposes of subsection (3) may be revoked at any time before or after the issue of the proclamation to which it relates.

Restriction on proclamation

39. (1) A proclamation shall not be issued under subsection 38(1) before the expiration of one year from the adoption of the resolution initiating the amendment procedure thereunder, unless the legislative assembly of each province has previously adopted a resolution of assent or dissent.

Idem

(2) A proclamation shall not be issued under subsection 38(1) after the expiration of three years from the adoption of the resolution initiating the amendment procedure thereunder.

Compensation

40. Where an amendment is made under subsection 38(1) that transfers provincial legislative powers relating to education or other cultural matters from provincial legislatures to Parliament, Canada shall provide reasonable compensation to any province to which the amendment does not apply.

Amendment by unanimous consent

41. An amendment to the Constitution of Canada in relation to the following matters may be made by proclamation issued by the Governor General under the Great Seal of Canada only where authorized by resolutions of the Senate and House of Commons and of the legislative assembly of each province:

(a) the office of the Queen, the Governor General and the Lieutenant Governor of a province;

(b) the right of a province to a number of members in the House of Commons not less than the number of Senators by which the province is entitled to be represented at the time this Part comes into force;

(c) subject to section 43, the use of the English or the French language;

(d) the composition of the Supreme Court of Canada; and

(e) an amendment to this Part.

(The box is continued on the next page.)

Amendment by general procedure

42. (1) An amendment to the Constitution of Canada in relation to the following matters may be made only in accordance with subsection 38(1):

(a) the principle of proportionate representation of the provinces in the House of Commons prescribed by the Constitution of Canada;

(b) the powers of the Senate and the method of selecting Senators;

(c) the number of members by which a province is entitled to be represented in the Senate and the residence qualifications of Senators;

(d) subject to paragraph 41(d), the Supreme Court of Canada;

(e) the extension of existing provinces into the territories; and

(f) notwithstanding any other law or practice, the establishment of new provinces.

Exception

(2) Subsections 38(2) to (4) do not apply in respect of amendments in relation to matters referred to in subsection (1).

Amendment of provisions relating to some but not all provinces

43. An amendment to the Constitution of Canada in relation to any provision that applies to one or more, but not all, provinces, including

(a) any alteration to boundaries between provinces, and

(b) any amendment to any provision that relates to the use of the English or the French language within a province,

may be made by proclamation issued by the Governor General under the Great Seal of Canada only where so authorized by resolutions of the Senate and House of Commons and of the legislative assembly of each province to which the amendment applies.

Amendments by Parliament

44. Subject to sections 41 and 42, Parliament may exclusively make laws amending the Constitution of Canada in relation to the executive government of Canada or the Senate and House of Commons.

Amendments by provincial legislatures

45. Subject to section 41, the legislature of each province may exclusively make laws amending the constitution of the province.

Initiation of amendment procedures

46. (1) The procedures for amendment under sections 38, 41, 42 and 43 may be initiated either by the Senate or the House of Commons or by the legislative assembly of a province.

Revocation of authorization

(2) A resolution of assent made for the purposes of this Part may be revoked at any time before the issue of a proclamation authorized by it.

Amendments without Senate resolution

47. (1) An amendment to the Constitution of Canada made by proclamation under section 38, 41, 42 or 43 may be made without a resolution of the Senate authorizing the issue of the proclamation if, within one hundred and eighty days after the adoption by the House of Commons of a resolution authorizing its issue, the Senate has not adopted such a resolution and if, at any time after the expiration of that period, the House of Commons again adopts the resolution.

Computation of period

(2) Any period when Parliament is prorogued or dissolved shall not be counted in computing the one hundred and eighty day period referred to in subsection (1).

Advice to issue proclamation

48. The Queen's Privy Council for Canada shall advise the Governor General to issue a proclamation under this Part forthwith on the adoption of the resolutions required for an amendment made by proclamation under this Part.

Constitutional conference

49. A constitutional conference composed of the Prime Minister of Canada and the first ministers of the provinces shall be convened by the Prime Minister of Canada within fifteen years after this Part comes into force to review the provisions of this Part.

Commons, the Senate, and the Supreme Court of Canada and that affect the use of the French and English languages in government affairs require the consent of Parliament and all the provinces.[8]

The *Charter of Rights and Freedoms* (see the appendix) was the most significant amendment to the constitution and will be discussed in more detail later in this chapter.

Despite patriation, Trudeau's vision of a unified Canada has yet to be realized. As the following sections will explain, more than two decades after patriation Canadians are still debating constitutional issues and attempting to win Quebec's signature to the constitution.

ONGOING CONSTITUTIONAL DEBATE

In spite of the events of 1982, the Quebec separatist movement could not galvanize public opinion sufficiently to achieve independence. After coming to power in 1976, the Parti Québécois had focused on social issues, rather than pursuing its separatist objectives. As well, a 1980 referendum on the issue of "sovereignty association"—only a step toward full nationhood—was lost when 60 percent of Quebeckers voted against the proposal. When the provincial Liberal Party won the election of 1985, it seemed as though the Quebec separatist movement was dead. In federal politics, Trudeau had retired, and in September 1984, Canadians elected the Progressive Conservatives, led by Brian Mulroney. A Quebecker himself, Mulroney wanted to bring Quebec back into the constitutional family.

The Meech Lake Accord

An apparent agreement was reached between Mulroney and the 10 provincial premiers at a first ministers' conference at Meech Lake, Ontario, in April 1987. The proposed amendments of the Meech Lake Accord met Quebec's minimum demands for signing the constitution:[9]

- Quebec would be recognized as a distinct society.

- Quebec would have a veto on any future constitutional changes.

- All provinces would have increased powers over immigration.

- All provinces would be able to opt out of any federal cost-sharing programs (for example, medicare and child care).

- Justices of the Supreme Court of Canada would be appointed from lists provided by the provinces.

In addition, the concerns of the other provinces were addressed with the following:

- Provincial demands for Senate reform would be met by giving the provinces the right to provide the federal government with a list of individuals from which to choose senators.

- Future constitutional amendments would be discussed at annual first ministers' meetings.

- All provinces—not just Quebec—would have the power to veto amendments.

Mulroney then announced that no amendments to Meech Lake would be considered—it had to be ratified within three years by Parliament and by all 10 provincial legislatures. Not a word could be changed.[10]

Despite the agreement of the politicians, many groups opposed the Meech Lake Accord. Some people were unhappy that ordinary Canadians had not been involved in the reform process in any way, arguing that the future of the nation should not be decided by only 11 men. People who were in favour of a strong federal government believed that the Accord gave too much power to the provinces. First Nations' hopes for a guarantee of the right to self-government were dashed. Many people, including Quebeckers, wanted to know exactly what "distinct society" meant in the legal sense, a definition that was not provided in the Accord. Many people were concerned about how this recognition of Quebec might affect the provisions of the *Charter of Rights and Freedoms* and how it would be interpreted by the Supreme Court when deciding issues related to the Charter. Mulroney countered that "distinct society" was mainly a symbolic term, thus basically confirming that it had little constitutional worth. Critics, many of them from Quebec, disagreed, however. Other critics of the Accord included women's groups and groups that were concerned that the ability of provinces to opt out of proposed shared-cost programs (for example, a national child-care program) would lead to the abandonment of such programs.

Another stipulation of the Meech Lake Accord was that all provinces and the federal government were to ratify the agreement within three years—that is, pass a statute accepting the Accord in their respective Parliaments within three years. Three years passed and, with them, brought political party changes in several provinces. When the deadline was reached, 2 of the 10 provinces had still not approved the agreement: Newfoundland and Manitoba. Newfoundland premier Clyde Wells, a lawyer and constitutional expert, was in favour of a strong federal government and an elected Senate with equal representation from all the provinces, and he was opposed to recognizing Quebec as a distinct society. In Manitoba, a member of the Legislative Assembly, Elijah Harper, in a stand for First Nations' rights, managed to delay a vote on the passage of the Accord.

The Meech Lake Accord died in 1990, as did hopes of obtaining Quebec's approval of the constitution. Quite the contrary happened—the debates surrounding Meech Lake had actually stirred up pro-separatist feelings. Quebeckers felt betrayed by the opposition to the distinct society clause and the switch from addressing Quebec's constitutional concerns to addressing the concerns of other groups. As a result, several Quebec members of the National Assembly formed a new federal political party—the Bloc Québécois, led by one of Mulroney's most senior Cabinet ministers, Lucien Bouchard—to defend Quebec's rights in Ottawa. Quebec premier Robert Bourassa announced plans for a referendum on separation for 1992. Facing growing support for Quebec separation, the federal and provincial leaders decided to resume negotiations toward a new accord before the referendum deadline.[11]

The Charlottetown Accord

The federal government began by announcing a Citizens' Forum on Canada's Future in November 1990. Sensing a looming national crisis, Prime Minister Mulroney wanted to consult a broad range of Canadians about how to deal with the situation. He described the commission as a way to create "a dialogue with people across the country and help create a consensus about Canada and our future."[12] The commission's subsequent report contributed to a larger effort at constitutional reform, already under way.

The Charlottetown Accord of August 1992 was two years in the making and included something for everyone: special status for Quebec in exchange for equal provincial representation in the Senate, recognition of Aboriginal rights to self-government, a social charter guaranteeing that existing social programs would be maintained by government, and more provincial powers. In addition, all Canadians would be involved in ratifying the Accord in a referendum scheduled for October 1992.

Despite polls suggesting that most Canadians would support the new Accord, 6 of the 10 provinces voted against it. It seemed that in trying to please everyone, the Accord managed to please no one and only fuelled Quebec separatist sentiments. Everyone was tired of constitutional wrangles and wanted to turn to other pressing concerns, such as the serious economic recession and rising unemployment. Meanwhile, separatists in Quebec seized on Charlottetown as additional proof to back their cause. Quebec finally held its referendum on separation in 1995, which was only narrowly defeated when 49.4 percent of Quebeckers said "Yes" to separation from the rest of Canada.[13]

Recent Constitutional Issues

Canada has experienced some very difficult economic and social ills since the attempt to amend the *Constitution Act*. Constitutional issues and the threat of Quebec separation, although important, have taken a back seat to other priorities—jobs, health care, and the state of the economy among them. When Parti Québécois leader Lucien Bouchard was re-elected premier of Quebec in 1998 with less than 43 percent of the popular vote, his government decided there was no pressing need for another referendum on separation. The Quebec Liberal Party, led by Jean Charest, won the provincial election of April 2003 and stated that, for now at least, it saw no need to revisit constitutional reform. Meanwhile, the provinces and the federal government have continued to discuss various constitutional issues.

One result of negotiations was the Calgary Accord of September 1997, in which the federal government and all provinces except Quebec (which boycotted the meeting) agreed to a set of seven principles that, it was hoped, would bring Quebec into the constitution. Unlike the Meech Lake and Charlottetown accords, the Calgary Accord was mostly a goodwill gesture that expressed some general principles rather than specific constitutional amendments. For example, Quebec was described as having a unique character, but this was alongside statements about the diversity and equality of all the provinces. The Calgary Accord emphasized cooperation, multiculturalism, and the partnership between the federal and provincial/territorial governments. To date, little has come of this effort.

In the same year, the federal government decided to pursue the issue of separation by challenging Quebec's right to separate. The government asked the Supreme Court of Canada to address the questions whether Quebec can legally make a unilateral decision to separate under the Canadian constitution (that is, decide on its own), whether Quebec can unilaterally separate under international law, and which law—Canadian or international—would apply if there were a conflict between the two.

In August 1998 the Supreme Court decided that Quebec had no unilateral right to separate under Canadian or international law, but also that the rest of Canada cannot deny Quebec's right to pursue separation if a majority of Quebeckers choose to do so. The court also decided that if a clear majority of Quebeckers voted for separation in a referendum, then the federal government has a "constitutional duty to negotiate" with Quebec. Note that the latter puts a reciprocal obligation on Quebec to negotiate.[14] After the court's ruling, the federal government introduced legislation in 1999 outlining how any separation vote must be conducted. The Quebec government countered with legislation of its own. The debate continues, as does the desire of some Quebeckers to secede.

Passions flared anew in 2006, when Prime Minister Stephen Harper introduced a motion in the House of Commons stating that Quebec forms a nation "within a united Canada." The motion was intended to pre-empt a looming Bloc Québécois motion that would call for Quebec to be recognized as a nation but would not include any reference to Canada. The prime minister's motion passed by a vote of 266 to 12, but not without repercussions for his minority government: a Cabinet minister resigned in protest of what he called Harper's "ethnic nationalism."[15] Although the nation debate has faded off the political radar, the larger issue of Quebec's place in Canada will remain one of the more challenging constitutional quandaries facing Canada's politicians.

THE CANADIAN CHARTER OF RIGHTS AND FREEDOMS

Canadian Charter of Rights and Freedoms part of the Canadian constitution that guarantees certain fundamental rights and freedoms to people in Canada

common law a body of law that has grown out of past court cases and is based on precedent or custom

As mentioned earlier in this chapter, probably the most significant aspect of the *Constitution Act, 1982* was the inclusion of the ***Canadian Charter of Rights and Freedoms***. Since Confederation, Canadians had enjoyed rights such as freedom of speech under **common law** (law based on past legal decisions, or precedents) and custom, but these rights were not entrenched in the BNA Act. In 1960, Prime Minister John Diefenbaker created the *Canadian Bill of Rights*, prohibiting discrimination according to race, national origin, colour, or sex. However, because it was passed as a normal piece of legislation, it remained vulnerable to change or repeal by any successive government. As a federal statute, it only applied to matters under federal jurisdiction. The provinces could do as they wished.

The Charter, the brainchild of then Prime Minister Pierre Trudeau, gave constitutional authority to a list of fundamental rights and freedoms enjoyed by all people in Canada (see the appendix for the full text of the Charter).

With the addition of the Charter, Canada saw its government structure shed some of its British tradition—in which Parliament is the greatest power in the land—and take on more of the American tradition, where the Supreme Court is the highest power because of its right to interpret the terms of the constitution.[16] The Charter guarantees certain fundamental freedoms and democratic rights to all Canadians, thereby expressing the basic values of our nation, and sets out rules that all levels of government must follow.

Section 2 of the Charter sets out the fundamental freedoms:

- freedom of conscience and religion;
- freedom of thought, belief, opinion, and expression, including freedom of the press and other media;
- freedom of peaceful assembly; and
- freedom of association.

The other sections set out various rights, declare Canada's official bilingualism, explain how rights and freedoms are enforced, and describe how the Charter applies to all levels of government. Sections 7-14 set out legal rights, which apply to anyone in Canada and are particularly relevant to law enforcement. These legal rights include:

- the right to life, liberty, and security of the person;
- the right to be secure against unreasonable search and seizure;
- the right not to be arbitrarily detained or imprisoned;
- on arrest or detention, the right to be informed promptly of the reason for arrest and the specific offence;
- the right to retain counsel;
- the right to be tried within a reasonable time; and
- the right to be presumed innocent until proven guilty.

The Charter is a fundamental piece of legislation that law enforcement officers need to understand and apply conscientiously. As part of the constitution, the Charter must be considered in concert with other Canadian criminal and civil laws and also applies to the actions of government and its representatives, such as law enforcement officers. Thus, anyone who believes that Charter rights are being contravened by any federal or provincial law can dispute that law in court and, conceivably, have it declared unconstitutional by the court. Similarly, if a court finds that an accused person's rights have been contravened at any step in the judicial process by any agent of the state—such as law enforcement officers—the charge against the accused may be stayed.

Limits on Charter Rights

Included within the Charter's guarantees of rights are some limits to those rights. We will discuss two of the most important qualifiers here. First is the "reasonable limits" clause in section 1:

> 1. The *Canadian Charter of Rights and Freedoms* guarantees the rights and freedoms set out in it subject only to such reasonable limits prescribed by law as can be demonstrably justified in a free and democratic society.

This means that Charter rights can be overridden if the government can prove that an apparent Charter violation is a reasonable limit. For example, when police officers conduct a RIDE (Reduce Impaired Driving Everywhere) program, they are allowed to detain motorists because doing so is seen as a reasonable limit that can prevent motorists and others from harm caused by drunk drivers. Similarly, the right of freedom of speech does not extend to spreading hate literature against a particular person or group in our society.

The "notwithstanding clause" in section 33 is another limit in the Charter, and one that has been the subject of much controversy.

> 33(1) Parliament or the legislature of a province may expressly declare in an Act of Parliament or of the legislature, as the case may be, that the Act or a provision thereof shall operate notwithstanding a provision included in section 2 or sections 7 to 15 of this Charter.

What this means is that a government can override a section of the Charter with one of its own laws by passing legislation declaring that it is doing so. Section 33 goes on to explain the time limits on such an action. This clause seems to have been a way for Trudeau to secure the provincial premiers' approval of the Charter. Shortly after the passage of the constitution in 1982, Quebec used the notwithstanding clause to exempt all of its legislation from the Charter, claiming that its provincial human rights code protected Quebeckers adequately. This has allowed Quebec to, for example, override the minority-language education rights that are set out in section 23 of the Charter. The province also invoked the clause in the late 1980s, in order to exempt Bill 178, Quebec's French-only sign law, from a Supreme Court decision declaring it unconstitutional.

An Expanded Role for the Courts

The Charter has effectively shifted some power from the government to the courts, whose role now includes interpreting the impact of any legislation on Charter rights. Individuals as well as special-interest groups are challenging legislation and government policy in ways that were not possible before 1982. What were once political issues are increasingly becoming legal issues, and some people see this new power of the courts—and of the people who challenge the Charter—as dangerous. In a democratic system that is based on representatives being elected by citizens, should judges, who are appointed, have the right to overturn laws and policies made by our elected representatives?

This complex question has no simple answer, and it is being hotly debated by academics, lawyers, concerned citizens, and others. Some believe that the courts, particularly the Supreme Court of Canada, have too much political power, while others believe that this new role of the courts is exactly what is needed to make sure our politicians uphold the laws of the land, including the rights of citizens.

Get Real!

FREEDOM VERSUS SECURITY, POST-9/11

The *Charter of Rights and Freedoms* is intended to protect Canadians from unfair treatment by governments and their representatives. It formed a key part of former Prime Minister Pierre Trudeau's vision for a "just society"—a place where individual difference could be accommodated within a larger framework of communal values. While such a goal sounds reasonable, in practice it is often difficult to achieve. For example, government legislation introduced since the World Trade Center terrorist attacks on September 11, 2001 challenges many of the protections Canadians enjoy under the Charter. Since the passage of Bill C-36,[17] "the right not to be arbitrarily detained or imprisoned" and "on arrest or detention, the right to be informed promptly of the reason for arrest and the specific offence" are no longer guaranteed. In June 2007, Canada followed the lead of the United States and implemented a no-fly list on all domestic commercial air travel (international flights would be included later). The program, called Passenger Protect, catalogues the names of people "reasonably" suspected of terrorist activity, people who have been previously convicted of crimes against aviation security, and people who have been convicted of more general "serious offences" and who "may attack or harm an air carrier, passengers or crew members."[18] A Transport Canada news release said the program "will not only make Canada's aviation system more secure, it will also keep the world's skies safe."[19] Critics say such a system is unavoidably vague and flawed (for example, several infants have been denied boarding in the United States) and a violation of Canadians' rights to privacy and freedom of movement.[20] The question then becomes: How much of our freedom are we willing to trade for security?

Consider the case of Maher Arar. In September 2002, the Ottawa software engineer was detained by US authorities during a stopover in New York City. They claimed Arar had ties to al-Qaeda, and, despite the fact that he carried a Canadian passport, deported him to Syria, where he was jailed and tortured during a year-long incarceration. After intense lobbying by his wife and other supporters, Arar was released and returned to Canada in 2003; a public inquiry was called into the case a year later. It concluded "categorically that there is no evidence to indicate that Mr. Arar has committed any offence or that his activities constitute a threat to the security of Canada."[21] In 2007, the Canadian government affirmed Arar's innocence, issued a formal apology, and awarded him $12.5 million in compensation. To date, the US government refuses to remove Arar from that country's no-fly list. Further, reports indicate that many other Canadians also have been imprisoned abroad, held without charge, denied access to lawyers, and tortured.[22] Activities such as these have led some Canadians to worry that Charter rights cannot be altered without endangering the principles that underlie the rule of law and democracy itself—the right to be presumed innocent until proven guilty, and the right to be treated in a fair and just manner by officials of the Canadian government, particularly those who enforce the law. Supporters of measures such as the no-fly list, however, contend that the rules have changed, and that the world we live in has become a very different one since 9/11. As one observer puts it, "the inconvenience of a few pales when weighed against the safety of many."[23] What do you think? Can we ensure public safety without endangering fundamental principles of justice?

SUMMARY

More than 100 years after Confederation, Canada finally brought home its constitution in 1982. The central documents of our current *Constitution Act, 1982* are the *British North America Act*, now called the *Constitution Act, 1867*, and the *Canadian Charter of Rights and Freedoms*. However, we are still struggling as a nation to reach a consensus on many related issues and particularly to get Quebec's signature to the constitution.

Several attempts have been made to incorporate the conditions that Quebec believes are necessary prerequisites to signing the constitution. These attempts included the Meech Lake and Charlottetown accords, both of which failed to win the support of a majority of provinces. Attempts at constitutional reform continue, but have taken a back seat to other issues in recent years.

The *Charter of Rights and Freedoms* has significance in our everyday lives and in the institutions of government. The Charter enshrines rights and freedoms in the constitution that previously existed only as part of Canadian common law and custom. As a result, it has had significant implications for our political system, particularly in terms of the increased power of the judiciary, which has, many argue, become a third branch of government (a topic that will be discussed in more detail in chapter 4). In a post-9/11 world, the challenge for Canadian government officials is to strike a balance between preserving Charter rights and freedoms and ensuring national security.

KEY TERMS

amending formula

Canadian Charter of Rights and Freedoms

common law

patriation

NOTES

1. Under federal and Ontario Liberal governments, an agreement had been reached, but before it could be enacted, the federal Liberals lost power. The new Conservative government ignored the previous agreement, and the ensuing legal wrangling eventually led both sides to appeal to the Judicial Committee of the Privy Council for a decision. The body ruled in 1883 that Ontario's western boundary should be fixed at its present-day location. See R. Douglas Francis et al., *Destinies: Canadian History Since Confederation*, 4th ed. (Toronto: Thomson Nelson, 2000), 82-83. See also Peter H. Russell, "Provincial Rights," in R. Douglas Francis and Donald B. Smith, *Readings in Canadian History: Post-Confederation*, 6th ed. (Toronto: Thomson Nelson, 2002), 21-33.

2. *Statute of Westminster*, 22 Geo. V, c. 4 (1931).

3. Francis et al., supra note 1, at 447.

4. Lester B. Pearson, address to the Empire Club at the Royal York Hotel, Toronto (October 15, 1964). Available online at http://archives.cbc.ca/ IDC-1-73-394-2226/politics_economy/constitution_debate_1/clip11.

5. *Canada Act, 1982* (UK), c. 11 (1982).

6. *Constitution Act, 1982*, RSC 1985, app. II, no. 44.

7. *Canadian Charter of Rights and Freedoms*, part I of the *Constitution Act, 1982*, RSC 1985, app. II, no. 44.

8. Alvin Finkel and Margaret Conrad, with Veronica Strong-Boag, *History of the Canadian Peoples, Vol. 2: 1867 to the Present* (Toronto: Copp Clark Pitman, 1993), 585.

9. Ronald H. Wagenberg, "The Institutions of the Canadian State," in Kenneth G. Pryke and Walter C. Soderlund, eds., *Profiles of Canada* (Toronto: Copp Clark Pitman, 1992), 102.

10. Finkel and Conrad, with Strong-Boag, supra note 8, at 593.

11. Ibid., at 592-598.

12. Spicer Commission 1991 Citizens' Forum on Canadian Unity. Available online at www.uni.ca/initiatives/spicer_part1.html.

13. Finkel and Conrad, with Strong-Boag, supra note 8, at 598-602.

14. Warren J. Newman, *The Quebec Secession Reference: The Rule of Law and the Position of the Attorney General of Canada* (Toronto: York University Centre for Public Law and Public Policy, 1999), ch. 4.

15. For more information, see Robert Benzie, "Premiers Hail Birth of Council of the Federation," *Toronto Star* (December 6, 2004), A6. The idea has come under criticism because it lacks regional credibility. See Robert Roach, "A 'Council of the Federation' Is Just the Beginning," *The Globe and Mail* (July 15, 2003), A15.

16. Wagenberg, supra note 9, at 112.

17. The text of Bill C-36 is available on the Parliament of Canada website at www.parl.gc.ca. For concerns about possible implications and a response to the bill, see A. Alan Borovoy, General Counsel of the Canadian Civil Liberties Association, "New Powers Aren't Really Necessary," *Toronto Star* (October 12, 2001), available on the Association's website at www.ccla.org/news/power.shtml.

18. Transport Canada, "Air Security Strengthened—Passenger Protect Ready to Take Flight" (May 11, 2007) (news release), available online at www.tc.gc.ca/mediaroom/releases/nat/2007/07-gc017e.htm.

19. Ibid.

20. See CBC News, "Canada's No-Fly List to Take Effect June 18" (May 11, 2007), available online at www.cbc.ca.

21. For more on the Maher Arar case, see CBC News, "Maher Arar: Timeline" (January 26, 2007), available online at www.cbc.ca, as well as Arar's own website at www.maherarar.ca.

22. For example, see Amnesty International Canada, "No Security Without Human Rights" (December 14, 2006), available online at www.amnesty .ca/themes/canada_no_security.php.

23. Rosie DiManno, "In the Wake of 9/11, We're Better Safe Than Sorry," *Toronto Star* (September 3, 2003), A2.

EXERCISES

Multiple Choice

1. Since 1982, government constitutional negotiations have centred on

   a. redefining federal and provincial government powers

   b. obtaining Quebec's signature to the *Constitution Act, 1982*

   c. reforming the Senate

   d. addressing the concerns of various groups in Canadian society

   e. all of the above

2. The Charter is a significant part of our constitution because it

   a. changed the Canadian political system from one based in British tradition to a system more like that of the United States

   b. is above all other law

   c. enshrines specific rights for all Canadians

   d. limits government legislation and policies

   e. all of the above

3. The rights and freedoms set out in the Charter

   a. can be limited by the federal and provincial governments

   b. can be limited by the "reasonable limits" and "notwithstanding" clauses

   c. have no limits

   d. can be ignored by the courts

   e. a and b

4. The *Charter of Rights and Freedoms* is relevant to law enforcement because it

    a. defines the rights of citizens, including those of persons accused of committing offences

    b. limits the actions of government and its agents in maintaining public order

    c. gives law enforcement officers the right to decide what constitutes reasonable limits on citizens' behaviour

    d. all of the above

    e. a and b

5. The expanded role of the Canadian courts since the passing of the Charter is controversial because now

    a. the courts are more powerful than the government

    b. appointed judges interpret the Charter and make decisions that affect laws and policies created by elected politicians

    c. the courts are responsible for making laws

    d. the courts can overturn any law or policy they don't like

    e. all of the above

True or False?

_____ 1. Under the BNA Act, the Canadian government simply passed legislation when it wanted to amend the Act.

_____ 2. Canada's current constitution is called the *Canada Act*.

_____ 3. Before the *Charter of Rights and Freedoms* was added to the constitution, Canadians enjoyed rights under common law and by custom.

_____ 4. The Charter has no effect on the justice system or on how law enforcement officers do their job.

_____ 5. The Charter grants unlimited fundamental rights and freedoms to all Canadians.

Short Answer

1. Explain why Quebec has not signed the *Constitution Act, 1982.* What are its main concerns?

2. In order to amend the constitution, what has to happen first?

3. Why have the federal and provincial governments attempted constitutional reform? What are they trying to achieve?

4. List some advantages and disadvantages of having a powerful judiciary as part of our political structure.

5. Describe how the *Charter of Rights and Freedoms* affects you now and will affect you in a future career in law enforcement.

CHAPTER 4

Welcome to the Machine: Canadian Political Structure and Its Operation

CHAPTER OBJECTIVES

After completing this chapter, you should be able to:

- Define and differentiate the terms "representative government" and "responsible government."
- Understand the structure and roles of the three levels of government.
- Explain how laws are enacted at the three levels of government.
- Describe the status of First Nations within our political structure.

INTRODUCTION

In the last chapter, we discussed the historical context underlying Canadian politics and how this evolution informs current government action. In this chapter, we turn to the "nuts and bolts" of political structure, that is, how various people and groups organize themselves within government to achieve political aims. What democratic traditions underlie Canada's parliamentary tradition? How are laws created and debated? What is the relationship among various systems of government and how do they compare with one another? How does Aboriginal government function in the Canadian political context? These and other questions will be addressed in this chapter.

WHAT IS REPRESENTATIVE GOVERNMENT?

Imagine for a moment that your college has decided to allow students to decide what colour to paint the classrooms. What is the most democratic way the institution could arrive at a decision? Your response might be "Ask every student." This sounds straightforward, but in schools where enrolment is literally in the thousands it would take a very long time, and worse, some students might change their minds. Further, by the time the entire student body had been consulted the year might be over, with an entirely new group of students arriving in the fall. In short, democracy taken to an extreme is simply too time consuming and achieves little in the way of results.

So, what is the most efficient way to decide what colour to paint the classrooms? Well, you could decide based on your individual preference, but this would be seen as blatantly undemocratic and would therefore lack the support of your fellow students. Another solution might be to select a number of students—say, one from each program—to poll their respective peers and bring the results to a meeting where a vote could be held on each colour. In this way, democratic consultation and administrative efficiency would be accommodated to an acceptable degree. Voilà! You have just created a representative system of consultation. Representative government works on the very same principle.

representative government
government that is based on members elected by citizens to represent their interests

In a **representative government** people are elected by geographic area to represent the concerns of the people living in that area. It is a fundamental principle of democracy. Canada has a representative government that is based on members elected by citizens to represent their interests. Similarly, the provincial and territorial governments have members elected by citizens to represent their interests. We will explain these government structures in detail.

Critics of Canada's system of representative forms of government argue that the tradition of party loyalty deters representatives from reflecting the views of their constituents on political issues. Further, they argue, the tendency of senior politicians (prime ministers, premiers, and Cabinet ministers) to dominate policy making and the legislative agenda subverts the original spirit of representative democracy. This, they contend, is responsible for growing public apathy about elections and a lack of respect for the functions of government.

As discussed in chapter 1, a move in this direction is very dangerous because it has a direct impact on respect for the rule of law and those who defend it (police and the courts). Recent moves by provincial and federal governments to address the "democratic deficit" suggest that they recognize the importance of protecting political integrity.[1] These initiatives are an encouraging sign, but whether they will reinvigorate public attitudes remains to be seen.

Elections in Canada

In Canada, elections are called at the discretion of the prime minister at the federal level, and, in most provinces, at the discretion of the premiers. In 2005, legislation was passed in Ontario that fixes a date for an election every four years, on the first Thursday in October.[2] British Columbia is the only other province with fixed election dates. In both cases, an election must take place no later than five years following the last election. In times of public emergency, such as war or domestic crises, exceptions can be made to the five-year rule at the federal level. Municipal election schedules vary from province to province. Ontario municipalities have elections every three years.

One of the major players in an election is the candidate who is running for office. (The other major player, the constituent or voter, is discussed in chapter 11.) The rules and regulations governing candidacy are contained in the *Canada Elections Act*[3] and its counterparts at the provincial and territorial levels. With a few exceptions, the rules are very similar. You must be a resident of Canada and be eligible to vote. You cannot currently be serving as a political representative at another level, and you must be innocent of any corrupt political practices for the previous five years. You are also disqualified if you are imprisoned or are an election officer. Most judges and some Crown attorneys are also prohibited from running.[4] Federal candidates must collect 100 signatures of fellow electors and make a deposit of $1,000. In Ontario, the same number of signatures is required, but the fee is $200, and for municipal elections, no signatures are required and the fee is $100.[5]

WHAT IS RESPONSIBLE GOVERNMENT?

The concept of responsible government is another central principle characterizing democratic countries such as Canada, where the system of government is based on a parliamentary model. The principle of **responsible government** requires that the government may govern only as long as it has the support of a majority of the state's elected representatives.

responsible government
government that is responsible to the wishes of its citizens, as embodied in their elected representatives

Majority or Minority?

If a majority votes against the government on a bill of major importance, then that government must resign, thus dissolving Parliament. In almost all cases, this results in an election call to allow voters to decide which party will form the next government. In Canada's 308-seat House of Commons, for example, a simple majority of 155 **members of Parliament** (MPs) voting against a major government bill would trigger this event.

In reality, however, this rarely happens because of another parliamentary tradition called party loyalty. **Party loyalty** demands that all members of a particular political party vote according to the wishes of their leader. In other words, they are not free to vote as they wish. This means that as long as the government—that is, the political party with the most elected representatives—can convince 155 or more MPs in the House of Commons to vote in its favour, it can continue to hold power.

Observing the principle of responsible government is particularly easy when 155 or more MPs belong to the same party. In this situation the party forms what is called a **majority government**, since its members constitute a majority in the legislature. But what happens when a federal political party ends up with more MPs but fails to achieve the number required for a majority? In this case, a **minority government** is formed. As you can probably tell, minority governments are much more unstable because opposition MPs outnumber, and can therefore outvote, the government on any bill.

member of Parliament
an elected representative in the House of Commons who represents a riding

party loyalty
the requirement that all members of a political party vote according to the wishes of their leader

majority government
a government that includes more than half of the total MPs in the House of Commons

minority government
a government that has the greatest number of MPs in the House of Commons but not more than half of the total MPs

There are advantages and disadvantages to each situation. Majority governments are much more productive in terms of the amount of legislation they produce because they can outvote opposition members as a bill makes its way through the legislative process (discussed later in this chapter). They also don't need to worry about losing their mandate through an opposition-sponsored non-confidence vote—a vote to replace the government because it has lost the confidence of the majority of the House. Thus, within the five-year limit, majority governments are free to decide when the next election will be held. Most governments typically wait about four years before issuing an election call. Majority governments are often criticized for being insensitive to different viewpoints and may be perceived by constituents as being arrogant and undemocratic.

Minority governments face almost the opposite set of challenges. They are forced to listen to opposition concerns, which often lead to political compromises or further consideration. But this situation also makes minority governments inherently unproductive and short-lived. The cooperative consultative practices inherent in minority governments can bog down the legislative process, and the opposition parties may outvote—and thus defeat—the government at any time. The result is a very unpredictable session. Historically, Canadians have tended to vote in majority governments. The minority Liberal government elected in June 2004 was the first one in 25 years. It was dissolved in 2005 after a non-confidence vote, and was replaced by a Conservative minority in 2006. Prior to 2004, the last minority government, led by Joe Clark, was elected in 1979 and lasted less than a year—from May 1979 to February 1980—before it was defeated.

STRUCTURE OF THE FEDERAL GOVERNMENT

In democratic countries such as Canada, power is usually separated into three main categories: executive, legislative, and judicial. We can think of the organization of the federal government in terms of these three branches (see figure 4.1).

The Executive Branch

executive branch (federal) the branch of government that includes the monarch's representative (governor general), the elected head of state (prime minister), and Cabinet

The **executive branch** of the federal government includes the Queen (or current reigning British monarch), the governor general (the Queen's representative in Canada), the prime minister, the Cabinet, and the ministries and departments that provide government goods and services. In a parliamentary system, the power to govern rests here.

Although officially Canada's head of state, the Queen in reality has no role in Canadian government except to formally appoint the governor general, who is always chosen by the prime minister. The governor general acts as the Queen's representative in Canada, although the relationship is entirely ceremonial in nature, hearkening back to our colonial ties to the British empire. The governor general mainly performs functions such as opening Parliament, and she or he is usually appointed for a term of five years.

The prime minister and Cabinet are the most important members of the executive branch and the people we usually think of as "government." The real locus of power lies here. As leader of the national party in power, the prime minister wields

FIGURE 4.1   Structure of the Federal Government

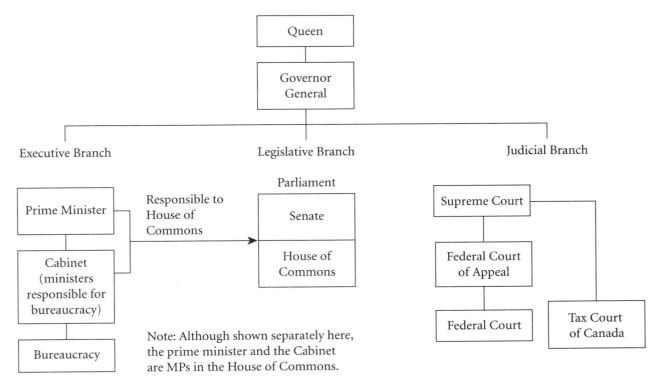

Note: Although shown separately here, the prime minister and the Cabinet are MPs in the House of Commons.

considerable power within this structure. He or she controls the appointment of Cabinet ministers, deputy ministers, senators, senior judges, and a host of other important government positions. The prime minister also has the power to dissolve Parliament, which results in an election call.

The **Cabinet**—chaired by the prime minister—is where government policies are developed, debated, and decided. The Cabinet is made up of MPs selected by the prime minister to represent the diverse population of the country. Cabinet ministers oversee individual government departments, communicating the political will of the Cabinet as it applies to each department.

When choosing Cabinet members, a prime minister considers several factors. The first is that the person be elected to the House of Commons. As well, a person's education, career, and experience in government are also considered. Choices are also influenced by the "theory of representativeness," which dictates that public officials should reflect the diversity and complexity of those they serve. Therefore, where MPs live, their ethnic background, gender, and other traits are factors in whether they will be chosen to become Cabinet ministers. Finally, individuals are chosen on the basis of their past relationship with the prime minister. Because Cabinet represents the locus of power in a parliamentary democracy, it is vital that the "team" work together under the direction of its leader, in good times and bad.

While individual Cabinet ministers may privately disagree with government policies, they are bound to support government action publicly. This reflects the principle of **Cabinet solidarity**, which allows the government to speak with one voice on given policy matters. The bureaucracy, or civil service, is responsible for implementing political will and will be examined in detail in part III of this text.

Cabinet
the government body that consists of MPs appointed by the prime minister who oversee government departments and act as advisers in major policy areas

Cabinet solidarity
the united front that Cabinet presents on given policy matters, although individual Cabinet ministers may privately be opposed

The Legislative Branch

legislative branch (federal)
the lawmaking branch of government (House of Commons and Senate)

Lawmaking is a major government role, and most legislation, or law, is the result of government initiatives that are designed to carry out election promises. The **legislative branch** consists of those government bodies that are responsible for passing legislation. At the federal level, this branch includes the two Houses of Parliament: the House of Commons (the lower chamber) and the Senate (the upper chamber).

Proceedings in each chamber are overseen by the Speaker, who is elected from among the current MPs, or, in the case of the Senate, selected by the prime minister. Once in that position, the Speaker assumes a neutral, non-partisan role, maintaining order and ensuring respect for the rules of Parliament.

HOUSE OF COMMONS

In 2007, the House of Commons was made up of 308 MPs representing the 308 geographic areas—called ridings or constituencies—into which Canada has been divided. Ridings vary in size according to population, with each containing approximately 100,000 Canadians. When an election is held, candidates in each riding compete to get the most voter support. The candidate with the most votes becomes the MP for that riding. This is known as a "first past the post" system of election.

The party with the second-highest number of MPs elected forms the Official Opposition. These MPs, along with the other non-government members of the House, hold the governing party publicly accountable and responsible for its actions. They also participate in passing legislation and represent their respective constituencies.

SENATE

There are 105 seats in the Senate (as of 2007). Senators, who are appointed by the prime minister rather than elected, approve decisions of the House of Commons. The Senate also reviews proposed legislation and may choose to reject it. For this reason, the Senate is known as the chamber of "sober second thought." Senators must be at least 30 years old, and they may hold office until aged 75. There are 22 senators from each of Ontario and Quebec; 6 from each of Alberta, Saskatchewan, and Manitoba; 5 from each of British Columbia and Newfoundland and Labrador; 9 from New Brunswick; 7 from Nova Scotia; 3 from Prince Edward Island; 1 from the Northwest Territories; and 1 from Nunavut. (At publication, there was no senator from the Yukon, and 12 senate seats were vacant.)

The Senate has come under increasing criticism in recent times because its members are not elected and are therefore not directly accountable to the Canadian public. As well, the Senate has become a patronage reward for friends of the prime minister and those loyal to his or her party. A general perception exists that as long as senators are appointed, this House has no legitimacy. This has led to calls

triple E Senate
a Senate that is equal, elected, and effective

for what has become known as a **triple E Senate**—one that is equal, elected, and effective. The logic is that, if an equal number of senators were elected from each province, then the Senate would function as it was originally intended and its integrity would thereby be restored. In the United States, for example, voters in each state, regardless of size or population, elect two senators to Congress to counterbalance the House of Representatives where state representation is determined by population. The first prime minister who has moved to make this change is Stephen

Harper, who has plans to implement reform measures that limit senate terms (Bill S-4) and also pave the way for the election of senators. Debate over Senate reform will likely continue.

HOW FEDERAL LAW IS MADE

A proposed law is called a **bill**. There are three different kinds of bills: government, private member's, and private. All bills are not created equal—successful navigation through Parliament's legislative labyrinth depends to a large extent on who has sponsored the voyage.

Government bills are introduced by Cabinet members and concern national matters. Only this category of bill can involve spending public money or imposing taxes. Not surprisingly, government bills almost always pass. This is because the legislation in question has the support of the governing party, which can take advantage of the principle of party loyalty to ensure passage.

Private members' bills are sponsored by either backbench MPs (members of the governing party who do not sit in Cabinet) or opposition MPs. These bills are normally used to propose an alternative to existing government policy or to embarrass the government into action, so they are usually defeated or sidelined by the governing party. It is only because of parliamentary reforms approved in 1998 that these bills are even allowed to be discussed. If a private member's bill ever hopes to pass into law it must have strong public support and relate to a national concern. For example, for years some people have believed that Canada should have a national holiday in February called Heritage Day. Every now and then a private member's bill surfaces to propose such a holiday.

Private bills are always introduced in the Senate and almost always pass. They deal with minor issues, such as professional designations, that concern a person or a group of people—for example, authorizing the Canadian Institute of Chartered Accountants to use the professional designation of "chartered accountant."

The overwhelming power of a governing party to control the legislative process has caused many MPs and members of the public to criticize this practice and has led to some parliamentary reform, but the Cabinet remains a dominant force in setting the legislative agenda.

The various kinds of bills must all pass through Parliament and the Senate for approval before becoming law. Figure 4.2 summarizes the process. Once a bill receives royal assent, the bill becomes an act and is given a statute number. In theory, the Queen, through the governor general, could withhold assent and refuse to sign the bill, preventing it from becoming law. This has never happened in Canada. The Queen could also withdraw her assent within two years, but this has never happened either. The relationship of the Crown to the political leader was clarified in 1926, through a series of events that became known as the King–Byng Affair. Prime Minister William Lyon Mackenzie King, leading a new minority government, asked Governor General Lord Byng to dissolve Parliament, after losing the support of the Progressive Party over a Custom Department scandal. Byng refused, and asked Conservative leader Arthur Meighan to form a government instead. Within days, the Meighan administration was defeated on a motion of non-confidence. In the election that followed, King's Liberals were vaulted into a majority. The incident ended any uncertainty regarding the deference of governors general to the wishes

bill
a proposed law

government bill
a bill proposed by a member of Cabinet

private member's bill
a bill proposed by a non-Cabinet MP

private bill
a bill proposed by a senator

FIGURE 4.2   A Federal Bill Becomes Law

First Reading

The bill is introduced by a minister in the House of Commons. It is printed and copies are given to all MPs.

↓

Second Reading

MPs debate the bill and take a vote on its general principles. If it passes, the bill is referred to a committee. If it is defeated, the bill is dead.

↓

Committee Stage

The bill is examined in detail by a committee made up of MPs. The committee may get experts to provide information related to the bill and help improve it.

↓

Report Stage

The committee returns the bill and proposed amendments to the House of Commons. MPs debate and vote on the amendments.

↓

Third Reading

The House of Commons debates and votes on the bill as amended. If it is defeated, the bill is dead.

↓

Senate Approval

The bill goes through the same process in the Senate. If amended by the Senate, the bill returns to the House of Commons to be passed again. If it is defeated, the bill is dead.

↓

Royal Assent

The governor general approves the bill, and it becomes law.

Note:

Bills of major significance that are defeated during the reading stages in the House of Commons are interpreted as the government losing the confidence of the House. Thus, the government is expected to resign, thus dissolving Parliament and triggering an election.

Bills defeated in the Senate do not imperil the sitting government, since it is responsible only to the House of Commons.

of Canada's elected representatives, and led to the passage of the *Statute of Westminster* (discussed in chapter 3).[6] As a result, royal assent is only a formality. The governor general's role is merely ceremonial and carries no political power.

The Judicial Branch

Courts exist to enforce the principle of the rule of law. This means that all government actions must be authorized by law and there must be specific legal authority for the actions taken by government. As explained in chapter 1, this principle is essential to our democratic system and ensures that no government official is above the law.

The **judicial branch** of government consists of the court system, which helps to legitimize the rule of law and also supports the powers of the federal and provincial governments as identified in the *Constitution Act*.[7] At the federal level, the judicial branch consists of the Supreme Court of Canada, the Federal Court of Appeal, the Federal Court, and the Tax Court of Canada.

judicial branch
the branch of government that consists of the court system

The Supreme Court consists of nine judges, including the Chief Justice, who are appointed by the federal government. Three judges must come from Quebec, but appointment of the rest is based only on custom: three are usually from Ontario, two from the West, and one from the Atlantic provinces. The judges may serve until they are 75 years old.

The Supreme Court is the final court of appeal in Canada, and its decisions are binding on all the lower courts, including those of the provinces. The Supreme Court also serves a political purpose in that it facilitates the operation of the federal system by deciding which level of government—federal or provincial—has constitutional jurisdiction, in addition to upholding individual and group rights guaranteed under the *Canadian Charter of Rights and Freedoms*.[8] In recent years, the Supreme Court has increasingly been hearing Charter challenges—that is, cases that deal with alleged violations of Charter rights and alleged unconstitutional legislation and government policy. One famous case in this regard has involved the legal right of Quebec to separate from Canada (discussed in chapter 3).

Supreme Court decisions, which are separate from and independent of government, occasionally force governments to either withdraw or modify proposed legislation, or to compensate individuals and groups whose constitutional rights have been violated. For example, in the past, prisoners were not allowed to vote in elections. Since the passage of the Charter in 1982, which lists voting as a democratic right of Canadian citizens, prisoners have successfully challenged the denial of this basic right and won the right to vote.

The Federal Court hears cases concerning such areas as federal taxes, patents, and copyrights. The Tax Court hears appeals on cases that concern the Income Tax Act,[9] the Canada Pension Plan, the goods and services tax, and so on.

STRUCTURE OF THE PROVINCIAL GOVERNMENTS

The structure of the provincial governments is parallel to that of the federal government, with the notable exception that there is no upper chamber in the legislative branch. It can be divided into the same three branches (see figure 4.3 for Ontario's government structure).

The Executive Branch

executive branch (provincial)
the branch of government that includes the monarch's representative (lieutenant governor), the elected head of state (premier), and the Cabinet

At the provincial level, the **executive branch** includes the lieutenant governor (who represents the Queen), the premier (sometimes called the "prime minister" in Quebec), and the Cabinet (sometimes called the Executive Council in Ontario). Cabinet members are chosen by the premier and must be elected members of the provincial legislative assembly. The lieutenant governor is formally appointed by the governor general, but the prime minister actually chooses the person for this position. The method of appointment hearkens back to Confederation. Federal politicians such as Prime Minister John A. Macdonald thought that by choosing the Crown's representative in each province, the federal government would be able to prevent provinces from acting contrary to the wishes of Ottawa. Under the *British North America Act* (BNA Act), lieutenant governors were given the power to reserve (hold) or disallow laws passed by provincial legislatures. However, provinces increasingly challenged this view, arguing that their relation with the Crown gave them political power that was similar, rather than subordinate, to that exercised by the federal government.[10]

Again, the lieutenant governor's role is mostly ceremonial (for example, he or she opens the Legislative Assembly), and key political decisions are made by the premier and Cabinet.

FIGURE 4.3   Structure of the Ontario Government

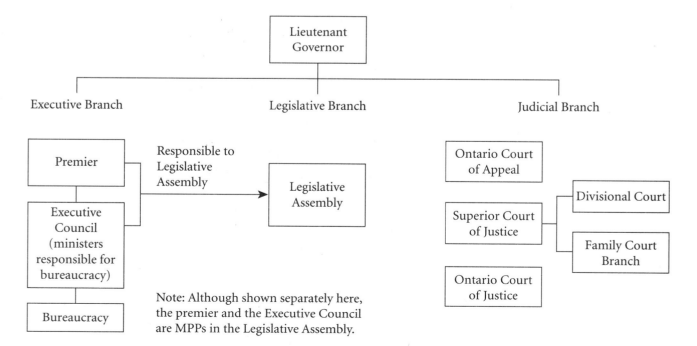

Note: Although shown separately here, the premier and the Executive Council are MPPs in the Legislative Assembly.

The three territories are officially administered by the federal government, which is represented by a commissioner for each territory. In reality, the commissioner has much the same role as that of the lieutenant governor of a province. The territories each have an elected Legislative Assembly made up of a premier and MLAs, but these governments operate based on consensus rather than on party-based confrontation. The premier and Cabinet are chosen by fellow members of the Legislative Assembly by secret ballot.

The Legislative Branch

The provincial **legislative branch** is called the National Assembly in Quebec and the Legislative Assembly in all other provinces. The provincial governments differ from the federal government in that they have a unicameral (or one-House) legislature. The Legislative Assembly has its counterpart in the federal House of Commons, but has no upper chamber that corresponds to the Senate.

Elected representatives of provincial governments are known as members of the provincial Parliament (MPPs) in Ontario, members of the Legislative Assembly (MLAs) in other provinces except Quebec, and members of the National Assembly (MNAs) in Quebec. The number of sitting members in each of the provinces and territories varies in proportion to the population of the province or territory. An Ontario provincial election occurring after August 2004 will reflect federal electoral boundary changes. These changes will increase the number of ridings and hence the number of MPPs to 107 from 103.

legislative branch (provincial)
the lawmaking branch of government, called the National Assembly in Quebec and the Legislative Assembly in all other provinces

HOW PROVINCIAL LAW IS MADE

The legislative assemblies of the provinces pass laws using much the same process as Parliament, except that there is no provincial equivalent to the Senate: there are three readings, a committee stage, final debate, final vote, and, finally, royal assent by the lieutenant governor. Government bills concern provincial matters and are introduced by Cabinet ministers. Private members' bills also concern provincial matters and are introduced by any other MPP. Private bills usually concern a person or corporation and can be introduced by any MPP, but are often introduced by the MPP for the particular person or corporation's riding.[11]

The Judicial Branch

This branch of government consists of the provincial courts, which do not have any real political power but uphold the laws made by the legislative branch. The judicial branch structure varies from province to province, so the names of individual courts and divisions also vary. Each province has a Superior or Supreme Court that has trial and appeal divisions. The trial division often includes small claims, family, and other courts. There may also be civil and criminal divisions. As well as the Superior Court there are provincial courts, which may also include family, small claims, youth, and other courts. Judges are appointed by the provinces.[12]

STRUCTURE OF MUNICIPAL GOVERNMENTS

The third level of government is municipal or local government. As mentioned in chapter 2, the Canadian constitution gives the provinces the responsibility for municipal governments—the municipalities themselves have no constitutional powers. It is at each province's discretion whether to create local governments and also what responsibilities municipal governments will have. Usually, local governments are responsible for such services as roads, police, firefighting, sewers, water, garbage collection, and so on. Schools are usually maintained separately by a school board. In Ontario, local governments are managed by a provincial law called the *Municipal Act.*[13]

municipal council
the governing body of a municipal government

Because municipal governments are a provincial responsibility, their structure varies widely. However, most tend to have a simple structure that includes only one elected body of representatives (generally with no political party affiliation)—the **municipal council**—which combines legislative and executive roles. Typically the municipal government consists of this council and its staff. The size of the council depends on the size of the municipality. There are several categories of municipality: city, town, village, rural municipality, county, or regional, district, or metropolitan municipality. Some councils have as few as 3 members, while in 2007 Toronto's council had one mayor and 44 members. Generally a mayor heads the council, although he or she may also be a reeve (in rural municipalities), a warden (in a county), or a chair (in a regional municipality). Council members are elected by ward (the municipal equivalent of a riding) and are known as councillors or aldermen (the term "aldermen" is falling out of favour since many are women). Municipal

bylaw
a local or municipal law

governments pass local laws, called **bylaws**, as well as supervise local services and hire staff for those services.

In recent years several provinces have taken measures to decrease the number of municipalities in an effort to cut costs and reduce duplication of services. Ontario is one province that is significantly decreasing the number of municipalities, as witnessed by the formation of the Toronto "megacity" by amalgamating seven municipal governments in 1997.

Councils can appoint citizens to various committees to make decisions on specific responsibilities, such as local roads, recreation, libraries, water, sewers, garbage collection, firefighting, police services, public transportation, and so on. The day-to-day running of the local government is generally handled by staff organized into various departments, which are managed by department heads reporting to either a clerk or chief administrative officer (CAO) of the municipality. The departments, for example, could be the recreation department, public works department (water, sewers, and roads), fire department, and so on. The clerk or CAO reports directly to council (see figure 4.4).

Local governments can be a major contributing factor to our quality of life since they are responsible for administering the services and programs we enjoy every day. In recent years some provincial governments have downloaded more and more responsibility for services to local governments without making sure they have adequate money to provide these services. Examples of areas in which this downloading has occurred include local roads, transportation, public housing, and emergency services such as ambulance. Unfortunately, despite their importance in our everyday lives, local governments are rarely given the credit and attention they deserve.

FIGURE 4.4   Example of a Municipal Government Structure

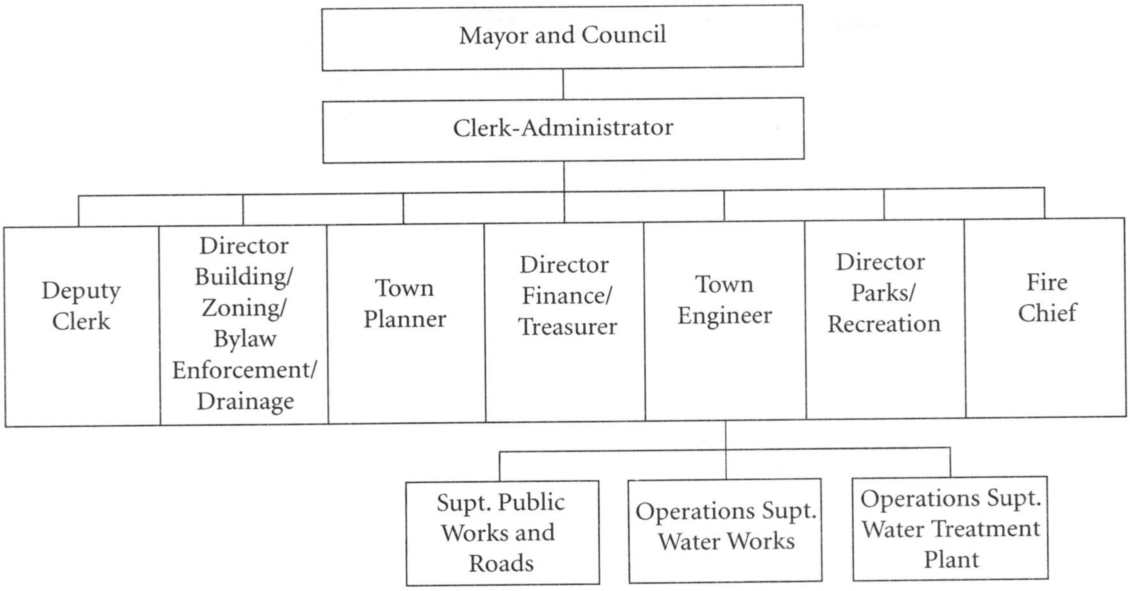

```
                        ┌──────────────────────┐
                        │   Mayor and Council   │
                        └──────────┬───────────┘
                        ┌──────────┴───────────┐
                        │  Clerk-Administrator  │
                        └──────────┬───────────┘
```

Deputy Clerk	Director Building/ Zoning/ Bylaw Enforcement/ Drainage	Town Planner	Director Finance/ Treasurer	Town Engineer	Director Parks/ Recreation	Fire Chief

Supt. Public Works and Roads	Operations Supt. Water Works	Operations Supt. Water Treatment Plant

Source: Reprinted with permission from *Bradford West Gwillimbury Community Profile* (Town of Bradford West Gwillimbury, 1998), p. 7.

This may be due, in part, to the tendency of mass media to focus on provincial and federal issues, in spite of the fact that the day-to-day operation of these levels of government remains at a distance from most citizens. Consider the impact that municipal services have on you every day. Did you shower this morning? The heat, electricity, and water you use most likely are managed by a local utility. By what routes do you travel to class each day? Most of the roads, traffic lights, and signs in municipalities have been established and maintained by them. Do you plan to clean the house or go for a bike ride in the park this evening? Garbage pick-up and the maintenance of local parks also constitute a significant part of the services provided by your municipality. Ironically, of the three major levels of government, municipal elections draw the lowest voter turnout. Consider this the next time municipal elections are held!

How Municipal Bylaws Are Made

The process of passing bylaws is not nearly as complicated as the process of passing federal and provincial laws. The municipal council votes on bylaws proposed by its members and staff of the municipality and passes those that have the support of a majority of council members.

Like their federal and provincial counterparts, municipalities pass legal statutes (laws) to carry out their activities. These statutes can manifest themselves either as bylaws or as resolutions. Although similar in most respects, bylaws are understood as more formal in character, whereas resolutions are understood as a statement of a council's intention respecting a specific subject. For example, it would make sense to pass a bylaw imposing fines for parking violations, whereas a resolution of council would suffice to recognize the achievements of a local sports team. Passing bylaws and resolutions is similar to federal and provincial processes already discussed.

In deference to these processes, the tradition of three readings is paid lip service, although in practice it is simply stated as having occurred, rather than actually taking place. Proposals are forwarded to council, either by councillors themselves, their constituents, or particular committees of council. The proposal may be discussed, debated, and referred to a committee for comment and report, and must ultimately receive the approval of a majority of council before it can be enacted.[14] The following vignette may help illustrate the point.

Your college is located in a high-traffic area, away from any traffic lights or pedestrian crossing. You and many other students are frequent users of a jogging trail across the street from your campus, but it is often too dangerous to attempt access. A crosswalk would go a long way to solving your dilemma. Being an astute political observer, you first gather a petition of fellow students, staff, and area residents to present to your local councillor. He or she, in turn, forwards the request to the city clerk, who places it on the agenda for the upcoming council meeting. Council, at the meeting, directs the department head of public works and roads to study the feasibility and cost of completing this project. Once completed, the report and its recommendations are sent back to council, and the matter is tabled for discussion at the next council meeting. It is budget-setting time and some councillors object to the cost, but your councillor points out that the popularity of the jogging path means that more and more students are crossing the road, and that their safety should be paramount in council's mind. At the same meeting, council hears a deputation from a local trucking firm opposed to the crosswalk, saying it will impede traffic flow in the area. Council agrees to refer the matter back to the roads department, so that it can study whether, in fact, this is the case. Will the bureaucracy never end!

After much passionate debate, and amid the din of cheering students, council approves the crosswalk. A bylaw is then prepared, establishing the crosswalk, setting out the offence if motorists do not obey the new law, and stating that the penalty will be pursuant to the *Provincial Offences Act*. Once the bylaw is presented to council, given three readings, and passed, the public works and roads department is instructed to install the appropriate signs and markings and the police service is advised that this new law is in place and enforceable.[15]

Although fictitious, this example demonstrates the ability of municipal politics to accommodate and respond to local concerns, and its receptiveness to grassroots participation, whether by individuals or groups. All the same, it remains political.

FIRST NATIONS IN THE CANADIAN POLITICAL STRUCTURE

Members of First Nations in Canada have a unique, and many would say extremely disadvantaged, status in our current political structure.

In chapter 2, in the section on the division of powers, you may have noticed that Aboriginal peoples came under federal jurisdiction. Otherwise, the *British North America Act* made no mention of First Nations. In recent decades Canadians have witnessed First Nations' growing frustration with government, sometimes erupting into violent confrontations when peaceful negotiations have been unsuccessful. The idea of Aboriginal self-government has been steadily gaining support and has been instituted in parts of Canada (for example, Nunavut and Labrador).

This topic will be discussed further in chapter 5, but here we will briefly discuss some of the relevant history and context of the First Nations' relationship with the federal government and the rest of Canada.

> According to the *Indian Act*, a "band" is a body of First Nations for whom the government has set aside lands for their common use and benefit; for whom the government is holding moneys; and who have been declared a band by the governor in council for the purposes of the Act. ... (Note: The federal government does not recognize the term "First Nations" but identifies Native communities as "Bands.")[16]

Keep in mind as you read this section that the term "First Nations" covers diverse peoples, cultures, and traditions, and that it is dangerous—as well as naive—to assume that all these groups are the same and have the same goals. Canada has over 633 First Nations communities within its borders.[17] As well, since detailed coverage of the status of First Nations in the Canadian political structure is beyond the scope of this book, this section greatly simplifies the history and issues that have led to their current status.

Historical Background

The history of First Nations since colonial times is a history of steady erosion of their rights and independence and of broken promises on the part of government. When the European colonists no longer needed the First Nations' help in war and trade, they began to see these peoples as liabilities and obstacles to expansion and development. Government initiatives in relation to Aboriginal peoples turned to assimilating them into the non-Aboriginal culture and "protecting" Native land by creating and controlling reserves on which Aboriginal peoples were to live. With the *Royal Proclamation of 1763*, Britain attempted to organize its newly acquired territory in North America after the defeat of the French in 1760. In this statute, the British government declared itself the only party that could make treaties with the Aboriginal peoples, and it also set down a treaty-making process.[18] This process accorded "nation" status to Aboriginal peoples, in essence legally recognizing them as autonomous, self-governing states.

After the new Canadian government was given responsibility for Aboriginal peoples under the BNA Act, it passed the *Indian Act*[19] in 1876, a statute that confirmed its control over their lands, the resources on those lands, and the lives of the people themselves. Under it, Native people became "wards of the Crown," diminishing their legal status to that accorded children and the mentally incompetent. Until the passing of this Act, First Nations had governed themselves and made their own decisions. Under the Act, the federal government imposed changes on how chiefs and councils were to operate, how bands were to select their leaders, and so on—basically, the government dismissed First Nations customs and replaced them with laws that were made without consulting the people they affected.[20] In addition, First Nations peoples were subject to the legislation of the province in which they resided.

The Act covered only registered or status Indians—the descendants of those people who were considered Indians when the Act was passed, a definition that excluded the Métis and Inuit peoples. Status Indians were entitled to certain services provided by the federal government (in the areas of health, education, and so on), but they could not vote in federal elections until 1961, when this condition was finally changed. Status could also be lost, as we will discuss below, with the result that some people were and still are excluded from the Act.

Revisions to the *Indian Act* in 1951 further restricted who was eligible for status. Status Indian women who married non-status men—even men of Aboriginal ancestry—automatically lost their status. The same condition did not apply to men who married non-status women. Losing status meant losing certain federal services, losing any private property on a reserve, and even losing the right to live on the reserve. This discriminatory condition was abolished in 1985 after much protest, and some First Nations members have regained their status.[21]

Over the years there have been many revisions to the *Indian Act*, but it continues to apply only to those people defined by the government as status Indians. It is no longer possible for status Indians to lose their status. You might think First Nations people would welcome an end to the status Indian category, but in fact most oppose abolishing it because they believe that doing so would lead only to more hardship for people who already face much higher levels of poverty, unemployment, and other socioeconomic problems than the non-Aboriginal population.

Treaties

In addition to federal statutes, First Nations' rights are based on their historical occupation of the land and on treaties signed with first the British and then the Canadian governments. These treaties—agreements between First Nations bands and the government of the day—first established peace and trade between the parties, and later increasingly involved transferring land to the government. With this loss of land—and the livelihood they made from this land—First Nations lost much of their autonomy.

Treaties fall into three main categories: pre-Confederation treaties, numbered treaties, and modern treaties. Pre-Confederation treaties were made with the British government before Canada became a nation. Many of the original documents have been lost or were poorly recorded. Eleven numbered treaties were made between 1871 and 1921 as Canada grew as a nation and built a national railway, and these required First Nations to accept settlement on reserves. Most of these treaties also promised the First Nations schools, farming equipment, money, and other benefits, many of which never materialized. Modern treaties are land claim agreements that have been signed since 1973.[22]

As you can imagine, the result is a patchwork of treaties across Canada, some of them dating back to the 1700s. Many of the promises made by the government have never been fulfilled, although government initiated the treaties. Nonetheless, the treaties continue to be recognized as legal documents by our judicial system. Treaty disputes continue to today and must be resolved on a treaty-by-treaty basis. Individual treaties are not always clear about the rights and responsibilities they confer. Further complicating matters are the following circumstances: some treaties contradict provincial regulations; written treaty provisions must be interpreted; unwritten promises that have survived as oral history have to be considered; and some provisions have since been overridden by federal legislation. These are only some of the factors that make settling disputes over land, Aboriginal rights, and other issues so complex.[23]

Funding

Most of the funding for services and programs provided to First Nations comes from the federal government, the majority of it from the Department of Indian Affairs and Northern Development. Some examples include educational programs (for example, band schools, First Nations culture and language programs), health care programs (for example, alcohol and drug awareness, mental health), child welfare, and economic development (for example, support for small businesses). Over the years, First Nations bands have been given more and more control over the day-to-day administration of these services, services that other Canadians receive through their provincial and municipal governments. However, funding for many First Nations programs, such as in the area of health care, still lags behind the level of funding that other Canadians enjoy.[24]

First Nations Rights

It is clear that the government's attempts over the years to assimilate First Nations into the non-Aboriginal population have failed.[25] Distinct Native groups still exist across Canada, just as the non-Native population is made up of distinct ethnic groups. After many years of resistance to and criticism of federal policy regarding First Nations, the Aboriginal and treaty rights of Indians, Inuit, and Métis were enshrined in 1982 in the *Charter of Rights and Freedoms* (section 25), although the nature of these rights and the definition of who is covered by this section of the Charter are not spelled out. The Meech Lake Accord and then the Charlottetown Accord—attempts at constitutional reform—proposed self-government for First Nations, but as we saw in chapter 3, both accords were defeated. A guarantee of the right to self-government—a major aim of First Nations—has still to be won.

Settling land claims is seen by many First Nations people as a way to gain some independence from the federal government, benefit from the resources of the land, and thus make some social and economic gains. The ability to make decisions at the band level, free of federal interference, is an important prerequisite to this independence. This does not mean that First Nations want to separate from Canada, but that they seek a new relationship with government that allows them to pursue their interests. Several local, regional, and national First Nations associations have been created to lobby for Aboriginal rights and to pursue the resolution of land and treaty claims. At the national level, the Assembly of First Nations is the most important organization. Some progress has been made, but much remains to be done for First Nations bands across Canada to achieve political, economic, social, and cultural independence.[26]

First Nations Government

The federal government recognizes First Nations government only at the band level, and the federal government defines what constitutes a band. The chief and band council make bylaws—called band council resolutions—for the community on a reserve.

Under the *Indian Act*, councils make decisions for the reserve in such areas as health, traffic, law and order, road and building construction and other local works, and so on. However, council resolutions may be denied by the federal government or negated by provincial laws. Enforcing resolutions is also difficult when there is no Native police force or other enforcement agency on a reserve.[27] For these and other reasons, the Assembly of First Nations and other Aboriginal organizations have made Aboriginal self-government their major goal.

Get Real!

FIRST NATIONS AND JUSTICE

I am a sovereign Mohawk man, and you have no jurisdiction over me.[28]

February 2007 marked the one-year anniversary of the standoff over a land claim in Caledonia, Ontario. Twelve months earlier, a small group of Aboriginal protesters from the Six Nations reserve began occupying the site of a housing development in that community, claiming that the land was theirs, and citing a 1784 land grant signed by the British Crown as evidence of that fact. (Their land claim was filed with the federal government in 1999 and is still pending. Currently, there are over 800 unsettled land claims in Canada.[29]) The provincial court granted the land developers an injunction compelling the protesters to vacate the site so that construction could resume, but when the Ontario Provincial Police tried to enforce it, the Aboriginals refused to leave their blockade. What followed was a tense and sometimes violent year of altercations, arrests, meetings (and cancelled meetings), court decisions (and reversals), and intense political debate.[30] One flashpoint was the arrest of Mohawk Trevor Miller for allegedly attacking a TV crew. Miller and his supporters refused to recognize the authority of the "colonial" courts and demanded instead he be released to his people. In June 2006, the dispute appeared to be moving toward a resolution when the provincial government bought the disputed land from the developers for $12.3 million and put it in trust until the land claim issue can be resolved. And in early August 2006, Ontario Superior Court Justice David Marshall ordered the provincial government to stop negotiating with the protesters until they had left the disputed land. A subsequent appeal by the province overturned Marshall's ruling. Since then, there have been periodic skirmishes between protesters on both sides, both peaceful and violent. Negotiations continue.

Why are disputes such as the Caledonia occupation so difficult to resolve? One reason centres on the question of jurisdiction: what government or agency is responsible for such matters? In Canada, First Nations (and their land claims) are governed at the federal level, but their communities are policed by the province. So when a protest is staged over a land claim issue (such as Caledonia, or Ipperwash and Oka before it), the police are called in to "keep the peace," and the provincial court system handles the legal manoeuvres, but neither entity has any power to address the larger problem of who has claim to the land. What's more, when the larger problem is a conflict over land ownership, protesters often feel they are not obligated to obey the rules of what they view as an oppressive and illegal occupying government (witness Trevor Miller's declaration of sovereignty). The result is often a frustrating and potentially dangerous impasse. In Caledonia, as the dispute drags on, the commissioner of the Ontario Provincial Police ultimately declared that resolving it is "beyond any scope that I could have," while the provincial government claims that such disputes are "solely the federal government's responsibility."[31] How do we reconcile Aboriginal legal issues when sovereignty, land claims, and traditional ideas of justice are at stake? Who is responsible? And what role should law enforcement play?

SUMMARY

Representative and responsible government are two fundamental principles of parliamentary democracy. These concepts manifest themselves in the structure of the federal and provincial governments, with their executive, legislative, and judicial branches of authority. Municipal governments are much simpler, though they affect our everyday lives more directly. Through the electoral process, Canadians have an opportunity to choose the party, platform, and person they feel will best represent their needs in the Canadian federation.

At the federal and provincial levels, proposed laws are called bills. There are various categories of bills, and the successful passage of a bill into law depends mainly on who initiates it. Similarly, municipalities enact bylaws and resolutions to put council decisions into action.

First Nations have a unique relationship with the federal government and in Canada's political structure, a relationship that has its roots in colonial history. Years of attempts to control Aboriginal peoples and assimilate them into the non-Aboriginal population have contributed to high levels of poverty, unemployment, loss of cultural identity, and other socioeconomic problems among First Nations. For these and other reasons, First Nations are seeking greater autonomy from government control and entrenchment of the right to self-government in the Canadian constitution. As we have seen in Get Real!, these demands are dealt with at both the local and national levels of government. We will be revisiting the topic of self-government in later chapters.

KEY TERMS

bill

bylaw

Cabinet

Cabinet solidarity

executive branch (federal)

executive branch (provincial)

government bill

legislative branch (federal)

legislative branch (provincial)

judicial branch

majority government

member of Parliament

minority government

municipal council

party loyalty

private bill

private member's bill

representative government

responsible government

triple E Senate

NOTES

1. Former Prime Minister Paul Martin made the "democratic deficit" a key issue for his government. See CBC News, "Martin Urges Parliamentary Reform, End to 'Democratic Deficit'" (October 22, 2002), available online at www.cbc.ca. Prime Minister Stephen Harper, for his part, has focused on Senate reform, election timing, and government accountability. See CBC News, "Harper Promises Bill to Elect Senators" (September 7, 2006), available online at www.cbc.ca. For Ontario government initiatives, see the Democratic Renewal Secretariat website at www.democraticrenewal .gov.on.ca/english.

2. However, the date can be changed if it conflicts with a "religious or culturally significant day." Such was the case with the 2007 election date, which was switched from October 4 to October 10 in order to avoid coinciding with an orthodox Jewish holiday. See CBC News, "Ontario 'Fixed' Election Date Moved Off Jewish Holiday" (February 7, 2007), available online at www.cbc.ca.

3. *Canada Elections Act*, RSC 1985, c. E-2, as amended.

4. For more details, see Elections Canada, *Election Handbook for Candidates, Their Official Agents and Auditors* (March 1, 2007), available online at www.elections.capol/can/ec20190_c2_e.pdf.

5. See Ontario, Ministry of Municipal Affairs and Housing, "Candidates," in *Municipal Elections 2006 Guide* (Toronto: Queen's Printer for Ontario, 2007), available online at www.mah.gov.on.ca/Page1510.aspx.

6. For a brief summary, see Claude Bélanger, "The King–Byng Affair" (2001), available online at www.marianopolis.edu/sites/library.

7. *Constitution Act, 1982*, RSC 1985, app. II, no. 44.

8. *Canadian Charter of Rights and Freedoms*, part I of the *Constitution Act, 1982*, RSC 1985, app. II, no. 44.

9. *Income Tax Act*, RSC 1985, c. 1 (5th Supp.), as amended.

10. Much of the early impetus for the provincial rights movement came from Ontario premier Oliver Mowat. For example, see Peter H. Russell, "Provincial Rights," in R. Douglas Francis and Donald B. Smith, eds., *Readings in Canadian History: Post-Confederation*, 6th ed. (Toronto: Thomson Nelson, 2002), 21-33; J.R. Miller, "Unity/Diversity: The Canadian Experience from Confederation to the First World War," in Francis and Smith, at 34-42. For a general overview, see R. Douglas Francis et al., *Destinies: Canadian History Since Confederation*, 4th ed. (Toronto: Thomson Nelson, 2000), 8 and 82-83.

11. For more information, see the website of the Legislative Assembly of Ontario at www.ontla.on.ca. Click on the link "Learning & Teaching."

12. Department of Justice Canada, "Provincial Courts" (October 20, 2005), available online at http://canada.justice.gc.ca/en/dept/pub/trib/pc .html#tp.

13. *Municipal Act*, RSO 1990, c. M.45.

14. Summary based on information from the Association of Municipal Managers, Clerks and Treasurers of Ontario (AMCTO).

15. This anecdote was put together with the assistance of Laura S. Lee, Clerk, Council Services, City of Orillia. The author wishes to thank her and the city for its permission to use its organizational chart.

16. Pamela Williamson and John Roberts, *First Nations Peoples*, 2nd ed. (Toronto: Emond Montgomery, 2004), 120.

17. Assembly of First Nations Brotherhood (www.afn.ca), cited ibid.

18. Williamson and Roberts, supra note 16, at 69-80.

19. *Indian Act*, RSC 1985, c. I-5, as amended.

20. Williamson and Roberts, supra note 16, at 106-108.

21. Max J. Hedley, "Native Peoples in Canada," in Kenneth G. Pryke and Walter C. Soderlund, eds., *Profiles of Canada* (Toronto: Copp Clark Pitman, 1992), 78.

22. Williamson and Roberts, supra note 16, at 80-82.

23. Williamson and Roberts, supra note 16, at 82-84; Hedley, supra note 21, at 75-77.

24. Williamson and Roberts, supra note 16, ch. 6.

25. Hedley, supra note 21, at 79.

26. Williamson and Roberts, supra note 16, ch. 7; Hedley, supra note 21, at 76.

27. Williamson and Roberts, supra note 16, ch. 7.

28. Quoted in Fiona Becker, "Mohawk Political Prisoner Challenges Jurisdiction of Colonial Courts," *Indymedia*, November 30, 2006, available online at http://publish.indymedia.org/en/2006/12/875953.shtml.

29. Figure cited by Indian Claims Commission. See CBC News, "New Law Expected to Speed Land Claims" (June 11, 2007), available online at www.cbc.ca.

30. For a timeline of the Caledonia land dispute, see CBC News, "Caledonia Land Claim: Timeline" (November 1, 2006), available online at www.cbc.ca.

31. Gregory Bonnell, "Keeping the Peace in Caledonia Need Not Mean Lawlessness: Fantino" (October 30, 2006), Canadian Press NewsWire.

EXERCISES

Multiple Choice

1. The structure and role of government can be divided into three major functions:

   a. to be elected, to carry out election promises, and to represent citizens

   b. to enforce the rule of law, to authorize government actions, and to give legal authority to those actions

   c. to uphold constitutional rights, to pass new laws, and to administer public services

   d. to govern, to make laws, and to enforce those laws

   e. to represent citizens, to make laws, and to hold elections

2. Canada's head of state is

   a. the governor general

   b. the Queen

   c. the prime minister

   d. the lieutenant governor

   e. the Senate

3. The judiciary exists to

   a. make laws

   b. uphold the legitimacy of government

   c. legitimize the law

   d. make constitutional amendments

   e. enforce the principle of the rule of law

4. Key political decisions are made by

   a. the prime minister or premier and Cabinet

   b. political parties

   c. the Senate

   d. the governor general

   e. the Queen

5. A majority government is formed when

    a. one party has more MPs in the House of Commons than any other party

    b. one party's MPs hold a majority of seats in the House of Commons

    c. the Official Opposition has a majority of MPs in the House of Commons

    d. the majority of MPs are backbenchers

    e. the majority of MPs are appointed to Cabinet

True or False?

_____ 1. If a political party does not win at least 155 seats in the House of Commons in an election, it automatically loses.

_____ 2. Cabinet solidarity refers to the principle of government members agreeing, at least publicly, on given policy matters.

_____ 3. Under the constitution, local governments are responsible for such services as roads, police, firefighting, sewers, water, and garbage collection.

_____ 4. The *Indian Act* and individual treaties govern the relationship between the federal government and First Nations.

_____ 5. Settling land claims is an important step toward Aboriginal self-government since this would give some First Nations economic gains and, ultimately, make them less dependent on the federal government.

Short Answer

1. Define "responsible government." How does it differ from "representative government"?

2. One criticism of Canada's political system is that far too much power is vested in the prime minister and Cabinet. What reforms might solve this problem?

3. What factors do you believe the prime minister should consider when choosing Cabinet ministers? What external factors might limit his or her choices?

4. Why has the Senate lost its credibility as an institution? What can be done to repair this image problem?

5. Why are First Nations seeking the right to self-government?

6. How do minority governments differ from majority governments? Which do you prefer, and why?

CHAPTER 5

Politics, Society, and Law Enforcement

CHAPTER OBJECTIVES

After completing this chapter, you should be able to:

- Describe how the three levels of government cooperate in law enforcement.

- Relate the evolution of public law enforcement in Canada to broader socioeconomic changes in Canadian society.

- Relate the political spectrum model to the major federal political parties.

- Describe the major characteristics of Canadian political culture.

- Demonstrate how political ideology informs the development of public policy.

- Describe some of the major issues currently facing the justice system.

- Use information in this chapter to forecast future trends for law enforcement in Canada.

- Analyze the impact of increased police activity on the political process and on democracy.

INTRODUCTION

Previous chapters have described how government structure and the political process have evolved in Canada and what this means in terms of the roles of the federal, provincial, and municipal governments. In this chapter we will see how these roles often overlap and affect one another in the area of law enforcement. We will then look at political and socioeconomic influences on law enforcement and the Canadian justice system. As we will discover, historical changes reveal much about current attitudes toward politics and the justice system.

Government activity should properly be viewed as organic in nature. It is a network where decisions in one area have consequences in another. Therefore, as you read, remain aware of these relationships. This will help you to put what you have studied into perspective.

GOVERNMENT RELATIONS

Recall from chapter 2 that the Fathers of Confederation anticipated a dominant role for the federal government, granting it blanket power over "peace, order and good government" and the ability to legislate in any areas not specifically mentioned in the constitution. The provinces were handed what were then considered to be minor areas of responsibility, such as education, health, and welfare. These were considered of little importance because at the time government usually did not fund or actively participate in running social programs. Instead, support for these areas was considered the responsibility of the individual, family, or local community and came from private charities and philanthropists. Increasing urbanization and industrialization after the turn of the 20th century and growing public expectations have subsequently enhanced the significance of these provincial areas. The federal and provincial governments are regularly at odds over which has jurisdiction in a particular area, and these increasing squabbles over political turf have come to characterize Canada's political culture.

Ironically, municipal governments are the weakest politically of the three levels of government, even though the public services they provide affect us more directly on a daily basis than either of the other two government levels. Further, even though municipal politics provides the greatest opportunity for citizen participation in government, it attracts little public notice most of the time.

The constitution provides for the coordination of law enforcement across Canada. The federal government is responsible for creating criminal law, while the provinces are responsible for administering and enforcing its provisions and for creating and administering civil law. Municipal policing services are an extension of this provincial authority. Disagreements over how to approach justice issues can put provincial initiatives at odds with federal ones; similarly, local initiatives can be at odds with provincial ones. The remainder of this chapter will examine some of the political, social, economic, and other influences on law enforcement.

Evolution of Government Services

Canada's population grew dramatically in the years following Confederation, from about 3.6 million to nearly 8.8 million in 1921.[1] As Canada moved into the 20th century and cities drew increasing numbers of people to industrial employment, the need for coordinated social services became acute. Existing private agencies lacked the resources and expertise necessary to meet the needs of urban-industrial society, and reformers began calling for government intervention in social services. Education in Ontario had become free, universal, and compulsory in 1871, and by the 1920s public health and social assistance were being regulated. The economic growth of Canada and the shift of the population to urban centres that began around the turn of the century were factors that led the provincial governments to assert themselves more. Provincial concerns about federal domination have existed ever since.

Public demand for government-funded social services considerably enhanced provincial authority in the federal system, since the vast majority of these areas fell within their constitutional jurisdiction. However, limited provincial taxing capacity made it difficult to fund the ever-increasing costs of providing these services. Matters grew worse during the Great Depression of the 1930s as unemployment and poverty dramatically increased and federal funds became necessary to meet the added costs of running relief programs. This set the stage for the later pattern of **cost sharing**, where the federal government "topped up" provincial programs in return for setting national standards in that area. During and after World War II, the federal government continued to dominate provincial actions by using its **federal spending power** to fund programs in areas outside its constitutional jurisdiction. Taken together, these events had the effect of centralizing power at the federal level, since the provinces subsequently became dependent on federal money for social program funding.

In the 1960s, the provinces began to reassert themselves in the Canadian federation, increasingly challenging Ottawa's dominant position. Beginning with Quebec's Quiet Revolution (see chapter 2) and spreading to other regions such as the West during the 1970s and 1980s, this more confrontational approach to federal–provincial relations has characterized Canadian politics up to the present day. Federal belt-tightening measures have aggravated the problem. As Ottawa has reduced its funding for social programs, provinces have called for more flexibility in the manner and means by which they deliver these services. Similarly, provincial government reductions in transfers to municipal governments have caused municipalities to either cut services or find new ways to fund them. In some communities, cost cutting has affected the quality of recreation programs, public maintenance, and emergency services as local politicians struggle to control costs while maintaining public services.

cost sharing
funding of provincial programs that combines federal contributions with provincial funding

federal spending power
the power of the federal government to raise the greatest share of tax revenues

Law Enforcement at the Three Levels of Government

As Canada grew and moved toward a more urban and industrial way of life, new social realities and subsequent public concerns spawned changes in the nature and operation of policing within the justice system.

Although jointly overseen by the federal justice and solicitor general departments and provincial attorneys and solicitors general, public law enforcement was for the most part left to individual communities to administer. The larger urban centres, such as Toronto and Montreal, were exceptions to the rule with their formal law enforcement systems. What has resulted from the constitutional division of powers is a sometimes confusing mix: the federal government creates laws governing the behaviour and activities of people and businesses; the provincial governments administer and enforce these laws, with some exceptions, through provincial agencies; and the municipal governments also enforce these laws through local police services, licensing, and so on.

The three levels of government often cooperate to safeguard the public safety of all Canadians. Better communication and coordination have become paramount concerns since the terrorist attacks on the World Trade Center on September 11, 2001. Thus, Canadian law enforcement participates in a larger international sphere, as a means of combatting threats from abroad. This cooperation provides for consistency and equity in enforcing the laws of Canada, especially in the prosecution of criminal offences. The federal enforcement agencies, described below, work in concert with the various provincial and municipal enforcement services in combined forces operations, a prime example of the three levels of government working together for the public good and sharing costs.

Governments determine the kinds of laws we have and to what degree they are enforced. Also, each level of government except the municipal level is permitted by the constitution to raise sufficient funds through taxes to pay for the cost of operating various programs and services. By provincial law, municipal governments can raise money through property taxes and through licence fees and fines.

The same applies to the administration of justice in the provinces. Again, by sharing in the operating costs, the federal government can greatly influence how justice is administered. At present, justices of the Supreme Court of Canada are appointed and paid for by the federal government; lower-court judges are appointed and paid for by the provinces. Other differences in the justice system exist in the areas of correctional services for adult and young offenders, and in public policy and protection relative to combatting organized crime, among others.

FEDERAL LAW ENFORCEMENT

As discussed in chapter 1, the evolution of the justice system in Canada was rather uneven up to Confederation. As the country matured, however, standardization and regulation were implemented to lend stability as the country grew and changed. Accompanying the economic and social changes was a gradual recognition of the importance of public policing to control crime and maintain civil order amid the transitions that were taking place in Canadian society. In 1873, Prime Minister John A. Macdonald, who was doing double duty as justice minister, supervised plans for a national police force "to bring law, order and Canadian authority to the North-West Territories (present-day Alberta and Saskatchewan)."[2] In doing so, Macdonald hoped to guard against American encroachment, maintain friendly relations with the First Nations peoples, and facilitate an orderly settlement of the region. Known initially as the North-West Mounted Police (NWMP), this national police force was renamed the Royal Canadian Mounted Police (RCMP) in 1920.

During World Wars I and II, the NWMP/RCMP conducted border patrols and surveillance of potential security threats. In 1932, it consolidated a number of other government services to form the Marine Section to give Canada a national presence in its territorial waters. The RCMP also helped to create and coordinate a national database providing resources such as fingerprints, a crime index, firearms registration information, a photo section, and forensic expertise to help police investigators across the country. Potential internal security threats, exemplified by the FLQ Crisis of 1970 in Quebec (in which radical Quebec separatists kidnapped British diplomat James Cross and Quebec labour minister Pierre Laporte and later killed Laporte), led to an expansion of security and intelligence operations. In

1984, these were formally separated from direct RCMP operations with the creation of the Canadian Security and Intelligence Service (CSIS). Today, the RCMP has policing responsibilities in every province and territory, including policing contracts in eight provinces, the three territories, and hundreds of municipalities.[3] The RCMP is administered by Public Safety Canada, formerly Public Safety and Emergency Preparedness Canada.

Other enforcement agencies organized and paid for by the federal government include the Immigration and Refugee Board of Canada, and Fisheries and Oceans Canada, which are administered by the appropriate ministries responsible for the area of jurisdiction. These agencies generally focus their efforts on their respective related federal laws, such as the *Immigration Act*,[4] the federal *Fisheries Act*,[5] and so on. Recently, the duties of Canada Border Services Agency officers have been extended to include enforcing *Criminal Code*[6] driving offences and other federal statutes. Along with other federal enforcement officials, customs officers have been given the powers and protection of peace officers as described in the *Criminal Code.*

It is clear that the policies developed by the federal government greatly influence the kinds of services provided by the provincial governments. Historically, the federal government, because it collects the majority of tax money, has determined the amount of money to transfer to each province for specific purposes. The lion's share is for social programs, particularly in the areas of health care and education, which are both provincial responsibilities. The amount of money transferred to the provinces generally depends on the provincial government's following the wishes of the federal government, which is often led by a different political party from the provincial government.

PROVINCIAL LAW ENFORCEMENT

Ontario and Quebec have their own provincial police services. The Ontario police service is administered through the provincial Ministry of Community Safety and Correctional Services, formerly the Ministry of the Solicitor General. Provincial police work through joint forces operations with the RCMP and municipal police services to ensure that major criminal activities such as drug trafficking, illegal immigration, and counterfeiting are investigated efficiently and cost-effectively.

The history of provincial policing in Ontario dates back to 1875, when the first full-time paid criminal detective was hired by the attorney general's office. The staff gradually increased, and in 1909 an order-in-council was passed in the provincial legislature officially creating the Ontario Provincial Police (OPP) force.[7]

The history of the OPP resembles that of the RCMP, most notably in the areas of professionalization and technological innovation. Pioneers in highway patrol, OPP officers used motorcycles, marked cruisers, and, after 1947, radio communication to enforce the province's *Highway Traffic Act*.[8] In fact, by 1956, 75 percent of provincial policing was taken up by this activity.[9] As with other government services, the OPP expanded greatly during the 1960s and 1970s. As we will see in coming chapters, the postwar period in Canada was a time of expansion in government services, including law enforcement. Police forces were able to keep up with technological changes as they emerged, and governments at all levels seemed ready, willing, and able to underwrite the additional costs. For example, this philosophy enabled the OPP to become the first force in North America to enforce traffic regulations from the air.[10]

Provincial governments seem to be intervening more and more in existing federal laws and policies. The federal *Young Offenders Act*,[11] for example, was widely criticized after its inception in 1984, leading eventually to its replacement with the passage of the *Youth Criminal Justice Act*,[12] which came into force on April 1, 2003. Now, young people who commit very serious criminal acts can be tried as adults. Less serious offences, however, may be settled through a number of alternative measures, such as local Youth Justice Committees. In 2001, the Ontario provincial government passed the *Parental Responsibility Act*,[13] which imposes a fine of up to $6,000 on parents to pay for property damage or loss caused by children under 18, unless the parents can prove that the damage or loss was not intentional or that they provided reasonable supervision of their children.

MUNICIPAL LAW ENFORCEMENT

police services board
civilian board that oversees a local police service

Municipal police services are administered by their **police services boards**, which consist of locally elected and appointed civilians. The board oversees the police service and establishes policies for managing the service, creates guidelines for dealing with public complaints against the police, approves operating budgets, and so on. It does not, however, deal with the day-to-day management of the police, which is done by the police service itself. A board can have as few as three members or as many as seven, depending on the size of the municipality.

INFLUENCES ON LAW ENFORCEMENT

Political Parties and the Political Spectrum

Do you think, like many people, that the only thing distinguishing one political party from another is its name? While some parties do share similar platforms, many observers use the terms **right wing** or **left wing** to describe a party's fundamental philosophy. These terms have their origins in France, after the revolution of 1789, when the new political assembly was shaped like a semicircle. Members who favoured the traditional social hierarchy and economic status quo sat on the right side, while those who supported social equality and the major economic changes this would necessitate sat on the left. Moderate members—ones who favoured a more balanced approach to government—sat in the middle. Over the years, these labels have been attached to broader political ideas, which can be portrayed in a linear model called the **political spectrum** (see figure 5.1).

right wing
a political attitude or philosophy that favours more individual freedom and less government intervention

left wing
a political attitude or philosophy that favours more government intervention to help achieve social equality

political spectrum
a model that shows political philosophy on a continuum from left wing to right wing

Today, "right" and "left" are generally associated with degrees of government involvement in the lives of citizens. Supporters of the right tend to prefer more individual freedom and less government intervention, particularly in the economy. This group thus supports measures such as the privatization of government-owned corporations and less government regulation of business in general. Those on the right—also known as neoconservatives—favour policies such as tax cuts, less social spending, and more emphasis on individual responsibility. This group also tends to support "law and order" agendas, including tougher law enforcement and stiffer

FIGURE 5.1   The Political Spectrum

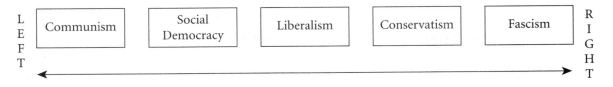

FIGURE 5.2   Major Canadian Political Parties on the Political Spectrum

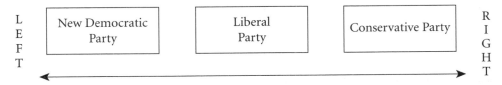

penalties for convicted criminals, a topic we will return to in the section "Law Enforcement and the Political Spectrum." Those on the left favour more government intervention, particularly in economic matters, with the aim of achieving greater social equality of citizens and mitigating the effects of an unpredictable economy.

Figure 5.2 shows where Canada's major federal political parties sit in relation to one another on the domestic political spectrum (the Bloc Québécois, because of its philosophy based on French ethnicity and nationalism, does not easily fit into this model but tends to lean toward the left). On the international political spectrum, Canada is considered to be slightly left of centre in relation to the rest of the world.

POLITICAL PARTIES AND THE HISTORY OF CANADA

Since Confederation, Canadians have witnessed the rise and fall of the major federal political parties. A historical context not only enables us to recognize some of the political, social, and economic factors that led to their creation, but also helps to explain why some parties have shifted their position on the political spectrum.

Only two parties have ever formed the federal government: the (Progressive) Conservative Party and the Liberal Party. Until almost the turn of the 20th century, federal politics was dominated by the Conservatives, created and guided by John A. Macdonald, Canada's first prime minister. Under his tutelage, the party took a pro-business attitude, combining an allegiance to Britain with a deep mistrust of the United States.

Conversely, the Liberals dominated Canadian federal politics during most of the 20th century, having held power for almost 70 of those years.[14] The party had its roots in a loose political coalition of reformers, who favoured more socially progressive policies than did the Conservatives and freer trade with the United States. Notable among their early leaders was George Brown, publisher of *The Globe* in Toronto. Despite its beginnings around Confederation, the Liberal Party did not really come into its own until Wilfrid Laurier assumed its leadership in 1887. Unlike the Conservatives, the Liberals were more open to relations with the United States and had a strong base of support in Quebec.

Aside from a smattering of protest parties, these two parties dominated the political landscape during Canada's first 60 years. English–French relations proved to be a sore point for both parties during this time. Episodes such as the execution of Louis Riel in 1885, the Manitoba Schools Question in the early 1890s (over the replacement of a dual Protestant–Catholic school system in Manitoba with a single Protestant one), and the Conscription Crisis of World War I created deep divisions between French and English Canada. Neither party seemed able to address this problem to the satisfaction of both sides. The Great Depression of the 1930s, however, temporarily shifted the political focus away from English–French tensions.

During the Great Depression, many people became frustrated with the inability of the established parties to deal with the economic hardships. This eventually led to the creation of a new party in 1932—the Co-operative Commonwealth Federation. This decidedly left-wing party evolved into the New Democratic Party in the early 1960s, and although it has never formed a federal government, many of the social policies it supported were adopted by governing parties (the Canada Pension Plan and universal health care, for example).

After World War II, many Western countries instituted social programs in health care, education, and social assistance. In Canada, the growth of social welfare was due to many factors, including a widespread fear of the economy sinking to Depression-level depths again after the war, labour shortages during the war that helped labour unions become more powerful, and a booming wartime economy that could afford to institute more government services. This shift to the left of the political spectrum lasted until the 1970s, when the political winds of conservatism began to reappear. Once more, the slow reaction of the existing political parties to this change proved to be the catalyst for the creation in 1987 of the Reform Party, which changed its name in the spring of 2000 to the Canadian Alliance and then merged with the Progressive Conservative Party in 2003 to become the Conservative Party. Created originally as a party supporting Western Canadian concerns, the Conservatives espouse right-wing policies such as cuts to taxes, cuts to social programs, smaller government, and stricter controls on immigration.

The right wing has continued to gain momentum in recent years, although it has not yet won the allegiance of the majority of Canadians. Following the sponsorship scandal under Jean Chrétien's government, the Liberals, led by Paul Martin, held on to a shaky minority for a little over three years, before a non-confidence vote in the House of Commons triggered a federal election. That government was replaced by another minority, this time a Conservative minority under Stephen Harper. Harper's victory ended 12 years of Liberal rule in Canada.

LAW ENFORCEMENT AND THE POLITICAL SPECTRUM

"Tough on crime." "Law and order candidate." "Victims' rights."

Perhaps you have noticed such slogans and similar ones during recent political campaigns in your community. Where do they come from, and what informs their message? Most of us would agree that criminal behaviour in Canadian society is indeed a bad thing and every attempt should be made to prevent crime and preserve civil order. How a government chooses to go about these tasks reveals a lot about its ideological preferences.

The moral viewpoints of the political party in power have always had a major impact on the kinds of government services provided to Canadians. Each political party has its own views on how Canada should be managed and which government services should be given priority, including those that apply to public safety. For example, in spite of the current Conservative government's tough talk, federal corrections is moving away from mega-jails toward smaller institutions and rehabilitation, while some provinces have shut down smaller jails, opting for private mega-jails and a "get tough" approach, particularly in the area of young offenders. These different philosophies reflect ideological disagreements over how to deal with crime in society. These become clear when we look at where each political party in power sits on the political spectrum.

Right-wing ideology tends to emphasize self-reliance, individual responsibility, and a "survival of the fittest" attitude toward society. Therefore, issues of crime and punishment focus on making individuals accountable for the choices they have made—that is, "Do the crime, do the time." On the other hand, left-wing ideology emphasizes collective responsibility and sees the state as a means through which to overcome inequality and look after those who are unable to look after themselves. Thus, left-wing proponents see criminals as products of a social system that prevents them from achieving their potential. In the eyes of the left, "It's the system that's at fault."

Should governments spend more money on tracking down, prosecuting, and incarcerating criminals, or should they focus on improving the social conditions that lead to criminal acts? Left-wing ideology emphasizes the social problems, institutions, and policies that create an environment for crime. For example, in the fiscal year 2000–1, the latest year for which figures are available, it cost Canadians more than $11 billion to operate the criminal justice system. This included the costs of policing ($6.8 billion), adult corrections ($2.5 billion), the courts ($1 billion), legal aid ($512 million), and criminal prosecutions ($335 million). That works out to $362 for every Canadian citizen.[15] In 2004–5, the average cost to keep someone in a federal prison was $85,927 per year for men and $166,642 for women.[16] In Ontario in 2002–3 the costs were $56,000 for adult inmates and almost $124,000 for youth.[17] It is interesting to note that the average cost of maintaining offenders in the community (that is, keeping people out of the prison system by imposing sentences not involving prison time) is about $20,000 annually.[18] Research also shows that it can cost seven times more tax dollars to process an offender through the justice system and related government services than to invest in social programs that help at-risk youth. Such programs can reduce serious crime by 10 percent.[19]

There is no right or wrong answer here; rather, it is a question of resource allocation. Crime will always be a part of society. The question we as citizens should consider is what is the most efficient and effective way to mitigate crime and its consequences?

Canadian Political Culture

What does it mean to be Canadian? Beyond the obvious stereotypes of beer, hockey, and winter, people often find it difficult to define a national sense, or identity. While Canada is recognized internationally for the creation of, and continued participation in, peacekeeping, it also is well respected as a nation that embraces justice and respect in a multicultural context. Several political observers have suggested that we have developed these national character traits through experiences and realities that have forced us to compromise and cooperate, in order to accomplish tasks that would prove insurmountable to any one part of the country. This instinctive sensibility about ourselves helps shape our political culture.

political culture
the basic attitudes people
have toward each other,
the state, and authority

Political culture refers to "the basic attitudes people have toward each other, the state and authority, that in essence reflect the impact of history on a society's beliefs."[20] Canadian political culture has been and continues to be influenced by a number of factors. Our political views have been shaped by our history and geography and by the diversity of our population.

Canada evolved from former French and British colonies, all of which were carved from lands once occupied by First Nations peoples. The mutual agreement and cooperation necessary for Confederation and coexistence between these two dominant linguistic groups have infused Canadian politics with a tendency toward compromise, rather than confrontation, when disagreements appear.

REGIONALISM

Regional loyalties have always coloured the Canadian political landscape. Within our immense geography are several regions—notably, Atlantic Canada, Quebec, Ontario, the West, British Columbia, and the North—all with differing interests and viewpoints as to how the Canadian political system can and should function. These feelings have even manifested themselves through the formation of formal political parties, such as the Reform Party (now the Conservative Party) in the Western provinces, and the Parti Québécois and Bloc Québécois in Quebec.

Regionalism has been strengthened by economic disparity, some of which dates back to the time of Confederation. For example, the residents of such regions as the North, the Atlantic provinces (particularly Newfoundland and Labrador), and the predominantly agricultural prairie provinces (for example, Saskatchewan) face limited opportunities because of an inhospitable climate, a lack of development, diminishing natural resources, and other factors. Canadians have thus tended to relocate to areas that promise better opportunities, creating large urban centres whose residents have high expectations for a better life. The majority of immigrants also tend to settle in the major urban centres, where jobs and housing, schools, and other facilities are more plentiful. This concentration in a few major cities poses many challenges and creates social problems, not the least of which is a growing gap between the "haves" and the "have-nots." We see this shift occurring in the lower mainland of British Columbia, in the large cities of Alberta, and also in Southern Ontario, which is experiencing a dramatic growth in population. These regions tend to have low unemployment and a high cost of living. They also tend to have growing numbers of homeless people and more complex social problems.

AMERICAN INFLUENCE

Another way many people define "Canadian" is with the glib reply, "not American." This being said, they are often hard pressed to explain their statement in any more detail. Yet there is little doubt that Canada's geographic proximity to the United States has had a part in informing Canadian identity. Historically, Canada has adopted both bilateral and multilateral arrangements in its external relations, in an attempt to find a national position that both serves its interests and preserves relations with its powerful neighbour to the south.

Bilateralism is a political term referring to a relationship between two powers—in this case, Canada and the United States. We see this in operation when both countries sign agreements to coordinate border security or form commissions to fight pollution in the Great Lakes. *Multilateralism* refers to relations involving more than two powers. Canada has adopted this policy in circumstances where it feels that its interests might be overshadowed by American influence in a particular area. This was the case internationally, following World War II. Concern about overzealous anti-communist American policies prompted the Canadian government to foster alliances with other nations. Good examples of this approach are found in Canada's contribution as a founding member of the United Nations in 1945, and membership in NATO (North Atlantic Treaty Organization), in 1949.[21] Because our interests remain closely tied to those of the United States, it is sometimes assumed that we will follow their lead. However, as demonstrated by our refusal to support American military action in Vietnam in the 1960s, and more recently in Iraq in 2003, differences of opinion do exist. These can extend to areas of trade and culture.

The overwhelming barrage of American culture and the United States' close economic relations with Canada have blurred traditional differences between what is considered cultural preservation and what is considered economic protectionism. For example, after hearing a case brought to it by the United States, the World Trade Organization ruled in 1997 that Canadian laws aimed at protecting the Canadian magazine industry from American competition in the form of split-run magazines (US magazines that publish a Canadian edition) violated international trading rules. Subsequent agreements allow American publishers to sell up to 18 percent of their advertising space to Canadian advertisers, and as a whole the Canadian magazine industry continues to thrive.[22]

MULTICULTURALISM

Canada's political culture has also developed out of a long tradition of immigration, from the arrival of the First Nations to today. Our constitution recognizes two dominant European cultures—French and English—and confirms that Canada has two official languages. Although English–French conflict still exercises considerable influence on Canadian politics, Aboriginal voices, as well as those of many more cultures and communities, add new flavours to the political mix.

Traditional politics has also been influenced tremendously by the *Canadian Charter of Rights and Freedoms*,[23] which enshrines **multiculturalism** as a characteristic of Canadian society that is to be maintained and enhanced. The Charter has permitted citizens and individuals to participate in political decision making through the courts, forcing politicians to recognize constitutional guarantees in policy matters. Some critics have charged that this change has removed the spirit of compromise that characterized the politics of earlier times.[24] This debate demonstrates the ongoing evolution of political culture in Canada, and serves to remind us that although political culture is informed by past events, it cannot be held prisoner by them forever.

multiculturalism
cultural and racial diversity; in Canada, a constitutionally enshrined policy that recognizes the diversity of our population

Canada's multiculturalism policy aims to promote the full participation of *all* Canadians in our society, tolerance for diversity, and a reduction in prejudice. In spite of this, minorities still struggle for recognition and representation in a number of social areas. For example, of the 103 MPPs in the Ontario legislature, only 26 are women, and only 7 are visible minorities;[25] and of the 308 seats in Parliament, only 62 are held by women. Multiculturalism applies to everyone, not just to recent immigrants or particular ethnic groups. Note, however, that many First Nations members are not in favour of being lumped under multicultural policies (as they are in the Charter) because of the unique problems they face as a result of a history of colonization.[26]

FIRST NATIONS

Chapter 4 introduced some of the history of First Nations' relations with government, including some of the reasons for increased Aboriginal activism and desire for self-government. In the last decade Canadians have witnessed some serious confrontations between First Nations bands and law enforcement agents over land claims, traditional hunting and fishing rights, logging rights, and other issues. The standoff between police and Aboriginal protesters at Oka, Quebec over a land claim in 1990 and the dispute over fishing rights in Burnt Church, New Brunswick in 1999–2000 are only two examples.

It is important to remember that although the term "First Nations" encompasses many groups, it does not include the Inuit and the Métis. The Inuit people of the Far North, for example, have a very different lifestyle and cultural traditions from the Plains Indians bands. Even today, with the growing Aboriginal movement to address the social, economic, and other ills that have characterized the lives of many bands since colonial times, there are widely differing views on how to achieve these aims, including whether civil disobedience is justified to make their voices heard.

Aboriginal self-government
greater autonomy of First Nations to pursue their own political, social, cultural, and economic objectives with limited interference from the federal government

A substantial shift of responsibility for First Nations, including the administration of reserves and of government-funded services to reserves, is occurring as more and more bands win the right to **Aboriginal self-government**. We have witnessed this in Western Canada in the settling of large land claims and in the creation of First Nations police services on some reserves (for example, the Dakota-Ojibway Police Service of Brandon, Manitoba). More recently, the mostly Inuit Nunavut territory created its own court and corrections infrastructure and is planning its own police service.[27] These are truly historic steps in the First Nations fight for self-determination, but we must keep in mind that these steps do not solve the serious problems—low life expectancy, lack of basic infrastructure and government services, high unemployment, and low education levels, to name only a few—faced by Aboriginal peoples.

What exactly does Aboriginal self-government mean? It means that bands are allowed to pursue their own policies rather than government-imposed ones. Instead of reserves being simply places set aside by government for the purpose of controlling people, the reserves become communities that develop economic activities, services, infrastructure, and so on, for the benefit of their residents—just like any other community in Canada. However, note that overall control of reserve policy is still in the hands of the federal government as set down in the constitution. The right to self-government has yet to be added to the constitution (although

First Nations groups have been fighting for such an amendment for years). Despite obstacles, some of which go back almost 400 years, First Nations continue to strive for greater political, economic, social, and cultural independence.[28]

In practical terms, self-government will have effects on law enforcement and the justice system. Some of the changes already include Aboriginal police services (see below), which have been replacing the RCMP and OPP on reserves. Efforts are being made to recruit more people of Aboriginal descent as court workers, paralegals, justices of the peace, legal clinic staff, and so on. These measures are intended to bring elements of First Nations culture and custom to the justice system and make it more responsive to the needs of First Nations offenders. A new form of alternative justice—the sentencing circle—has been set up on some reserves. Sentencing circles, composed of community members, hear cases involving First Nations offenders that are considered better addressed at the community level than in the court system. The circle may impose a sentence that includes community service, counselling, or restitution to the victim in some form.[29]

First Nations Policing   First Nations policing is a relatively recent innovation in public law enforcement. It has evolved out of a desire on the part of Aboriginal communities to police themselves and a growing public understanding of the need for and benefits of policing that recognizes the unique traits of the many Aboriginal cultures. Beginning in the 1970s as a series of joint pilot projects, Aboriginal policing has developed into a complex system of operations that can involve individual communities, and the federal and provincial levels of government.

In 1991, the federal government passed legislation setting up the legal and bureaucratic framework for self-policing in Aboriginal communities across Canada. In 2000, 127 agreements were in place across Canada to facilitate these police services. The variety of treaties and diversity of communities defy absolute bureaucratic standardization; however, there are some general principles upon which all policing agreements are based. Because Aboriginal relations fall within federal jurisdiction, it is ultimately the responsibility of the federal solicitor general to work with Aboriginal communities to set up and manage policing services in each community. However, in many instances, provincial governments assist in funding, training, and administration.

Increasingly, First Nations police services are developing into organizations similar in structure and authority to those in non-Aboriginal areas. In northern Ontario, for example, the Nishnawbe-Aski Police Service is regarded as a regional service similar to those of York, Peel, and South Simcoe–West Gwillimbury. Although not subject to the provincial *Police Services Act*, the force trains its recruits at the Ontario Police College. Fifty-two percent of Nishnawbe-Aski's funding comes from the federal government, while the Ontario government makes up the remainder. In 2006–7, its budget totalled $18 million. The Nishnawbe-Aski Police Service currently employs 134 officers and over 30 civilian staff.[30]

SPECIAL INTEREST GROUPS AND CITIZENS' ORGANIZATIONS

In Canada, social movements have tended to be based around "region, workplace, and household."[31] For example, French nationalism (and the desire for Quebec separation) is probably the most significant regional movement in Canada. Other important movements include the labour (union) movement, environmentalism, multiculturalism, the women's movement, and the gay and lesbian rights movement. In recent years, globalism—the interrelationships among cultures and economies around the world—has been gaining momentum. Important political decisions cannot be made without considering their effects on others.

It has been said that "[t]he ideal of democratic governance is to ensure [that] citizens 'enjoy an ability to participate meaningfully in the decisions that closely affect their common lives as individuals in communities.'"[32] We have already discussed the danger of growing public apathy about politics. The perception that average citizens simply can't make a difference in politics has spawned a number of initiatives that attempt to reclaim political power. Known collectively as *direct democracy*, these activities seek to actively engage voters in holding politicians accountable between elections, and provide an avenue for citizen-driven legislation. For example, a *recall* allows voters who are not happy with their elected representative between elections to hold a vote on whether or not that representative should be allowed to continue to hold office. The vote occurs once a certain percentage (say, 20 percent) of signatures is gathered in that constituency. The *referendum* and *plebiscite* provide a means through which people vote directly on a specific issue. Normally, a referendum is considered as binding on a government; that is, politicians will follow the wishes expressed by the majority. A plebiscite is understood as providing information and guidance to officials, and the result is not considered as binding. Canada's most recent use of a national referendum came in 1992, when Canadians were asked to vote on whether to adopt the constitutional changes contained in the Charlottetown Accord. An *initiative* allows citizens to present a proposal directly to fellow citizens, who vote to decide whether it will become law. Again, a certain number of signatures must be gathered in order to get the proposal on the ballot.

While proponents of direct democracy argue that it empowers citizens, the concept is not without fault. Critics point out that in some respects, direct democracy hinders, rather than aids, representative democracy. For example, a recall prevents sitting politicians from making tough but necessary decisions such as tax increases or changes in services. It also undermines the fundamental principle of party loyalty, vital to parliamentary democracy. Referenda, while useful in some circumstances, often artificially polarize debate into a yes/no proposition, overshadowing equally important, but more complex, issues for consideration. Likewise, initiatives can in effect "seize the agenda" from an elected legislature, by introducing laws that may interfere with larger government policies and directions. In addition, initiatives speak to single issues; thus, their objectives may produce unintended consequences that negatively impact citizens, hindering them from achieving their intended purpose. One example of the ambiguity of direct democracy was evident in the 2003 voters' recall of California Democratic governor Gray Davis, which resulted in the election of movie star and Republican candidate Arnold Schwarzenegger. Davis was recalled because of California's crumbling public services, in spite of the fact that prior citizen initiatives contributed to the state's financial problems![33]

In a democratic state, politicians are supposed to consider all points of view, but there remains the danger that when some voices become too loud they drown out other voices or cause them to be ignored altogether. As we have seen throughout the first half of this text, Canada owes much of its enviable quality of life to its tradition of consultation and compromise. It is important to keep this in mind when considering the viability of direct democracy here.

Government Downsizing and Public Opinion

We pay various forms of taxes to the three levels of government to pay for the services they provide. Federal and provincial income taxes are based on the income earned by individuals and businesses. Other taxes include the federal goods and services tax (GST), provincial sales tax (PST) in all provinces except Alberta, and local property taxes based on an assessment of the municipal property residents own, which is generally determined by the market value. Governments also raise revenue by assessing fees for various licences and permits, including business, vehicle, hunting, fishing, and firearms, among others. As well, special programs such as employment insurance and the Canada Pension Plan are funded by employer–employee payroll deductions.

It seemed in past years that the cost of operating government programs was of no concern and that the money necessary to pay for them was easily attainable. Only in recent years have Canadians begun to realize just how indebted they are due to government spending and taxation, and only recently have governments begun to balance their budgets. Interestingly, municipal governments, by provincial law, cannot run deficits (spend more than they collect in taxes)—they establish a working budget and then assess the cost against the local ratepayers (taxpayers).

There exists a widespread perception that government waste and inefficiency during the 1970s and 1980s led to large annual deficits and accumulated public debts during this time. While this is partly the case, there were other factors that led to the fiscal crisis, resulting in government cutbacks and downsizing in the decade that followed. First, the extremely high interest rates of the '70s and early '80s (at one point, 21 percent) greatly compounded the charges governments had to pay on the money they borrowed. Secondly, the burden of taxation shifted from the corporate sector to individual taxpayers. Thus, citizens have found themselves shouldering a larger share of the tax burden than was previously the case. As other countries have lowered their corporate tax rates, Canada has been forced to follow suit. Finally, an ideological swing to the political right during the late 1980s and early 1990s changed public perceptions about the role and purpose of government. The public embraced tax cuts and less government involvement in our lives, resulting in the downsizing and privatization of many public services.[34]

Policing in Canada has not been immune from these government initiatives to save money. Police budgets are now coming under much more scrutiny than in the past, while police forces are expected to maintain service and adapt to increasingly sophisticated criminal activities. The threats of organized crime and Internet fraud require cutting-edge computer technology and surveillance equipment—expensive propositions for cash-strapped agencies.

As an example, in 2007, Toronto faced what the mayor termed a budget crisis—a deficit so severe that the local president of the Board of Trade said, "We are frightened for Toronto's future."[35] This led to severe cost cutting, a lawsuit designed to win more support from the provincial government, and a 3.8 percent increase in property taxes. By contrast, funding to the Toronto Police Service increased from

$752 million in 2006 to $785 million, a 4 percent increase. Of the $2,174.60 paid in property taxes by the average Toronto homeowner in 2007, $531.52 went to policing.[36] As argued by the police service, preserving law and order costs a lot of money. The salary for a first-class constable in Toronto in 2007 was $71,522.[37] Salaries account for over 90 percent of the service's budget. To put this in perspective, a leap year's extra day (February 29) can cost the police service an additional $1 million to operate!

The issue of "blank cheque" funding for police services is often justified with the adage "Crime doesn't take holidays." While this is no doubt true, we as citizens have to remember that our tax dollars pay for policing and other services, and bigger budgets in the public sector present politicians with the dilemma of either cutting service in other areas or raising our taxes to cover the additional cost.

At the same time, reductions in the number of criminal offences in Canada have caused some politicians to question the need for increased police budgets. Statistics show that Canada's overall crime rate has been declining for more than 10 years, with 2005 figures showing a further 5 percent drop from the previous year.[38] However, as experts point out, this trend may be due to Canada's aging population and the current economic boom. Statistically, crime rates tend to be higher in the 15-24 age group, which is now a relatively small percentage of Canada's population.

Despite these data, concern for public safety and security have remained hot issues. Booming sales of alarm systems and anti-theft devices, as well as a marked growth in private security (for example, corporate and private security guards), suggest that Canadians are feeling less, not more, safe. An aging workforce and budget restraints have led to chronic shortages of police officers, accelerated the growth of private law enforcement, and forced large police services to reorganize in an attempt to cut costs and improve efficiency. For example, the OPP has reconfigured its operations from 17 to 6 regions (encompassing 93 detachments) across the province, while the RCMP has created 4 regions and eliminated subdivisions, creating geographical districts. Despite recent hiring, past budget cuts have left the number of Toronto police officers fewer than what it was in 1993.[39] While cost savings and efficiency lie at the heart of these initiatives, it is still too early to assess whether they are achieving these goals.

POLICE RESPONSES TO A CHANGING SOCIETY

community policing
approach to policing
based on the police and
the community working
together

The influences mentioned have caused policing services to rethink and reorganize the way they do business, and to recruit personnel that mirror the people they serve. In addition, **community policing** has become commonplace all across Canada. Community policing is based on a belief that the officer on the street and members of the community can work together to prevent crime and resolve disputes. This approach emphasizes greater communication between police and residents, more input on local issues from rank-and-file officers and the public, the importance of having a police force that reflects the diversity of the surrounding community, and a more people-oriented approach to policing in general.[40]

The Ontario *Police Services Act*[41] sets out six principles on which police services are based. Note how the spirit of community policing is contained in these principles.

1. **Declaration of principles.** Police services shall be provided throughout Ontario in accordance with the following principles:

   1. The need to ensure the safety and security of all persons and property in Ontario.

   2. The importance of safeguarding the fundamental rights guaranteed by the *Canadian Charter of Rights and Freedoms* and the *Human Rights Code.*

   3. The need for co-operation between the providers of police services and the communities they serve.

   4. The importance of respect for victims of crime and understanding of their needs.

   5. The need for sensitivity to the pluralistic, multiracial and multicultural character of Ontario society.

   6. The need to ensure that police forces are representative of the communities they serve.

Following these principles benefits police services as well as the community, because officers who reflect their community and behave professionally receive more respect and cooperation from the public. Also note that being representative of the community not only means having more officers who share the cultures and ethnicities of community members, but also having more female officers.

Most citizens have a limited understanding of how different policing is in the 21st century from what it was a generation ago. Policing is no longer simply a matter of responding to crimes after they have occurred. Officers are involved in school and community-based programs, such as Crime Stoppers and Neighbourhood Watch, to deter crime, and in victim assistance programs that provide support for victims of crime. In addition, police services have made concerted efforts to be sensitive to, and representative of, the social and ethnic diversity of the citizens in their respective communities. In Toronto alone, in 2006, police officers completed over 6,400 community relations presentations.[42] Efforts are ongoing to actively recruit officers from historically underrepresented groups, including people of colour, women, and Aboriginal peoples. Police forces in large urban centres are attempting to form positive links with community groups representing a wide range of interests in an effort to gain their support. In 2007, the Toronto Police Service carried out recruitment drives in the city's Asian, gay, lesbian, and transgendered communities.[43]

Police officers have expressed concern that politicians are out of touch with the reality of police work. Police want to have greater input and influence in political decisions that affect them. Politicians and members of the public have been slow to acknowledge the greatly increased workload now expected of individual officers. Groups such as the Canadian Association of Chiefs of Police, the Ontario Association of Chiefs of Police, the Ontario Provincial Police Association, and the Ontario Association of Police Officers are making their positions known on a variety of justice-related issues. Through these and other associations, the police are now taking a much more active role by publicly questioning political decisions. However, this political activity has its limitations in a free and democratic society. As will be discussed in chapter 8, critics charge that this greater political activism threatens the integrity of civilian authority over police and the fundamental principles of elected representation.

Get Real!

DO POLICING AND POLITICS MIX?

A police state is one where police eschew any thought of political neutrality and indeed intervene on the side of those who do what the police want.[44]

Eye Weekly magazine called it "Prelude to a Police State." In *Eye's* October 9, 2003 edition, former Toronto mayor John Sewell lambasted the Toronto Police Association Board for its decision to take out a full-page ad in *The Globe and Mail* endorsing Ernie Eves in the upcoming provincial election. The controversial ad copy read: "Help Keep Ontario Safe. On October 2nd, vote for Ernie Eves and the P.C. candidate in your riding." Sewell cited the ad as evidence of the "politicization of the Toronto police" and filed a formal complaint at City Hall. It went nowhere, but the Police Services Board later determined the endorsement was illegal under the *Police Services Act*.[45] Section 46 of the Act states: "No municipal police officer shall engage in political activity, except as the regulations permit."[46] Additionally, regulation 554/91 states that police officers can speak freely about any issue "as long as the police officer does not, during an election campaign, express views supporting or opposing ... a candidate in the election or a political party that has nominated a candidate in the election."[47] It seems cut and dried. But in 2006, the Ottawa Police Association said it would publish a list of candidates it supported for the upcoming mayoral and city council races.[48] Later that year, Prime Minister Stephen Harper announced plans to appoint police officers to the panels that recommend candidates for judges to be appointed by the federal government. Harper said he wanted to appoint judges who would further his law-and-order agenda and make the country's communities safer.[49] The Toronto Police Accountability Coalition responded that it was "very bizarre to think that the way to be tough on crime is to give police more power and more influence in society."[50] What do you think?

SUMMARY

Politics and history have had and continue to have a significant role in the development of public law enforcement in Canada. In the country's early years, law enforcement agencies, like other government departments, were limited in both scope and size, due in large part to the sheer size of the country and the contemporary understanding of what constituted effective law enforcement.

As Canada was transformed from a rural-agricultural society into an urban-industrial one, new realities and the resulting new demands imposed themselves on public law enforcement agencies. The arrival of mass communication, more sophisticated transportation networks, and technological innovations has challenged and changed the justice system.

The political spectrum informs the ideologies of the major federal parties in Canada. Each government is influenced by the political and moral views of its elected body, and these views inform the analysis of, and proposed solutions to, social issues. This is especially true in relation to policing services, crime, and the administration of justice. The three levels of government often have interrelated and overlapping roles and responsibilities. We see this particularly in the area of law enforcement. This situation can be beneficial, as in the case of joint efforts to combat crime, but it can also result in government agencies working against, rather than with, one another.

Popular demand for greater government accountability and fiscal restraint has affected police services, resulting in reorganization and fresh dialogue with individuals and groups representing a variety of backgrounds, including First Nations and other cultural groups, citizens' organizations, and so on. Part of this new strategy is an attempt to communicate to the public how policing has changed over the years so that the communities being served understand better the realities of the job and the demands being placed on rank-and-file police officers. Deciding how far to push this message is at the centre of current debates, such as the one concerning political activism by police.

KEY TERMS

Aboriginal self-government

community policing

cost sharing

federal spending power

left wing

multiculturalism

police services board

political culture

political spectrum

right wing

NOTES

1. Statistics from R. Douglas Francis et al., *Destinies: Canadian History Since Confederation*, 5th ed. (Toronto: Thomson Nelson, 2004), 133.

2. Royal Canadian Mounted Police (RCMP), "Historical Highlights" (January 1, 2001), available online at www.rcmp-grc.gc.ca.

3. RCMP, "Contract Policing" (May 16, 2006), available online at www. rcmp-grc.gc.ca.

4. *Immigration Act*, RSC 1985, c. I-2.

5. *Fisheries Act*, RSC 1985, c. F-27.

6. *Criminal Code*, RSC 1985, c. C-46, as amended.

7. OPP, "A Brief History of the Ontario Provincial Police" (2006), available online at www.opp.ca/Community/Museum/opp_001071.html.

8. *Highway Traffic Act*, RSO 1990, c. H.8.

9. OPP, "A Brief History."

10. Ibid.

11. *Young Offenders Act*, RSC 1985, c. Y-1, as amended.

12. *Youth Criminal Justice Act*, SC 2002, c. 1.

13. *Parental Responsibility Act*, SO 2000, c. 4.

14. The exceptions were 1911–1921, 1930–1935, 1957–1963, 1979–1980, and 1984–1993. John Robert Colombo, ed., *1999 Canadian Global Almanac* (Toronto: Macmillan, 1998), 122-130 (based on information from Elections Canada).

15. Taken from Andrew Taylor-Butts, "Justice Spending in Canada," *Juristat* (Statistics Canada, 2002), catalogue no. 85-002-XIE 22:11.

16. Public Safety and Emergency Preparedness Portfolio Corrections Statistics Committee, *Corrections and Conditional Release Statistical Overview 2006* (Ottawa: Public Works and Government Services Canada, 2006). Catalogue no. PS1-3/2006E. Available online on the Correctional Service Canada website at www.csc-scc.gc.ca/text/publicsubject_e.shtml.

17. Costs vary because of varying inmate populations, programs, and facilities. The author wishes to thank Kath Underhill, Supervisor, Statistics Section, Program Effectiveness, Statistics and Applied Research, Correctional Service Canada, for her assistance with provincial data.

18. Public Safety and Emergency Preparedness Portfolio Corrections Statistics Committee, supra note 16.

19. For analysis, see University of Ottawa, Institute for the Prevention of Crime, "Support from Economists" (August 24, 2007), available online at www.socialsciences.uottawa.ca/ipc/eng/support_economists.asp.

20. Charles Hauss and William Smith, *Comparative Politics—Domestic Responses to Global Challenges: A Canadian Perspective*, 3rd ed. (Toronto: Nelson, 2000), 10.

21. For example, it was discovered only recently that the UN *Universal Declaration of Human Rights* was drafted by Canadian John Humphrey, a McGill University professor. See Francis et al., supra note 1, at 354. For a more general synopsis of Canada's position in the early postwar era, see Margaret Conrad and Alvin Finkel, *Canada: A National History* (Toronto: Pearson Education, 2003), 455.

22. See "The Split-Run Panic—Four Years Later," *National Post* (July 12, 2003), A17. For broader historical analysis, see John Herd Thompson, "Canada's Quest for Cultural Sovereignty: Protection, Promotion, and Popular Culture," in R. Douglas Francis and Donald B. Smith, eds., *Readings in Canadian History, Post-Confederation* (Toronto: Thomson Nelson, 2002), 404-416.

23. *Canadian Charter of Rights and Freedoms*, part I of the *Constitution Act, 1982*, RSC 1985, app. II, no. 44.

24. Hauss and Smith, supra note 20, at 63-64.

25. See Keith Lesbie, "All Parties Vow to Run More Women Candidates in Ontario Fall Election," *Canadian Press NewsWire* (February 20, 2007), and Myer Siemiatycki and Ian A. Matheson, "Suburban Success: Immigrant and Minority Electoral Gains in Suburban Toronto," *Canadian Issues* (Summer 2005), 69.

26. Shahé S. Kazarian, Wesley Chichlow, and Simon Bradford, *Diversity Issues in Law Enforcement*, 3rd ed. (Toronto: Emond Montgomery, 2007), 40.

27. Currently, the RCMP acts as Nunavut's police service. For more information on the activity of the RCMP in Nunavut, see Royal Canadian Mounted Police, "RCMP Nunavut—V Division" (February 12, 2007), available online at http://rcmp-grc.ca/nu/index_e.htm. For details on court and correctional services in Nunavut, see the Nunavut Department of Justice website at www.justice.gov.nu.ca/english. Under the "Divisions" menu, choose "Corrections" and "Court Services."

28. Max J. Hedley, "Native Peoples in Canada," in Kenneth G. Pryke and Walter C. Soderlund, eds., *Profiles of Canada* (Toronto: Copp Clark Pitman, 1992), 88.

29. Pamela Williamson and John Roberts, *First Nations Peoples*, 2nd ed. (Toronto: Emond Montgomery, 2004), ch. 7.

30. The authors wish to thank Nishnawbe-Aski Police Service Chief of Police B.W. Luloff for research and support materials. Thanks also to Allan R. Morrison, Education Officer/Special Projects Coordinator, at Windigo First Nations Council. See also the service's website at www.naps-net.org/home.php.

31. Barry D. Adam, "Social Inequality in Canada," in Pryke and Soderlund, supra note 28, at 64.

32. Darin Barney, quoted in Brenda O'Neill, "Democracy in Action: Elections, Referendums and Citizen Power," in Rand Dyck, ed., *Studying Politics: An Introduction to Political Science* (Toronto: Thomson Nelson, 2002), 262-289.

33. For further analysis, see Michael Green, "A Script Tailored for a Star," *The Globe and Mail* (August 13, 2003), A11.

34. Alternative views on the issue of government debt and taxation have been explored by several researchers. See, for example, Linda McQuaig, *Shooting the Hippo* (Toronto: Viking/Penguin Books Canada, 1995) and Murray Dobbin, *Ten Tax Myths* (Toronto: Canadian Centre for Policy Alternatives, October 1999).

35. Jennifer Lewington, "Toronto on 'Life Support': Budget Chief," *The Globe and Mail* (March 30, 2007), A14.

36. See City of Toronto, "2007 City Budget," available online at www.toronto.ca/budget2007/index.htm. Click on "Read more."

37. See Toronto Police Service, "Salary and Benefits" (2007), available online at www.torontopolice.on.ca/careers/salaryandbenefits.php.

38. Elaine Carey, "GTA Leads Way as Crime Drops Across Canada," *Toronto Star* (July 19, 2000), A1.

39. Uniform strength in 1993 was 5,450. In 2006, it stood at 5,376. See Toronto Police Service, "Statistical Reports," available online at www.torontopolice.on.ca/publications.

40. Kazarian, Crichlow, and Bradford, supra note 26, at 10-11.

41. *Police Services Act*, RSO 1990, c. P.15, as amended.

42. See Toronto Police Service, *2006 Annual Statistical Report* (2007), available online at www.torontopolice.on.ca/publications/files/reports/2006statsreport.pdf.

43. See Bruce DeMara, "Recruits for a New Age," *Toronto Star* (January 29, 2007), C2; "Police Try Recruiting Gays, Lesbians and Transgendered," *Toronto Star* (February 11, 2007), A4.

44. Taken from *Toronto Police Accountability Bulletin*, 4, October 2003. Available online at www.tpac.ca/bulletins.cfm.

45. See John Sewell, "Prelude to a Police State," available online at www.eyeweekly.com.

46. *Police Services Act*, RSO 1990, c. P.15. See also Dan Gilbert and Peter Maher, *Provincial Offences: Essential Tools for Law Enforcement*, 2nd ed. (Toronto: Emond Montgomery, 2008), 317.

47. Quoted in *Toronto Police Accountability Bulletin*, 5, November 2003. Available online at www.tpac.ca/bulletins.cfm.

48. See CBC News, "Reject Endorsements from Police Union, Chief Tells Candidates" (March 8, 2006), available online at www.cbc.ca.

49. See "Tipping His Hand?" (February 15, 2007), available online at www.macleans.ca.

50. Quoted in *Toronto Police Accountability Bulletin*, 34, February 2007. Available online at www.tpac.ca/bulletins.cfm.

EXERCISES

Multiple Choice

1. Public law enforcement is administered by

    a. the federal government

    b. the provincial governments

    c. the municipal governments

    d. all three levels of government

    e. none of the above

2. "Political culture" refers to

    a. the attitudes of politicians about government

    b. basic attitudes of citizens toward each another, the government, and authority

    c. political views that have been shaped by a country's history and geography

    d. a and b

    e. b and c

3. "Left wing" refers to

    a. a seat on the left side of the House of Commons

    b. a political philosophy that emphasizes tax cuts and smaller government

    c. a political philosophy that emphasizes social welfare and the collective good

    d. a political philosophy that emphasizes individualism and little government intervention

    e. all of the above

4. Only two parties have formed the federal government since Confederation:

    a. New Democratic Party and Progressive Conservative Party

    b. Liberal Party and New Democratic Party

    c. Canadian Alliance and Progressive Conservative Party

    d. (Progressive) Conservative Party and Liberal Party

    e. New Democratic Party and Canadian Alliance

5. Right-wing ideologists tend to believe that

    a. criminals should go to prison

    b. crime is a product of inequalities in the social system

    c. criminals must take responsibility for their actions

    d. a and b

    e. a and c

True or False?

_____ 1. Municipal policing services are an extension of provincial authority over the administration and enforcement of criminal law.

_____ 2. Through cost sharing, the federal government can greatly influence how justice is administered in the provinces.

_____ 3. Someone who supports right-wing ideology tends to view crime as a product of a social system that is inherently unequal.

_____ 4. Someone who supports left-wing ideology tends to view crime as an individual choice and therefore an individual responsibility.

_____ 5. The close proximity of the United States has no effect on Canada's political culture.

Short Answer

1. Explain how the different levels of government work together to provide policing services.

2. How do social realities affect decisions about what policing services are provided at the federal, provincial, and local levels and the nature of these services?

3. What is Aboriginal self-government? What is its purpose?

4. As a city councillor, how would you deal with proposed police budget increases? Explain your answer.

5. How might the principles of cooperation and compromise be employed to overcome current disagreements over the role of police in the political process?

6. Which side of the political spectrum most appeals to you? Why?

7. Choose the federal party you believe you will support in the next election. On what basis do you make this choice? Visit the party's website and see whether it has any information on the subjects you are interested in.

8. Using the framework of the political spectrum, choose three news items and analyze them from a left-wing and a right-wing perspective. How are the solutions to these issues coloured by the respective ideologies?

PART III

Public Administration

CHAPTER 6

A Cog in the Machine: Public Administration and Bureaucracies

CHAPTER OBJECTIVES

After completing this chapter, you should be able to:

- Define public administration and describe its relation to the political process in Canada.

- Explain and compare theoretical concepts of bureaucracy.

- Outline the benefits and drawbacks of each concept.

- Describe the degree to which each of these concepts has been adopted by private and public bureaucracies.

- Outline the differences between public and private enterprise.

- Understand the benefits and drawbacks of privatizing public services.

INTRODUCTION

"Prime Minister Promises $1 Million to Each Canadian."

Hold on! Before you drop this text and run off in search of your share of the cash, think for a moment about where exactly you'd be searching for this windfall. The prime minister's residence probably wouldn't be high on your list. You might visit the local federal government building or phone a federal government office in an attempt to discover how to receive payment. Now the bad news: as far as the author knows, there is no substance to this headline (but he could be wrong!). The good news is that, if you reacted to this headline as stated, you have already demonstrated an understanding of the difference between the political and administrative elements of government. Even though the prime minister announces that funding will be made available for all kinds of programs, the actual distribution of these funds or the services they provide is carried out by a vast and complex network of people and institutions referred to collectively as the public service.

Because of the close interaction between politics and public administration, it can be difficult to distinguish between them. Both are responsible for managing the day-to-day operation of government. Similarly, political and administrative bodies attempt to respond to citizens' needs by discussing and developing public policy. However, public administration differs from its political counterpart in several ways. First, we do not directly elect public servants. Instead, they are usually hired in much the same way as any other employee, although as we will see, some may be appointed by government to sit on a board or carry out a special duty. Second, public administration is, ideally, concerned with how to implement political will rather than with deciding what it is the public actually wants. Thus, in the above fantasy, it is the public service that would serve as the vehicle that would give each of us our money. In short, politicians make decisions while public servants implement, or carry out, those decisions.

THEORIES OF BUREAUCRACY

The model we have just described provides a general explanation of the relationship between politics and public administration, but this ongoing interaction is seldom this simple. The administrative side alone involves thousands of bureaucrats—basically, unelected government officials—intricate layers of communication, and an adherence to rules and regulations for the purposes of evaluation and accountability. This administrative machinery that supports government has been with us for as long as civilization itself. As humans began to congregate in larger and larger groups, structures of government developed; in turn, rulers depended on others to carry out their wishes. It is no surprise then that societies with highly developed bureaucracies were capable of considerable achievements. Though the word has many popular negative connotations, a **bureaucracy** is really just an organizational structure through which governments put their decisions into action. The word is a combination of the French *bureau*, for desk or office, and the Greek *cratie*, for rule. A **bureaucrat** is simply an employee of a bureaucracy—a public servant. Huge bureaucracies existed in ancient China and Egypt, societies whose legacy lives with us today in the Great Wall and the pyramids, respectively. Bureaucrats even had an effect on the location of Jesus' birth! Mary and Joseph went to Bethlehem in accordance with Roman policy, which decreed that people must return to their hometowns for taxation purposes. Thus, while they form an integral part of society, public bureaucracies have for the most part gone unnoticed or have been overshadowed by events with which most of us are familiar.

The nature and function of bureaucracies began to interest political thinkers during the 19th century. The field has expanded greatly since then, helped along by the theoretical ideas of several notable figures. These people can be categorized according to three general schools of thought: classic, structuralist, and human relations or humanist. We will deal with each category separately.

bureaucracy
the organizational structure through which government exercises its power

bureaucrat
public servant

Classic Theories of Bureaucracy

KARL MARX (1818–1883)

> From each according to his abilities, to each according to his needs.[1]

Karl Marx is best known for developing the political ideology of communism. In general terms, this way of thinking about society proposed that **capitalism**[2] creates two classes of people: the poorer class, collectively known as the proletariat, and the wealthier class, which Marx called the bourgeoisie. Marx argued that this class division occurs because competition in the free market forces bourgeois employers to exploit their proletariat employees—that is, work them as hard as possible for as little money as possible. Marx observed the terrible working conditions spawned by the Industrial Revolution of the late 1700s through the mid-1800s. This was a time of major economic changes as new machinery and technology revolutionized industry. The mainly rural population of Europe and other parts of the world moved to the cities in greater and greater numbers in search of jobs in the new factories. A new—and poverty-stricken—working class developed that worked under sometimes appallingly dangerous conditions and Marx became convinced that it was just a matter of time before workers would overthrow these capitalist oppressors, creating a society with no social classes or private ownership.

> **capitalism**
> an economic system based on private ownership and competition in a free market

Marx speculated that eventually there would be no need for government because people would work toward a common good and share equally in resources. As far as Marx was concerned, government was nothing more than a tool of the wealthy classes that they used to maintain their positions of social and economic privilege. Bureaucracy was merely an extension of this apparatus, a means of legitimating state oppression of the working classes while perpetuating an illusion of fairness, justice, and objectivity. Recall from chapter 1 that these are all vital elements underpinning public confidence in the rule of law and the political system in which it functions. Marx reasoned that as workers collectively became aware of their situation, conflict would increase between workers and the dominant classes. The latter would respond by resorting to more violence to keep the lower classes in line. For example, the police or army might be called upon to break up demonstrations or intervene in labour disputes. Thus, for Marx, the civil service was part of a systemic social problem of one class over another, and bureaucracy became more complex as government attempted to deal with class conflict.

Many scholars have attempted to interpret Marxist theory and explain its relevance to current events. Referred to as neo-Marxists, this group argues that the state exists for three major purposes. First, it accumulates and concentrates wealth and power within the wealthy classes. For example, the state may give the rich favourable tax treatment or provide corporations with generous job creation subsidies. Second, the state serves to legitimize the disadvantaged position of the working classes by pretending that social inequality is simply the result of the natural superiority of the upper classes. In other words, those on top deserve to be there by virtue of the fact that they are there. Finally, the state exists to quash any social unrest that may emerge as a result of worker dissatisfaction with the status quo.[3]

CRITICISM OF MARXIST THEORY

One criticism of Marxist social analysis is that it cannot adequately explain the social mobility that takes place among members of different classes. For example, some people who are born into a disadvantaged class are able to work their way up to a higher class. Marxism also stereotypes people according to their class and therefore cannot accommodate individual differences. In addition, notions of social class are difficult to define. Most Canadians like to think of themselves as middle class; however, the definition of what this actually means, even in terms of income, varies widely across the country.

During the federal election campaign of 2006, the Conservative Party defined a middle-class household income as between $70,000 and $80,000 a year, and Tory polls indicated that over 85 percent of Canadians were in that range. This data was key to the development of such Conservative platform planks as tax breaks and funding for childcare.[4] However, Statistics Canada, which defines "middle-class" according to how incomes are distributed on either side of the median income, paints a different picture. In its most recent numbers (2004), StatsCan reported that middle-class families represented 47 percent of Canadian households, down from 52 percent in 1989.[5] Many observers report that the majority of Canadians define themselves as middle class, whether they earn over $75,000 (as is the case with just over 2 million Canadians) or under $5,000 (2.2 million).[6]

Still, Marxist philosophy does provide some insights about how and why public bureaucracies function as they do, particularly when it comes to public law enforcement. Marxist analysis imbues a negative view of government, and this has implications for institutions that are charged with preserving public safety and civil order. It casts state armies and police forces as defenders of an unfair and self-serving regime, protecting and preserving the property and entitlements of the dominant classes. Thus, when workers attempt to force any changes on the existing social order, the upper classes can call on these law enforcement agencies to counter the perceived threat. They can also use other government institutions, such as the legal system, to deal with resistance. As a result, neo-Marxist theory puts little faith in the integrity of law enforcement, viewing it with suspicion and as an institution in need of constant monitoring.

MAX WEBER (1864–1920)

> The state is a relation of men dominating men, a relation supported by means of legitimate (i.e. considered to be legitimate) violence.[7]

Max Weber was a German scholar who studied social issues using systematic methods. As we have learned, bureaucracies have existed for as long as human civilization; however, it was Weber who pioneered the study of bureaucratic structure, function, and behaviour. His work remains relevant today because it offers insights into the ways public policy is developed and implemented.

Weber began his study of bureaucracy by relating it to his previous work in the field of political sociology. He identified three sources of authority that can form the basic power structure in a society: traditional authority, charismatic authority, and legal authority. **Traditional authority** refers to the right of someone to rule based on heredity, religion, or divine right (a right sanctioned by a higher spiritual power). A good example of this is the British monarchy, which has claimed legiti-

traditional authority authority based on heredity, religion, or divine right

macy to rule using all of these criteria at different periods in history. **Charismatic authority** refers to the unique talents and popular appeal that make an individual particularly attractive as a public leader. These attributes may or may not be related specifically to the political arena (witness the election of movie star Arnold Schwarzenegger to the California governorship in 2003); however, they are definitely an asset. **Legal authority** means that authority to govern is legitimated by the rule of law—that is, the laws and regulations that must be obeyed by all members of a society, the rulers as well as those they rule. Thus a queen, president, prime minister, or film star turned state governor is subject to the law. It is the law we trust and hence obey that legitimates the power of our leaders. Weber argued that modern bureaucracies are necessary parts of regimes whose power rests in legal authority.[8] Because of this, a government can tell us what to do ("men dominating men"), and can resort to coercive measures in order to ensure that we comply ("legitimate (i.e. considered to be legitimate) violence").

You can probably think of several examples in which one, some, or all of these sources of authority exist. Pierre Trudeau, for example, came to power in 1968 riding a wave of popularity known as "Trudeau-mania." Many observers pointed to a similar phenomenon when then Quebec premier Lucien Bouchard led the "Oui" forces in the 1995 sovereignty referendum. Still, the reason that these leaders and others like them continue to govern after the hoopla has subsided is because this power is ultimately vested in legal authority.

Weberian theory contends that, by its very nature, legal authority relies on bureaucratic organization to maintain itself. This is not meant to suggest that bureaucracies do not exist in other expressions of political authority; rather, Weber emphasized that legal authority cannot exist without a bureaucracy to support it. He went on to describe what he considered to be the fundamental components of an "ideal" bureaucracy, which could then be used to assess the development of systems of organization in the real world. While Weber himself cited eight separate components, more recent interpretations have consolidated these into four main areas:[9] hierarchy, continuity, impersonality, and expertise.

In this context, **hierarchy** refers to an organized system of labour where it is clear who reports to whom in a superior–subordinate relationship. **Continuity** means that the people working within the organization are full-time employees and can make a career out of what they do. **Impersonality** means that jobs and routines are based on written rules and records, which guard against favouritism. **Expertise** refers to hiring practices that are based on merit rather than patronage, and the ability to control and access information and knowledge specific to a particular area. Weber concluded that the more closely an organization approximates these ideals, the more rational and efficient it will be. In short, organizational efficiency occurs when people are hired for what they know rather than for who they know. And, as these employees work their way up through the ranks, they will develop expertise that can be used to improve the operation of the organization.

CRITICISM OF WEBERIAN THEORY

The major flaw with the Weberian view of bureaucracy is that it attempts to explain this type of human organization by measuring it against an ideal, or perfect, model. Weber asserted that the closer a bureaucracy came to approximating this

charismatic authority
authority based on the unique talents and popular appeal of an individual

legal authority
authority based on the rule of law

hierarchy
an organized system of labour characterized by a superior–subordinate relationship

continuity
the long-term or ongoing nature of a bureaucracy; continuity means that the people working within an organization are full-time employees who can make a career out of what they do

impersonality
the objective nature of jobs and routines in a bureaucracy, based on written rules and records

expertise
knowledge of or ability in a particular area or subject

model, the more efficient it would become. This is often not the case in the real world. In fact, strict adherence to the Weberian model can sometimes result in a very inefficient organization. For example, hierarchy and continuity can deter initiative and produce apathy as workers begin to feel insignificant and underappreciated. Expertise and strict adherence to formal rules can create a work environment that detracts from the organization's overall aims as employees focus on career advancement rather than on collective organizational needs.

Formal rules that are put in place to ensure fair treatment for everyone may paradoxically achieve the opposite effect. For example, in the past many police forces required prospective officers to meet certain height and weight requirements. These criteria were seen as objective requirements of the job. However, these standards inadvertently discriminated against certain groups of people. Since the standards reflected the average for white males, women and some cultural minorities faced unintended discrimination if they chose a career in policing. An argument can be made that physical size is important in law enforcement; however, an opposite argument can be made for equality of opportunity for employment. Thus, rules that at first appear neutral and non-discriminatory may produce the opposite effect.

These criticisms aside, Weber's analysis does provide insight into organizational behaviour, and as we will discover later in this chapter, plenty of evidence exists to support his observations.

Structuralist Theory of Bureaucracy

FREDERICK WINSLOW TAYLOR (1856–1915)

> No one can be found who will deny that in the case of any single individual the greatest prosperity can exist only when that individual has reached his highest state of efficiency.[10]

Whereas Max Weber was interested in the general aspects of bureaucratic organization, Frederick Winslow Taylor focused on its key elements. Taylor wanted to find out how best to use human and mechanical resources—workers and machines—to maximize productivity and minimize waste. This approach is called **scientific management**.

scientific management
management approach based on using resources in ways that maximize productivity and minimize waste

A mechanical engineer by trade, Taylor began his career on the factory floors of late 19th-century America. These experiences prompted him to consider ways to improve the efficiency of factory work. His observations of the workers led him to draw two conclusions: (1) they were prone to slacking off, and (2) their jobs were inefficiently organized. Taylor argued that a scientific approach could be used to solve both of these problems, and the result would benefit both workers and employers. His method involved having a trained observer watch an above-average employee perform his or her task, identify and time each component of that task, and then teach that employee's method to others in similar jobs. This would provide an empirical, objective standard against which employers could measure employee productivity. Taylor proposed solving the awkward organization of the jobs themselves by rearranging them so that each worker would be responsible for one or two clearly defined tasks, rather than doing piecework, which was a common practice during his day.[11] As industrialism pervaded society, Taylor gained a considerable following, and in 1911, he published a book entitled *The Principles of Scientific Management*,[12] in which he outlined several theories of organization modelled on his ideas.

Taylor's approach coincided with the emergence of a new group of managerial professionals, who supervised the increasingly complex operations of factories and other large businesses. Scientific management transformed skilled work previously done by one person or a small group (for example, shoe-making) into simple, repetitive tasks, done by a team of workers. In so doing, productivity and efficiency were greatly improved. This approach became a template for the assembly-line model of production so familiar today. Hence, "scientific managers" were to think of their workers as part of the "company machine," to be utilized by them in the most efficient way possible, at the least cost.[13]

CRITICISM OF TAYLOR'S SCIENTIFIC MANAGEMENT APPROACH

Taylor's theories of scientific management have drawn criticism for several reasons. First, he asserted that there should be a clear distinction between management and labour. Implicit in this division was an assumption that managers should be responsible for setting standards and making decisions, which would then be carried out by workers. This has been referred to as the "strong back and weak mind" principle by some critics, who also point out that Taylor's approach prevents workers from having any meaningful say in the duties that are expected of them. To be fair, Taylor recognized the importance of cordial labour–management relations, but his ideas suggest that he believed proper results could be achieved only when management dominated the relationship.

Later theorists criticized this approach for its emphasis on strictly material rewards for workers who performed well. This one-dimensional, mechanistic view of workers as mere cogs in the factory machine was certainly not lost on workers themselves. Much of the labour unrest of the early 20th century occurred as a result of attempts to implement principles of scientific management without workers' consent. Thus, Taylor's view of labour as but one (expendable) resource in industrial capitalism cannot address the non-economic human aspects of work—such as job satisfaction, morale, and loyalty—as motivating factors that contribute to overall efficiency.

Human Relations Theory of Bureaucracy

GEORGE ELTON MAYO (1880–1949)

> [T]he relation of working groups to management [is] one of the fundamental problems of ... industry.[14]

Problems arising from the top-down nature of hierarchical organizations (the approach embraced by Max Weber and Frederick Winslow Taylor) encouraged a search for other theoretical approaches to better understand individual organizational behaviour and find a way to maximize organizational efficiency. Through the work of a variety of individuals in business, psychology, and sociology, another perspective emerged known popularly as **human relations**. This approach recognizes the importance of attending to the personal and social needs of individuals to

human relations
management approach that recognizes and addresses the personal and social needs of individuals

promote desired outcomes. George Elton Mayo, a professor from Harvard University, was one of several researchers who applied this school of thought to the workplace. He is best known for conducting workplace experiments in 1924 at the Western Electric plant in Hawthorne, near Chicago. Along with two other researchers, Mayo hypothesized that improving workplace conditions (for example, lighting) would improve worker productivity. While the original experiments failed to achieve any conclusive results, they did lead to research into what became known popularly as the Hawthorne effect. Simply put, this principle states that workers who feel that they are appreciated and valued by their employers will be more productive.[15]

Mayo believed that modern industrial capitalism had disrupted more traditional forms of human support and interaction, such as family, community, and traditional work environments. These had functioned as informal meeting places for people and had facilitated feelings of identity and belonging. The modern workplace was not conducive to this informal social interaction, which was just as important a motivator as wages and career aspirations. In short, a workplace that is attentive to human needs results in better productivity. This can be achieved, Mayo argued, by involving workers in organizational decisions, teaching managers to be better listeners, and replacing overbearing supervision techniques with a more casual system of two-way communication.

CRITICISM OF MAYO'S HUMAN RELATIONS APPROACH

The human relations school of management drew criticism because its precepts appeared counterintuitive to the confrontational nature of labour–management relations. How much say should employees have in organizational decisions? What if these decisions run against those proposed by management? How much time and energy would have to be devoted to this exercise, and at what cost to organizational efficiency? For these and other reasons, the human relations approach has enjoyed limited success in the real world, although its influence is evident in such participative management strategies as management by objectives (MBO) and total quality management (TQM).[16]

Still, there remains little evidence in the Canadian public sector that the human relations approach has been able to entrench itself in employer–employee relations. Many observers believe that during the heyday of organizational humanism from the 1960s to the 1980s, Canadian governments were still characterized by rigid hierarchies and job structures, little employee participation in decision making, top-down communication, and other elements of scientific management.

THEORY VERSUS PRACTICE: CONTRIBUTIONS TO PUBLIC LAW ENFORCEMENT

We have just completed a cursory survey of some of the fundamental theories that address the nature and function of bureaucracies, as well as how they can be managed to maximize efficiency and effectiveness. We can also employ these philosophies as analytical tools to study public law enforcement. As we will discover, each perspective contributes in different ways to an overall understanding of why and how the rule of law operates in Canada.

Marxist ideology is considered left wing on the political spectrum. So, you might be tempted to conclude that in keeping with its tradition of active government social intervention Marxist thought should embrace large, well-funded police and military establishments. Recall, however, that Marxism—and the socialist sensibilities it spawned—harbours a deep mistrust of law enforcement agencies because they are the means by which those in power preserve their privileged positions. Although this reasoning may sound dated, its influence still permeates socialist views of society. Therefore, people on the political left favour a limited role for agents of state force. They prefer to focus public resources on remedying social inequities that they see as the root cause of crime and civil unrest.

This way of looking at events is also used in other political contexts. For example, the pepper spraying of protesters at the Asia-Pacific Economic Cooperation (APEC) summit in Vancouver in 1997 could be viewed as use of force (RCMP officers) by the state (the Prime Minister's Office) to quash a legitimate expression of protest by members of the public (student activists) against perceived human rights violations. Although Marxist analysis has faded somewhat from popular culture, it does offer a useful, if somewhat pessimistic, set of principles with which to judge the actions of politicians and bureaucrats.

Weber's ideas on bureaucracies give us a more rational view of the role of this type of human organization in society. Weber would recognize many of his bureaucratic ideals in today's complex system of public law enforcement. Officer ranking and the intricate reporting and communications networks among police forces demonstrate a clear hierarchy, providing opportunities for merit-based promotion in accordance with clearly articulated codes of professional conduct. On the other hand, in spite of possessing all of these traits, the system of law enforcement can fall prey to many of the criticisms associated with the Weberian model. For example, would any of the many chiefs of police in Canada be willing to assert that the bureaucracy under their control is flawless? Again, the gap between theory and practice can at times be large, but there is little doubt that the intricate network of law enforcement in Canada represents a highly developed and modern society, just as Weber claimed.

Scientific management principles have become so much a part of private and public bureaucracies that most of us simply take them for granted. Managers search constantly for ways to improve the way tasks are accomplished given the resources available to them. For example, how should police officers be distributed across a city to maximize efficiency? To be fair to all citizens, officers might be assigned to patrol certain geographic areas, dividing the city into equal sections. But what if some areas have higher rates of crime? What about public education to prevent crime? As you can see, there are many variables at play in any given decision, and they all have implications for people inside and outside the organization. Still, scientific management continues to exert considerable influence. As a police chief, you might consult empirical data such as crime statistics to help you make decisions. You might draw on the experience of other jurisdictions to assess the success of techniques they have adopted to meet local challenges. In short, the essential elements of scientific management have become part of the management of all bureaucracies, including law enforcement.

As previously noted, the school of human relations has not been adopted to any great extent in private or public administration. However, the importance of human resource departments and cooperative, team-based management strategies proves that this approach has not been totally rejected. Many government agencies whose members are exposed to dangerous or traumatizing events now provide crisis counselling and support to employees. Efforts like these suggest that this approach does in fact have benefits for an organization and its workers.

A good example of this is the Employee and Family Assistance Program (EFAP) for the Toronto Police Service. Developed in 1984, the program provides a broad range of services to police officers, staff, and their relatives in areas such as gambling, drug and alcohol addiction, marital and legal counselling, critical incident stress, and lifestyle management. The EFAP estimated its potential client base in 2007 to be about 30,000.[17]

Get Real!

PRIVATE VERSUS PUBLIC ADMINISTRATION: A TALE OF TWO PRISONS

"Why don't they run government more like they run a business?" You have probably heard someone ask this question, or perhaps you have asked it yourself after hearing yet another media report of alleged government waste and inefficiency. As we have seen in this chapter, there are many theories about how best to structure and manage a bureaucracy, how to make it more equitable and productive, and who ultimately benefits from such administrative practices. From now on, when you see a media report on or are involved in a discussion about bureaucracy, you can refer back to the ideas of Marx, Weber, Taylor, and Mayo to critically analyze the issues and weigh the advantages and disadvantages of the various perspectives. There are rarely any easy answers.

Consider a recent example: Canada's prisons. In 1997, the Ontario government announced the construction of a pair of "super-jails," one in Penetanguishene, the other in Lindsay. The first prison was privatized and came under the control of an American company; the Lindsay facility remained under provincial control. Controversy seemed to dog the private facility from the start. Unions representing corrections workers opposed the "sell-off" of their prison,[18] while community residents worried about safety being compromised for the sake of profit. The group Citizens Against Private Prisons (CAPP), composed of business representatives from Penetanguishene and surrounding communities, was especially vocal in lobbying the government to reconsider its decision. They cited increased violence and inmate deaths as evidence of the serious downsides of privatization.[19] It would seem their concerns were well founded: In 2006, the private contract for operating the Penetanguishene jail expired and it was subjected to a comparative performance evaluation by the government. The review concluded that the private prison lagged behind its public counterpart in security and prisoner health care, and had higher repeat offender rates. The Ontario community safety minister said, "We found that in basically every single area, the outcomes were better in the publicly run facilities." Control of the Penetanguishene super-jail has now been returned to the provincial government, with the transfer costing taxpayers an estimated $4 million.[20]

Should this failed experiment in privatization affect future decision making on how to administer Canada's prison system? Proponents of the public administration facility maintain that the existing prison system is not working either, and that privatization can not only reduce overcrowding in public facilities but also lighten the burden on taxpayers. One survey of prisons in the United States found that cost savings could be as high as 20 percent.[21] What's more, the issue is not going away any time soon: observers believe that the law-and-order agenda of the current Conservative government will spark a building boom in private prisons as a crackdown on crime leads to increased demand for correctional services.[22] With this in mind, what do you think the future of Canadian prisons should look like? What would Marx think? Or Weber?

Supporters of private and public administrations continue to argue the merits of their respective sides, and since every case is different, it is difficult to decide which perspective is best. Overall, it is important to keep in mind that while governments and private bureaucracies do many of the same things, their goals are very different. In business, the ultimate aim is economic efficiency: private administrations exist to maximize profit and minimize expense. Government, on the other hand, exists to respond to, maintain, and defend the public good. Its aim is necessarily to benefit everyone, regardless of their ability to pay for goods or services, and it is accountable to a far greater number of people than is a private enterprise. What we as the public have to ultimately consider is whether society is any better off as a result of privatization. Will promised financial savings contribute to the public good? Should we delegate this kind of power to the private sector? Can a private company be held accountable in the same way as a government? Is the move to privatize based on solid research, or is it a manifestation of right-wing ideology? These are only a few of the many questions that need to be addressed in judging such shifts in public policy.

SUMMARY

Public administration refers to the vast and complex network of people and institutions that is collectively called the public service. Public administration is ideally concerned with how to implement political will rather than deciding what the public actually wants. The administrative machinery that supports government is called the bureaucracy. Fundamental theories of bureaucratic organization help us to better understand why bureaucracies have become an essential part of all modern societies.

Karl Marx believed that bureaucracies existed to legitimate inequities among social classes, while Max Weber saw them as central to the emergence of modern nation states. Administrative pioneers such as Frederick Winslow Taylor and George Elton Mayo changed the arrangement and management of tasks and people in order to maximize overall productivity. All of these theorists have had an impact on the nature and functions of bureaucracies and on those who are responsible for managing them. Each theory has contributed to a greater understanding of both private and public bureaucracies, although not all have enjoyed the same degree of acceptance in the real world. What is clear is that bureaucracies remain necessary, if often misunderstood, parts of civil society.

Theories of bureaucratic organization can be employed to explain the nature and operation of government agencies, as was just seen in the discussion of prison privatization in Ontario. Doing so provides a variety of perspectives to help understand what happened and why, and to guide future practices.

KEY TERMS

bureaucracy

bureaucrat

capitalism

charismatic authority

continuity

expertise

hierarchy

human relations

impersonality

legal authority

scientific management

traditional authority

NOTES

1. Karl Marx, quoted in the *Oxford Dictionary of Quotations*, 4th ed. (New York: Oxford University Press, 1992), 452:5.

2. The term "capitalism" refers to an economic system based on private ownership. Individuals or corporations use what they own (land, factories, resources) to produce goods and services, competing with one another in the free market. This means simply that we as consumers are free to choose from among these offerings, based on such things as price, quality, reputation, and so on.

3. This set of principles is based on one found in David Kernaghan and David Siegel, *Public Administration in Canada*, 3rd ed. (Toronto: Nelson, 1995), 33.

4. Anne Marie Owens and Justin Mean, "Deflating a National Notion," *National Post* (October 21, 2006), A17.

5. Figures available from Statistics Canada, "Income Equality and Redistribution," *The Daily* (May 11, 2007), available online at www.statcan.ca/Daily/English/070511/d070511b.htm.

6. Owens and Mean, supra note 4.

7. Max Weber, quoted in the *Oxford Dictionary of Quotations*, supra note 1.

8. Max Weber, *Economy and Society* (New York: Bedminster Press, 1968).

9. Gregory J. Inwood, *Understanding Canadian Public Administration: An Introduction to Theory and Practice* (Toronto: Prentice-Hall, 1999), 33-35. For earlier interpretations, see H.H. Gerth and C. Wright Mills, eds. and trans., *From Max Weber: Essays in Sociology* (New York: Alfred A. Knopf, 1970), 178.

10. Frederick Winslow Taylor, *The Principles of Scientific Management* (New York: Harper & Brothers, 1911), available online at http://melbecon.unimelb.edu.au/het.

11. "Piecework" refers to a method of employment where workers are paid for the amount they produce rather than for the amount of time they work. For example, the use of this practice in law enforcement might mean that a police officer would be paid according to the number of traffic tickets given or people arrested!

12. Taylor, supra note 10.

13. For a summary of the application of scientific management and the development of the Canadian economy, see R. Douglas Francis et al., *Destinies: Canadian History Since Confederation*, 4th ed. (Toronto: Thomson Nelson, 2000), 136-141.

14. George Elton Mayo, quoted in "People Whose Ideas Influence Organisational Work," available online at www.onepine.info/pmayo.htm.

15. The experiments are explained in detail in F.J. Roethlisberger and William J. Dickson, *Management and the Worker* (Cambridge, MA: Harvard University Press, 1964).

16. In the management by objectives approach, employees set goals for themselves, in consultation with management, and their performance is measured against these goals. Total quality management is an approach that emphasizes a commitment to quality throughout a company. Employees are seen as an important element in ensuring this quality in everything they make or do. The origins and consequences of these management approaches are explored further in Peter F. Drucker, *The Practice of Management* (New York: Harper & Row, 1954); George S. Odiorne, *Management by Objectives* (New York: Pitman, 1965); and W. Edwards Deming, *Quality, Productivity, and Competitive Position* (Cambridge, MA: Massachusetts Institute of Technology, Center for Advanced Engineering Studies, 1982).

17. Many thanks to Tom Gabriel A.C.A.D. D/Constable #3792—Addictions Coordinator, Employee and Family Assistance Program, Toronto Police Service. Information on EFAP available online at http://efap. torontopolice.on.ca.

18. See "No Private Jails," *Our Ontario* (Winter 2000), 9, 14-15, available online at www.opseu.org/ourontario/ontario.pdf. *Our Ontario* is the official newsletter of the Ontario Public Service Employees Union.

19. See CBC News, "Ontario to Take Back Control of Private Super-Jail" (November 10, 2006), available online at www.cbc.ca.

20. Ibid.

21. Geoffrey F. Segal, "Private Prisons Save Money, Boost Productivity, Studies Find" (November 17, 2003), available online at www.reason.org.

22. Sue Bailey, "Even a Gentler Law-and-Order Platform Could Lead to Private-Prison Boom, Experts Say," *The Gazette (Montreal)* (April 3, 2006), A4.

EXERCISES

Multiple Choice

1. Public administration is concerned with

   a. deciding what the public wants

   b. making decisions for politicians

   c. managing government

   d. implementing political will

   e. making decisions for citizens

2. Marxists see law enforcement officers as

   a. authorities whose work is legitimated by the rule of law

   b. agents of the privileged classes who exist to quash social unrest

   c. bureaucrats who are a necessary part of the machinery of government

   d. agents of the working class who exist to quash unrest among the privileged classes

   e. members of the bourgeoisie who hold a privileged position in society

3. According to Weberian theory, the three sources of authority in a society are

   a. legal authority, bureaucratic authority, and political authority

   b. traditional authority, scientific authority, and charismatic authority

   c. charismatic authority, hierarchical authority, and legal authority

   d. hereditary authority, legal authority, and traditional authority

   e. traditional authority, charismatic authority, and legal authority

4. The following result is inherent in attempting to achieve Weber's ideal bureaucracy:

   a. hierarchy encourages worker initiative

   b. hierarchy deters worker initiative

   c. hierarchy makes workers feel important

   d. hierarchy makes workers feel appreciated

   e. hierarchy makes workers focus on organizational needs

5. Under the scientific management approach,

   a. workers do piecework

   b. employers measure worker productivity against a subjective standard

   c. resources are used in ways that maximize productivity and minimize waste

   d. workers are responsible for only one or two clearly defined tasks

   e. c and d

True or False?

_____ 1. Marx believed that government was necessary because it would eventually ensure that everyone would share equally in a country's resources.

_____ 2. A major flaw in Marxist thought is its inability to explain individual differences and the social mobility that takes place among members of different classes.

_____ 3. Traditional authority is authority that is legitimated by the rule of law.

_____ 4. In Weberian bureaucratic theory, "impersonality" refers to the nature of huge corporations that treat their employees like cogs in a machine rather than like people.

_____ 5. The Hawthorne effect contributed to the field of human relations theory.

_____ 6. Success in the private sector is based on economic efficiency.

Short Answer

1. Define what is meant by "public administration," and describe its role in the political process in Canada.

2. What are the central elements of bureaucracy, according to the following theorists?

   a. Karl Marx

b. Max Weber

c. Frederick Winslow Taylor

d. George Elton Mayo

3. How might each of the above theorists view public law enforcement?

4. Using examples from current events, determine the effect these theories have had on both the public and private sectors.

5. Which of the theoretical approaches do you believe would be most effective in public law enforcement? Why?

6. Outline the proposed benefits of privatization. What are the potential drawbacks?

CHAPTER 7
Evolution of Public Administration

CHAPTER OBJECTIVES

After completing this chapter, you should be able to:

- Understand the historical conditions that led to the development of public administration as a distinct field of academic study, and describe the evolution of the public service in Canadian history.

- Relate this evolution to broader social, economic, and cultural changes in Canadian history.

- Define and compare the advantages and disadvantages of the Keynesian approach to government policy.

- Define and compare the benefits and drawbacks of neoconservatism, noting its effect on Canadian public administration.

- Assess the benefits and drawbacks of privatizing the public sector, with examples.

- Define "whistle-blowing" and its impact on government employees, the public service, and the public go\od.

INTRODUCTION

Guidelines for bureaucrats: (1) When in charge, ponder; (2) When in trouble, delegate; (3) When in doubt, mumble.

—James H. Boren, American bureaucrat[1]

The above satirical set of instructions for senior civil servants does little to challenge popular perceptions of the civil service. And yet, without these people our towns, cities, and indeed entire country would grind to a halt.[2] How did our public service wind up with such a tarnished reputation? One can argue that derogatory public attitudes toward politicians and bureaucrats have always existed. To a point, this is certainly the case. However, by examining the growth of the public sector in the context of larger historical events, it soon becomes apparent that recent criticism may have more to do with the larger currents of political culture than with actual ineptitude.

PUBLIC ADMINISTRATION AS MODERN ACADEMIC DISCIPLINE

Most scholars cite 1887 as a benchmark for the emergence of public administration as an academic discipline. In that year, future American president Woodrow Wilson wrote an essay entitled "The Study of Administration." In his essay, Wilson emphasized that a disciplined, academic study of public administration would result in more accountable and efficient government. Wilson wanted to make a clear distinction between the administrative and political elements of government because he believed that improving the former would correct corruption in the latter. This may seem a little odd given what you already know about the power of elected over non-elected officials in a democracy. Keep in mind, however, that Wilson wrote this paper at a time in American history when the political system of urban "party bosses" and vote buying was in its heyday.[3] As one of the first advocates of reform in this area, Wilson declared that only a professional bureaucracy—one based on formal rules of conduct and hiring practices based on meritocratic principles— could clean up existing corruption.

politics–administrative dichotomy
theoretical framework that views politics as the decision-making apparatus of government and administration as performing the implementation function

Wilson's ideas also laid the foundation for a theoretical framework known as the **politics–administrative dichotomy**. This framework views politics as the decision-making apparatus of government and administration as the implementation function of government. In other words, politicians should decide *what* to do, and bureaucrats should then figure out the most efficient way to do it. The main problem with this theory, of course, is that it is too simple. As we have learned, politicians and bureaucrats are inextricable parts of an overall process, and neither can claim exclusive ownership of public policy development. But while the concept in its pristine form has come under considerable criticism—it assumes, for example, that bureaucrats are politically neutral players in the art of government when in fact they are often central in the process of making public policy (as you will see in chapter 8)—it remains useful in some quarters.

While public administration quickly gained recognition as an academic discipline in the United States, Canadian universities were slower to grant it similar status in the realm of political science. In fact, it wasn't until 1936 that a Canadian university, Dalhousie, offered a degree program in the field. However, public administration became widely accepted in the years following World War II, and today at least 18 Canadian universities offer programs in public administration, some at the master's level.[4] Despite this success, in recent times, public administration has been subjected to severe public criticism. To see why this is so, we need to retrace its evolution in the context of Canadian history.

THE HISTORY OF THE PUBLIC SERVICE IN CANADA

As you learned earlier, Canada's past reveals a lot about who we are and why our country's political system operates as it does. It is also important to keep in mind that outside events, issues, and trends have influenced the shape and direction of our political culture. The evolution of public administration in Canada can be used to illustrate both of these ideas.

Pre-Confederation

Before Confederation, colonial administration dictated the structure and operation of public service. Even 100 years after the decisive battle on the Plains of Abraham between the French and English forces in September 1759, the civil and political fabric of Quebec society retained the influences brought from France. Its bureaucracy reflected a hierarchically based military order, one steeped in patronage appointments doled out (or denied) by local authorities. The British colonies operated on similar principles, with delegates of the Crown rewarding those in the King's favour with government perks and positions. This practice remained commonplace after Confederation, but as Canada settled into nationhood, new challenges and ideas changed the nature and perception of the public service. One aspect of this came from Max Weber's "ideal bureaucracy" model (see chapter 6), which at that time was gaining popular acceptance in Europe and the United States.[5] Weber's ideal emphasized the importance of hiring people based on their qualifications rather than on who their friends were. Of course, the temptation to reward political allies did not disappear overnight, but as merit-based hiring became standard practice elsewhere, its advantages soon made themselves apparent to Canadian government officials.

The Minimalist State

As we will see below, Confederation heralded changes in the nature and size of Canada's public service. In comparison with today, however, the public service remained very small.[6] This can be partially attributed to beliefs at the time regarding the nature and function of government. These bear a direct relation to classic theories regarding political studies (as discussed in chapter 1) that explained state legitimacy and public deference to authority—how and why people allow government to have power over them. Thus, beyond very simple needs such as security and conflict management, the role of the state in society remained limited. As commerce and industry developed during the 19th century, governments assumed more responsibility for economic matters.

Most people looked to their governments for defence and order and as a provider of infrastructure. All of these were ultimately in the interest of business, trade, and commerce, which were assumed to be the real power behind any great nation. While these pursuits required some public administration, they were limited to what were considered essential or minimal services. This approach to government—common to Canada and most other nations at the time—was illustrative of a **minimalist state**. State resources were used in the interest of the business, or capitalist, classes to promote individual wealth and economic growth, while social services such as health and welfare were to be handled by private charities and individual philanthropists.

As the 19th century drew to a close and modern-day Canada began to take shape, the civil service began to grow, not only to keep up with the country's expanding geography but also to meet new demands brought on by the new challenges of urbanization and industrialism. While only 20 percent of Canada's population lived in urban communities of more than 20,000 people in 1867, this figure had increased to almost 50 percent by 1921.[7] Employment opportunities were created for such occupations as postal clerks, customs and excise officials, public educators, and

minimalist state
approach to government in which state resources are used in the interest of the business, or capitalist, classes, to promote individual wealth and economic growth

public law enforcement personnel. These, as well as a host of other positions, presented alternatives to the traditional work of farming and other resource-based employment. The public service also offered the emerging middle classes opportunities to improve their economic position by moving up through the ranks of the public service, something they were unlikely or unable to achieve in other sectors. In short, the public service promised these people upward social mobility.

As we have already noted, this expansion in the public service was accompanied by a growing interest in the serious academic study of public administration. Likewise, Frederick Winslow Taylor's scientific management principles (discussed in chapter 6) were beginning to show up in the public sector in an attempt to find the "one best way" of managing its people and resources to achieve maximum efficiency. In response to challenges such as immigration and the settlement of the West, governments were increasingly forced to adopt Weberian principles of professionalism and hiring based on merit to ensure accountability and effective communication among the many departments, outposts, and employees being organized to carry out increasingly complex tasks.

In 1908, the Canadian government created the Civil Service Commission, marking the drive toward a more professional civil service. It reinforced this trend by passing further reforms in this area in 1918. These laws gave the commission the power to oversee all appointments to the public service, thereby thwarting political interference in hiring practices. As well, candidates now had to compete for positions by writing exams and, once hired, were prohibited from any political activity. A new job classification system was introduced, and following World War I, special provision was made to favour returning soldiers for these positions. During the 1920s, there was little change in government's approach to public administration, but events that would drastically alter the nature, philosophy, and function of both politicians and bureaucrats were on the horizon.

The Keynesian State

Following the Great Depression and World War II, there was a major change in the way government operated. Many events and people contributed to this shift, but it is commonly accepted that no one played a more significant role than British economist John Maynard Keynes. Keynes laid the theoretical groundwork for a conceptual transformation of the role of government from one of limited intervention to one of active intervention.

Keynes first came to prominence for his predictions about the harsh peace terms dictated to Germany after World War I.[8] The stock market crash of 1929 and the Great Depression that followed provided Keynes with another opportunity to pitch his unorthodox economic views. First, he asserted that traditional **laissez-faire capitalism**, or free-market capitalism, had led to the economic catastrophe of the 1930s; thus, the market could not and should not be left unregulated. Rejecting the tradition of minimalist government, Keynes also argued that government was the only entity capable of intervening in economic affairs, because only government had the power and public authority to do so.

Traditional economic remedies such as **protectionism** and **isolationism** seemed incapable of curing the economic misery for most of the 1930s. Although some Keynesian-style approaches were initiated, it wasn't until after World War II that

laissez-faire capitalism
free-market capitalism with minimal government interference (French for "let act")

protectionism
an economic remedy characterized by protecting domestic products with tariffs, import quotas, and other barriers to trade with other countries

isolationism
an economic remedy characterized by refusing to trade with other countries

they came into common usage.⁹ At its heart, Keynesianism argued that government intervention in the economy was necessary to prevent the extreme economic cycles of boom and bust, with a view to reaching full employment. For example, when the economy was slowing down, governments could create temporary employment opportunities and spend money on public works to "prime the pump" of the country's economic engine to stimulate growth. Governments could also lower taxes and interest rates to encourage consumers and businesses to buy goods and make investments, thus further promoting a healthy economy and getting people back to work. Likewise, when the economy was drawing near to full employment and beginning to overheat, governments could alleviate inflationary pressure by raising taxes and/or interest rates (see figure 7.1). This cursory explanation greatly simplifies the Keynesian approach, but the widespread adoption of this philosophy in Canada and elsewhere after World War II had a dramatic effect on public policy and the civil service.

Accompanying these economic policy shifts was a growing public demand for government services in other areas of Canadian society. Taken together, these forces spurred growth in the public sector. Each new government program required staff, resources, and infrastructure. As Canada's social safety net took shape during the 1950s and 1960s, the public sector likewise expanded to accommodate the increasing responsibility. Most of the initial recruitment took place through an affirmative action program that gave returning war veterans preference in hiring. Although this influx was to triple the size of the public service in Canada, it had little effect on public sector organization and operations. In fact, it wasn't until the baby boom generation entered the workforce in the late 1960s and early 1970s that a substantial transformation occurred. This new group of university-educated professionals saw themselves as more than just tools of policy implementation—they were also instruments of change, and as such should be actively involved in creating and evaluating public policy. These public servants were eager to apply current business strategies and the latest in technical analysis to the practice of government. As their skills became accepted, recognized, and respected, the public service in Canada greatly enhanced its power and influence within the political process.

Some critics feared that bureaucratic influences were threatening the integrity of the political process because unelected technocrats appeared to be supplanting the authority of elected representatives. Democratic principle dictated that politicians be held accountable to their constituents for the policy decisions they made, but how could this happen when these decisions were in reality being made by an unelected bureaucratic elite? This debate was only one among several that contributed to the emergence in the early 1970s of a political philosophy that drew on both new and traditional concepts of governance for its platform. As before, this development would result in dramatic changes in the nature and operation of the public service.

The Neoconservative State

The Keynesian welfare state came under increasing attack for both theoretical and practical reasons during the 1970s. First, a phenomenon known as **stagflation** cast doubt on the Keynesian economic strategy. Stagflation refers to an economic situation of high unemployment and high inflation at the same time, something that

stagflation
a situation where an economy experiences high unemployment and high inflation at the same time

FIGURE 7.1a   Classic Free-Market Business Cycle

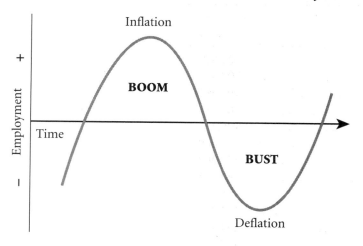

Economic Boom

During periods of accelerated economic activity, demand for goods and services creates upward pressure on prices (inflation). As the economy reaches full employment, prices become too high, and demand falls off. As this occurs, the need for labour also decreases, resulting in growing unemployment.

Economic Bust (Recession)

As unemployment rises, demand for goods and services drops, and prices continue to fall (deflation). As the economy sinks into recession, high unemployment causes social upheaval, as individuals struggle to survive (rising crime, family breakup, etc.).

FIGURE 7.1b   Keynesian Business Cycle (Government Intervention)

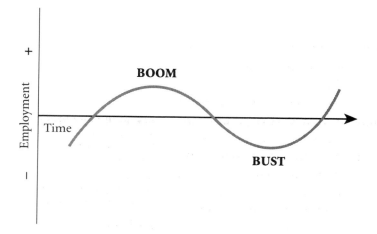

Keynes and subsequent followers argued that governments could lessen the extremes of the business cycle by actively intervening in their country's economy.

Boom with Government Intervention

1. Higher taxes increase cost of goods and services, thus curbing demand more quickly.
2. Raising interest rates increases cost of borrowing money (car loans, mortgages for homes, etc.), thus slowing consumption.

Bust with Government Intervention

1. Lower taxes and interest rates encourage consumption and investment.
2. "Priming the pump" stimulates economic activity —for example, funding make-work programs or extending cheap loans to aid private enterprise.

the Keynesian model had determined to be impossible (see figure 7.1). Second, the public began to lose faith in government's ability to solve social problems and increasingly viewed its activity as invasive, ineffective, and meddlesome. In addition, the media began to scrutinize the actions of government much more aggressively. The widely publicized Watergate scandal in the 1970s, during which US government officials, including then President Richard Nixon, used wiretapping and other undercover means to find damaging evidence against opposition Democrats, highlighted the potential abuse of political power and cast doubt on the integrity of politicians and bureaucrats. Stories of government waste and excess now received sensational media coverage, and governments faced mounting pressure to account for the tax dollars they spent.

Collectively, the general public malaise with government that was characteristic of the mid-1970s led to calls for a return to a more traditional role for government. The ensuing ideological discussion eventually produced a hybrid political philosophy. **Neoconservatism** ("neo" meaning new) criticized the Keynesian approach to

neoconservatism
a conservative political philosophy that argues that government should revert to the limited role it played at the beginning of the 20th century, particularly in social and economic areas

TABLE 7.1   Employment in the Federal Public Service, 1995–2007

Year	Number of employees
1995	225,619
1996	207,977
1997	194,396
1998	187,187
1999	186,314
2000	146,689
2001	155,360
2002	164,221
2003	168,864
2004	171,457
2005	171,125
2006	177,971
2007	180,986

Source: Canada Public Service Agency. © Canada Public Service Agency. Data for 2006 and 2007 taken from Public Service Commission of Canada, "Public Service Commission 2006-2007 Annual Report—Highlights" (2007), www.psc-cfp.gc.ca.

government, arguing that government should revert to the limited role it had played at the beginning of the century, particularly in social and economic areas.

Neoconservative ideas prompted academics and others to search for new ways of thinking about government's role in society. What resulted became known as the **new public management** (NPM). The general premise of NPM was that government had overextended itself—that is, it was doing too much and had become preoccupied with bureaucratic procedure. As one source put it, government was doing "too much rowing, not enough steering"[10] in its pursuit of the **public good**. In practical terms, this meant shrinking the size and scope of government activity, deregulating various economic sectors, and privatizing the public sector in many jurisdictions.

Neoconservative government first surfaced in Great Britain under Margaret Thatcher, then in the United States during Ronald Reagan's presidency. In Canada, Prime Minister Brian Mulroney's Progressive Conservative government introduced this new approach. The Liberals under Prime Minister Jean Chrétien continued this trend and, as we will see below, prolonged and even accelerated it.

The impact of neoconservative policies on the Canadian public service over the past two decades has been dramatic. Because of layoffs, budget cuts, and downsizing, the public service has not only shrunk in size (see table 7.1), but also had to redefine itself to stay current and continue to meet the needs of all Canadians.

Today's Public Service

The public service in Canada has very little in common with its 1867 counterpart. Today its hiring practices are based on merit rather than patronage, and it is vastly more complex and professional. Employment is handled by the Public Service Commission, an administrative agency reporting to Parliament ensuring "that persons appointed to positions in the federal Public Service meet all of the required job qualifications."[11]

new public management
an approach based on the belief that government has overextended itself by doing too much and becoming preoccupied with bureaucratic procedure

public good
the complex fabric of publicly funded goods and services that contribute to the collective well-being of a state

The goal, however, remains the same—to serve the public interest. So, who are the people behind the monolithic term "bureaucracy"? How are they organized? Let us begin by noting the difference between the public service of yesterday and today. In 1867, approximately 2,700 people worked for the federal government. Today, the federal government employs more than half a million Canadians in a variety of capacities both inside and outside the public sector proper, as defined earlier. In spite of recent cutbacks, the municipal, provincial, and federal governments collectively employ some 3.2 million people, constituting 19 percent of Canada's workforce.[12]

Federal public servants work in one of six major occupational categories: operational, technical, foreign service, administrative, administrative support, scientific and professional, and executive. Each classification denotes certain jobs and pay rates, and these hold true for an employee regardless of the area in which he or she is employed. In addition to general qualifications, other factors such as language, regional interests, and equity affect the hiring process. These determinants reflect a desire on the part of government to respect the **theory of representativeness**. The theory asserts that a representative public service should include employees from all the major ethnic, religious, and socioeconomic groups in Canada. In other words, if the public service is to be responsive to the needs of all Canadians, it should represent a cross-section of Canadian society. For example, police services across Canada want to attract more women and visible minorities to the profession to correct the overrepresentation of white males in their ranks. This aim has been criticized by those who argue that efficiency and effectiveness may be compromised by these initiatives. Should selection favour less-qualified candidates from underrepresented groups? Does one have to be from a certain background to be sensitive to the needs of people of the same background? The issue is complex, and the debate surrounding it will likely continue for some time.

Linguistic and regional representation have played a significant part in shaping who we are as a nation, and this in turn affects the public service. Federal government offices are distributed across Canada to equitably distribute employment opportunities and to provide a local presence for a central government that may be thousands of kilometres away. This manifestation of federal activity demonstrates to citizens that their taxes are, in fact, being used in their area.

The historical importance of the French language and culture in Canada has already been noted, and it is for this reason that the federal government has actively recruited French Canadians to work in the public service. Up to the 1960s, English Canadians constituted the vast majority of federal public servants. Steps were taken to reflect the French presence in Canadian political culture. Through progressive policy action such as the formation of the Royal Commission on Bilingualism and Biculturalism in the late 1960s and the passage of the *Official Languages Act* in 1969,[13] the federal government succeeded in increasing the number of French Canadians in its public service. They now represent about 32 percent of the federal public service. This rate has remained relatively stable over the past five years.[14]

Federal public servants won the right to collectively bargain in 1967, long after this right had been granted to workers in the private sector.[15] The unionization of the public sector since then has resulted in some interesting dilemmas for the unions and the government. Unlike in the private sector, where the interests of labour are pitted against profit maximization, collective bargaining in the public sector incorporates the dynamics of political power and the public good. We already

theory of representativeness theory that if the public service is to be responsive to the needs of all Canadians, it should represent a cross-section of Canadian society

know, for example, that governments raise revenues through taxation to fund public services. Therefore, it is the public that ultimately pays for any new expenses incurred as a result of negotiations taking place between government and a public sector union. Beyond this, however, lies a deeper implication. Some observers note that public sector unions may restrict or subvert government policy options by making demands that force their employer to do things it might otherwise reject. For example, a government may wish to give its citizens a tax cut or to cut its deficit and debt, but may be forced to abandon such an endeavour because of the increased wages and benefits it has just negotiated with a union. Further still, the precedent set by one union may serve as the benchmark for all subsequent collective bargaining. For example, a 5 percent wage increase for one police service may be used by other services as their wage demand.

Although there is always a danger that this sort of policy manipulation may occur, public sector unions seem to experience far less success than their counterparts in the private sector. For example, a 2003 study of trades workers in the public service showed that federal employees earned 20 percent less than their counterparts in the private sector, or at the provincial and municipal levels.[16] Under Prime Minister Stephen Harper, the Conservative government has flagged improving relations with the public service as a priority, but morale remains low and funding cuts continue.[17] It comes as no surprise, then, that the public sector is experiencing difficulty in attracting people, who no longer see it as a challenging career option. This trend must be reversed if the integrity of public service in Canada is to be preserved.

Get Real!

WHISTLE-BLOWERS IN THE PUBLIC SERVICE

The size, structure, and function of the public service in Canada have changed a great deal over time, and they continue to evolve as we re-evaluate and redefine the role of both government and administration in this country. Many questions remain: Should the services currently administered publicly be privatized? (See the previous chapter for related discussion.) Should the public service continue to be downsized? How do we ensure that the public service is a professional and effective entity? Should the political and administrative apparatuses of government be kept separate? Is it even possible to do so? And, finally, to whom is a public servant ultimately accountable? This question of accountability has been at the centre of efforts to improve the public service in Canada in recent years, especially as it concerns the rights of whistle-blowers.

A whistle-blower, in this context, refers to a public servant who speaks publicly about alleged wrongdoing in his or her government department or agency. For example, in 1999, a 26-year veteran of the RCMP, Corporal Robert Read, went public with allegations of corruption involving Canada's diplomatic mission in Hong Kong. Read was one of six investigators leading an RCMP investigation, which found that members of the mission were accepting bribes from wealthy Chinese families in exchange for Canadian visas, and that potential criminal charges were being swept under the rug in order to maintain good relations between the RCMP and Foreign Affairs. Read alleged that when these conclusions were brought before a joint committee of RCMP officials and various government departments, he was urged to keep the findings secret. Instead, he blew the whistle by granting media interviews to publicize the investigation. He was charged with disgraceful conduct and fired for violating the RCMP oath of secrecy. An external review committee determined that Read had the right to go public, but the RCMP refused to reinstate him. He took his case to the Federal Court of Canada, which supported the RCMP's decision to dismiss him, citing Read's "lack of loyalty to the government." In May 2007, the Supreme Court of Canada refused to hear Read's appeal. [18]

Ironically, the Supreme Court dismissal of the Read case came less than a year after passage of the *Federal Accountability Act*, a legislative package introduced by the Harper government that, among other things, aims to protect whistle-blowers in the public service. Of particular note in the legislative package is the *Public Servants Disclosure Protection Act* (PSDPA). The government has summarized the purpose of the PSDPA as follows:

> The Public Service of Canada is a multifaceted institution staffed by professional, dedicated, and highly skilled people. Its employees play a crucial role in supporting the Government's agenda and helping it deliver programs and services to citizens. Canadians have every right to expect that public office holders and public sector employees behave ethically and in accordance with their legal obligations. The public sector must, therefore, foster an environment in which employees may honestly and openly raise concerns without fear or threat of reprisal. [19]

Any piece of legislation that encourages a more ethical approach to administration would seem straightforward, yet as the Read case demonstrates, the issue is not always quite so black and white in practice. In fact, there are many opponents of the *Federal Accountability Act*, among them an alliance of some of the most well-known whistle-blowers in recent Canadian history. The group Federal Accountability Initiative for Reform (FAIR) was founded in 1998 by whistle-blower Joanna Gualtieri, whose says her public service career was derailed after she exposed "extravagant" Foreign Affairs overspending violations. Gualtieri and FAIR agree that "there are serious problems of mismanagement and corruption within the Canadian public service," and that this "corruption and mismanagement strike at the heart of our prosperous, free and democratic way of life." Whistle-blowers, they say, "play a vital role and need protection." However, FAIR does not feel that Harper's 2006 legislation is up to the task. Among their criticisms: whistle-blowers are not in fact permitted to voice their concerns publicly, in that they must first go through an intensive internal process of report and review. In the case of the RCMP, for example, members wishing to "do the right thing" cannot go directly to the federal integrity commissioner, but must instead bring their concerns to the RCMP commissioner for an internal investigation. Further, FAIR charges, the PSDPA contains a "duty of loyalty" clause, which states that public servants owe a duty of loyalty to their employer (recall the Federal Court's admonishment to Robert Read). They want the Act amended to reflect that public servants owe an equal duty of loyalty to the Canadian people. [20]

What are your thoughts on accountability and loyalty within the public service? To whom should public servants answer, and how might this affect the integrity of government services? Does legislation like the PSDPA actually give public servants the avenues they require to address wrongdoing without reprisal? Or is it mere window dressing?

SUMMARY

The evolution of public administration coincided with the development of a merit-based, professional public service in Canada. The nature and operation of the public service were also affected by socioeconomic changes taking place at home and abroad. Before World War II, Canada's public service existed within a minimalist state: government activity was limited in scope, so the public service was relatively small.

As the ideas of John Maynard Keynes took hold after the war, government's role expanded greatly as public demand for services increased and state involvement in social services became commonplace. The expansion continued until the early 1970s, when several events contributing to general public dissatisfaction with government resulted in the emergence of a hybrid political philosophy called neoconservatism. The practice of neoconservatism in the public sector, called the new public management, has led to a retrenchment of government activity in many areas and the privatization and deregulation of various sectors of the economy. The public service has thus undergone many changes since Confederation. It has evolved into a complex organization employing thousands of people that attempts to reflect a regional and cultural diversity that is uniquely Canadian.

Comparing and contrasting the public and private sectors helps to illustrate what can happen when the rules of private enterprise are applied to public institutions. The results of such policy choices deserve further scrutiny to properly assess both the short- and long-term consequences for society as a whole. As we have seen in the "Get Real!" section, the blurring of the line between public and private administration creates challenges in determining who is ultimately accountable to citizens, and how problems are to be addressed.

KEY TERMS

isolationism

laissez-faire capitalism

minimalist state

neoconservatism

new public management

politics–administrative dichotomy

protectionism

public good

stagflation

theory of representativeness

NOTES

1. Quoted in *Oxford Dictionary of Quotations*, 4th ed. (Oxford: Oxford University Press, 1992), 136-137.

2. A survey done in 1992 ranᵒked public service at the municipal, provincial, and federal levels 5th, 7th, and 8th, respectively, in a study of impressions of service quality among eight private and public sector organizations. Insight Canada Research, *Perspectives Canada*, vol. 1, no. 4 (Fall 1992), 36.

3. This period in American history is referred to as the Progressive Era. It is perhaps most notable for the widespread reform of public services such as health, education, and welfare, particularly in urban areas. See Paul S. Boyer et al., *The Enduring Vision: A History of the American People* (Lexington, MA: D.C. Heath, 1990), 752-789.

4. For a complete listing, see the SchoolFinder.com website.

5. Laurent Dobuzinskis, "Public Administration," in Michael Howlett and David Laycock, eds., *Puzzles of Power: An Introduction to Political Science*, 2nd ed. (Toronto: Oxford University Press, 1998), 156.

6. During the time of Sir John A. Macdonald, for example, the number of civil servants numbered only about 2,700. Ralph Heintzman, "Introduction: Canada and Public Administration," in Jacques Bourgault, Maurice Demers, and Cynthia Williams, eds., *Public Administration and Public Management: Experiences in Canada* (Sainte-Foy, QC: Les Publications du Québec, 1997), 4.

7. Alvin Finkel and Margaret Conrad with Veronica Strong-Boag, *History of the Canadian Peoples, Vol. 2: 1867 to the Present* (Toronto: Copp Clark, 1985), 12-19, 285.

8. Keynes was among the British delegation at the peace negotiations, and he argued against punitive measures against Germany. The ensuing hyperinflation that accompanied the drastic drop in value of the German currency and the rise of the Nazi party in Germany were seen as proof that he was indeed correct. See J.M. Keynes, *The Economic Consequences of the Peace* (New York: Harcourt, Brace and Howe, 1920).

9. One of the most widely publicized approaches was that carried out by US President Franklin Roosevelt, whose "New Deal" and its offspring "National Recovery Administration" attempted to influence wages, work hours, and prices. See Frank Friedel and Alan Brinkley, *America in the Twentieth Century*, 5th ed. (New York: McGraw-Hill, 1982), 221-261.

10. David Osborne and Ted Gaebler, *Reinventing Government* (Reading, MA: Addison-Wesley, 1992).

11. Electronic communication with Diane Rhéaume, Communications Adviser, Media Relations, Public Service Commission, June 2004.

12. See Statistics Canada, "Public Sector Employment," *The Daily* (August 30, 2007), available online at www.statcan.ca/Daily/English/070830/d070830c.htm.

13. *Official Languages Act*, RSC 1985, c. 31 (4th Supp.).

14. See Public Service Commission of Canada, "Public Service Commission 2006-2007 Annual Report—Highlights" (2007), available online at www.psc-cfp.gc.ca/index_e.htm. See also Canada Public Service Agency, "Annual Report on Official Languages—2005-06" (2007), available online at www.psagency-agencefp.gc.ca/reports-rapports/ol-lo/arol-ralo05-06-1_e.asp#Toc04.

15. Trade unions were illegal in Canada before 1872, and afterward governments remained reluctant to grant any meaningful right to bargain collectively. Leo Panitch and Donald Swartz, *The Assault on Trade Union Freedoms: From Wage Controls to Social Contract* (Toronto: Garamond Press, 1993), 17.

16. Public Service Alliance of Canada, "Joint Study Confirms That Federal Trades Workers Are Underpaid" (October 23, 2003), available online at www.psac.com.

17. Kathryn May, "The Spending Brakes Are On," *The Ottawa Citizen* (May 3, 2006), A8.

18. Joan Delaney, "Whistleblower Legislation Needs More Work, Say Critics," *Epoch Times* (May 17, 2007), available online at http://en.epochtimes.com/news/7-5-17/55413.html.

19. See Government of Canada, "Providing Real Protection for Whistleblowers" (August 7, 2007), available online at www.faa-lfi.gc.ca.

20. For more information, see the website of the Federal Accountability Initiative for Reform at www.fairwhistleblower.ca.

EXERCISES

Multiple Choice

1. The politics–administrative dichotomy views

   a. politics as the implementation function of government

   b. politics as the decision-making apparatus of government

   c. administration as the decision-making apparatus of government

   d. administration as the implementation function of government

   e. b and d

2. The following factor(s) had an impact on the evolution of the Canadian public service:

   a. the urbanization and industrialization of Canada in the late 1800s

   b. events and issues in other countries, such as the United States

   c. growing public demand for government services

   d. theoretical ideas, such as those of Max Weber, Frederick Winslow Taylor, and John Maynard Keynes

   e. all of the above

3. Stagflation is a situation where an economy experiences

   a. high unemployment and low inflation at the same time

   b. low unemployment and high inflation at the same time

   c. low unemployment and low inflation at the same time

   d. high unemployment and high inflation at the same time

   e. no change in unemployment or inflation

4. Neoconservatism argues that

   a. government should intervene heavily in social and economic areas

   b. government should have a limited role in social and economic areas

   c. government should increase the size of the public service

   d. government should increase the scope of its activity

   e. government should regulate various economic sectors

5. The theory of representativeness basically holds that

   a. the public service should reflect the ethnic, religious, and socioeconomic diversity of Canadian society

   b. the public service can be more responsive to the needs of all Canadians if it represents a cross-section of Canadian society

   c. linguistic and regional representation in the public service is important

   d. a local presence for federal government, in the form of offices across Canada, is desirable

   e. all of the above

True or False?

_____ 1. According to the politics–administrative dichotomy, bureaucrats should decide *what* to do, and politicians should figure out *how* to do it.

_____ 2. In the minimalist state, social services are not considered a responsibility of government.

_____ 3. The Keynesian model offers a solution to stagflation.

_____ 4. Canada's official bilingualism is an example of the theory of representativeness in action.

Short Answer

1. What is the politics–administrative dichotomy? What is its major shortcoming?

2. Define "minimalist state." What factors led to changing this approach?

3. Explain the major concepts of the Keynesian welfare state. Why did this approach to government come under attack in the 1970s?

4. Explain the theory of representativeness in your own words, and give examples of how the theory is put into action.

5. How is politics involved in public service union collective bargaining? Why do public servants face more challenges in changing their work conditions than their private sector counterparts?

6. Outline the benefits and drawbacks of enacting whistle-blower legislation.

CHAPTER 8

The Art of Government: Making Public Policy

CHAPTER OBJECTIVES

After completing this chapter, you should be able to:

- Define the term "public policy" and describe the process of formulating, implementing, and evaluating it.

- Distinguish among a variety of policy instruments, and determine why governments choose to use one rather than another in a given situation.

- Using recent examples, analyze and assess the changing role of police associations in the public policy process.

- Understand the difficulties politicians face in instituting public policy while attempting to satisfy various stakeholders.

- Propose public policy alternatives to address rising costs in the justice sector, in the context of larger government initiatives.

INTRODUCTION

[W]hat begins as a failure of perception among intellectual specialists finds its fulfilment in policy and action.

—Lionel Trilling, literary critic[1]

How often have you heard politicians make promises at election time and then fail to fulfill them once they're elected? Dalton McGuinty promised no new taxes during the election campaign of 2003. Yet, in his first budget as premier, he announced that people in Ontario would have to pay a health care premium to help cover shortfalls in provincial revenue. McGuinty also increased taxes on alcohol and tobacco (commonly known as "sin taxes"). Likewise, there remains a popular belief that the former Ontario government of Mike Harris did only what it said it would do when, in fact, several major initiatives implemented under its direction were never mentioned during the election campaign of 1995.[2] Former Prime Minister Jean Chrétien promised Canadians he would abolish the hated goods and services tax (GST) during the federal election of 1993. Yet, over a decade later it remains with us. It is easy (and, to a certain degree, occasionally appropriate) to blame individual politicians for making promises they cannot keep. But it is too shortsighted and simplistic to conclude that the "say one thing, do another" phenomenon is a character flaw exclusive to politicians.

The foregoing raises some interesting questions about the process that shapes public policy. Why does it appear to most of us that there never seems to be any one definitive answer to problems facing government? This chapter will provide you with at least a partial answer to this question.

WHAT IS PUBLIC POLICY?

public policy
what government does or does not do

The art of government is based on several key elements, among them leadership, integrity, and the ability to articulate an overall vision that has the support of the population. This requires a great deal of coordination, discussion, debate, planning, and evaluation on the part of officials. The result of this interaction is **public policy**. Defining this term is a challenge, and there are several definitions to choose from.[3] Simply put, however, "Public policy is whatever governments choose to do or not to do."[4] This statement is intentionally broad. Public policy encompasses the "big picture"; it resists being distilled into a single act or law. In addition, public policy reflects what government does rather than what it says it will do. Statements made by politicians on a particular issue do not always produce policy. Again, however, public policy also reflects what a government chooses *not* to do.

MAKING PUBLIC POLICY

There are three fundamental stages to executing almost any exercise: formulation, implementation, and evaluation. The public policy process is no different. However, accomplishing these tasks within an organization as vast and complex as government constitutes a significant challenge for a number of reasons. Let's examine each step to see why this is so.

classical technocratic
a model of public policy in which decisions originate with politicians, who then provide bureaucrats with clear direction as to what should be done

bureaucratic entrepreneur
a model of public policy in which bureaucratic experts within government come up with policy ideas and then approach elected officials to obtain the resources and public legitimacy necessary to implement their programs

Formulation—What Is It We Want To Do?

The two major stakeholders in formulating, implementing, and evaluating public policy are politicians and bureaucrats. The relative power of each of these players can significantly affect the nature and shape of public policy. The theoretical continuum in figure 8.1 provides a general framework as to where policy originates and the effect this can have on government as a whole.

At one extreme, known as the **classical technocratic** linkage, broad public policy decisions originate with politicians, who then provide bureaucrats with clear direction as to what should be done. This model draws on the Weberian bureaucratic ideal, where structure and communication are hierarchical and instruction is commonly understood and accepted. At the other extreme, the **bureaucratic entrepreneur** approach, bureaucratic experts within government come up with policy ideas, and then approach elected officials to obtain the resources and public legitimacy necessary to implement their programs. There are any number of points

FIGURE 8.1   Public Policy Continuum

Classical
Technocratic

Bureaucratic
Entrepreneur

along this continuum sharing influence between these partners.[5] You may also notice that as one moves toward the bureaucratic entrepreneur end of the continuum, democratic input decreases.

Although very simple, this model is useful because it helps illustrate that it is not politicians alone who are responsible for bringing policy ideas to public attention. Take, for example, the McGuinty government's apparent flip-flop on taxes. A classical technocratic analysis of this phenomenon might suggest that Liberal politicians were forced to change course because, once assuming power, they realized that the province was forecasting a $5.6 billion deficit. Public demand for improved public services expressed during the campaign left the new government with only one option. Rather than cut services, it decided to raise taxes, and told the bureaucracy (government departments and agencies) to come up with ideas as to how to increase revenues.

If, however, the bureaucratic entrepreneur analysis is employed, the scenario changes. In this instance, one might imagine senior public servants coming to the newly elected government and informing them of the fiscal reality, accompanied perhaps by estimates of just how much their campaign promises, if implemented, will add to the deficit. Senior bureaucrats might then present a variety of options (cuts to or elimination of public services, selling government assets, tax increases) to their political masters, with a view to protecting the public service from more cutbacks and downsizing. The end result might be that, given these unpalatable choices, the least offensive route for politicians to follow might be increasing taxes.

Although this greatly simplifies the reality of the relationship between these two key players, it does shed considerable light on the interdependence of both parties involved. Neither should we forget that each represents a vastly complex organization of individuals and groups, each of which may or may not support policy options as they develop. As you may have already guessed, several other actors also influence the policy-making process. The media may focus public attention on issues that in turn prompt some action or response by public officials. Interest groups and lobbyists may also intervene, providing input to advance or deter a course of action, or to propose alternatives.

The term "interest group" covers a wide variety of people and organizations concerned with influencing the actions and policies of government. Many are organizations with objectives that normally do not involve government, but who can become politically active when a proposed or existing public policy affects them. For example, a local historical association whose mandate it is to preserve and protect local history might decide to persuade its area politicians to prevent destruction of a heritage building. Others exist for the express purpose of monitoring and influencing government policy. These are sometimes referred to as "pressure groups."[6] Their primary focus is on how the actions of government affect the issue with which they are concerned. For example, People for Education is a citizen-based organization that monitors the quality of public education in Ontario. It tracks changes to educational policy and funding, releasing periodic reports for discussion and recommending policy initiatives to government.[7]

Although interest groups and pressure groups "lobby" government for their causes, the term "lobbyist" may be understood as potential "political persuasion for hire"—that is, a lobbyist is a paid professional who provides research, advice, and varying degrees of access to government decisions. The practice is not new, nor should it be understood by definition as undesirable. Information supplied by lobbyists can aid politicians and bureaucrats in defining and designing public policy desired by citizens. The danger is that because there is a degree of self-interest involved, lobbyists may also subvert or distort popular attitudes to achieve their purpose. In an attempt to monitor this situation, both the Ontario and federal governments have enacted legislation requiring lobbyists to register with the Office of the Integrity Commissioner and the Office of the Registrar of Lobbyists, respectively, but even these agencies capture but a small fraction of this activity.[8]

Implementation—Let's Do It!

Once a policy decision is made, it must be carried out if it is to be of any use. Implementation refers to policy in action. It poses some of the biggest challenges for government, for it is at this stage that intent and consequence often become separated. Increasingly, citizens, interest groups, and the media have been calling on governments to account for discrepancies between policies and subsequent actions and results. Consequently, governments have begun to pay more attention to implementation. Leaving evaluation aside for a moment, let us consider some of the reasons implementation can fail to achieve desired aims.

With government as complex as it is, the margin for conscious and unconscious error in the areas of organization, coordination, communication, and time lag can alter the original intent and the ultimate success of a policy decision. Much has been written about these pitfalls and how to avoid them, but their detail is beyond the scope of this text. It may be easier to illustrate the message by using a scenario based on the implementation of a law-and-order promise by an incoming provincial government.

You have just been hired as a police constable in Goodville, a town of about 5,000 in a largely rural area of the province. Having been a diligent student, your knowledge of law and its enforcement extends beyond simple academics to include pertinent issues that affect your job. Reading the newspaper one morning, you observe that the premier has announced that the province is getting tough on crime. You think this sounds positive, but without specifics, you have no way to judge what this statement means to you and your profession. At the division, other officers and the chief discuss the policy and draw similar conclusions. Should your professional demeanour change? You decide that unless new directives are issued, you will carry on as usual.

A few days later, you are told that the province is drafting a bill to articulate its policy, but the chief confides to staff that politicians are not listening to police chiefs and that she does not support the move. You hear from colleagues in other divisions that other chiefs are opposed as well. Meanwhile, the draft legislation has been criticized as being too costly by the finance department, so changes are being made that will save money but alter the bill's intent. The police chiefs are still unhappy and have recommended other changes to the bill. The media weigh in on the policy, pointing to falling crime rates and questioning the government's actions. After much tinkering and amendment, the bill is passed into law. Your chief declares that she will "interpret" the new legislation for the rank and file, but her perspective on some of its aspects seems at odds with its intent. To complicate matters, the staff and resources required to handle new tasks are being held up in legislative debate. By the time you receive a revised code of conduct, the government has decided not to pursue this matter because health care has become the focus of popular attention thanks to several media stories on the topic. Your chief is happy, but her abrupt retirement a few weeks later results in the appointment of someone who favours the government's abandoned initiative. It's all getting so political that you begin to wonder how anything is accomplished in government.

Before you throw up your hands in frustration, take some comfort in the fact that any large organization faces these challenges every day. But the task of getting things done in the private sector is less complicated than in the public sector. Public accountability and democratic sensibilities add layers of coordination and communication that necessarily encumber efficiency. Often by the time one policy initiative has worked its way through the system it has changed or has produced an unintended consequence. Governments therefore monitor this process through various stages and techniques of evaluation.

Evaluation—Did It Work?

Evaluation can be conducted during the implementation phase or following its completion—that is, once its outcomes are known. Evaluating the success of a government program isn't as simple as measuring tangibles, such as cost-effectiveness and efficiency, as might be done in the private sector. Because their ultimate goal is to serve the public good, government agencies must look for additional ways to evaluate what they do. Evaluation is all about accountability—demonstrating to interested parties that you are meeting organizational goals in a way that is acceptable to all concerned. In a private company, shareholders tend to focus on profit, so evaluations, whether they are about customer satisfaction or corporate image, ultimately refer back to maintaining or increasing profit. As citizens, we demand accountability from governments because it is we who pay the taxes that enable them to function. But measuring the effectiveness of public sector activity is not simply a matter of a financial cost–benefit analysis. Providing for the public good may mean operating some programs at a loss.

The other challenge facing public service managers is that it is sometimes difficult to identify specific criteria for measurement. How, for example, does one quantify national defence or measure the quality of justice? How would we know that these had improved over time? This problem of intangibility is not unsolvable, nor should it be used to justify abandoning any attempt at public accountability. However, it does highlight some of the challenges of public sector evaluation.

Remember, too, that evaluation costs time and money. For example, hiring or assigning civil servants or outside agencies to audit government programs can add significantly to their cost, meaning less money for the programs themselves, and can divert scarce human resources required to maintain a high quality of service. Thus, governments must strike a balance between the need to evaluate their activities and the real costs they will incur as a result.

The success or failure of a policy initiative lies ultimately in the hands of bureaucrats. After all, they are the experts who have supplied much of the information necessary for their political masters to make these critical decisions. Likewise, the ability of public servants to present or withhold certain information in the formulation, implementation, and evaluation stages of the policy process places them at a distinct advantage over their political colleagues. As Reginald A. Whittaker notes:

> [I]t is the permanent officials who normally have greater access to information resources. Ministers, after all, are also MPs and party politicians who spend much of their time giving speeches, travelling, attending political functions, and engaging in activities quite remote from the business of their ministerial portfolios. In many cases, they have no previous training or experience in the policy fields of their departments, little time to gain such knowledge while there, and a relatively short span in one portfolio before they move on. ... The bureaucracy, on the other hand, was there before, and will be there long after.[9]

The politics–administrative partnership that Whittaker alludes to can be either creative or debilitating, yet it represents a key element without which government would cease to function. Evaluating government activity is one way of ensuring that both sides are acting in a responsible manner. As citizens have demanded more accountability from government, evaluation has become an important part of public sector programs. Public acceptance of policy decisions is one significant indicator of their success. There are several ways to monitor public compliance with government policy.

POLICY INSTRUMENTS AND DEGREES OF REGULATION

policy instrument
method employed by governments to ensure compliance with public policy and to achieve their goals

Once a policy decision is in place, governments have a range of options to choose from to ensure general compliance. Referred to as **policy instruments**, these are methods employed by governments to achieve their goals. The choice of instrument depends on a number of factors and can range from non-coercive inactive involvement (essentially, letting individuals and businesses regulate themselves) to coercive active involvement—in short, it is a question of the extent to which government wants to intrude into and influence private decisions.

This level of intrusion is best described on a continuum of state coercion (see figure 8.2). At one end, the state is largely absent from decision making. Individuals may be encouraged to voluntarily comply with a government objective. For example, municipalities might ask citizens to reduce the amount of water they use, for conservation reasons. Similarly, groups may be allowed to regulate themselves, such as in the case of the law and medical professions. Actions such as these cost very little and may signal relative indifference or reluctance on the part of the state to become involved in a particular area.

Next along the continuum are expenditure instruments, such as social spending (in the form of welfare, pensions, private sector assistance, and so on) or tax breaks offered to encourage individuals and companies to change their behaviour. For example, a policy to reduce poverty among the elderly might increase social assistance payments to needy senior citizens. Likewise, people may be encouraged to save for their retirement through the creation of tax-sheltered retirement savings plans.

After expenditure instruments comes regulation, which is the use of all civil and criminal laws of a state, including rules created by government agencies and

FIGURE 8.2   Continuum of State Coercion

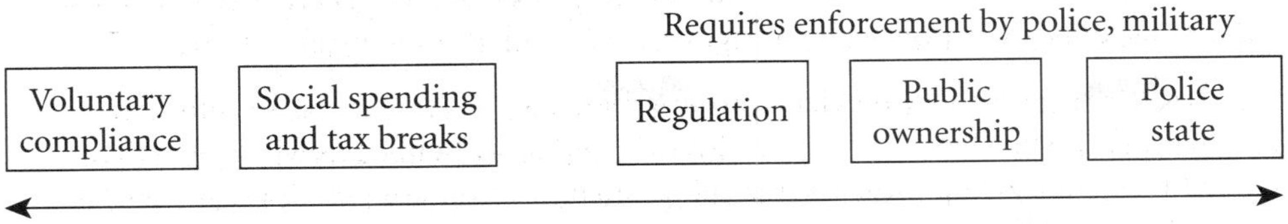

Requires enforcement by police, military

Voluntary compliance	Social spending and tax breaks	Regulation	Public ownership	Police state

rules dealing with taxation. It is at this point that public law enforcement begins to come into play. Governments may use police forces, the military, or both to coerce citizens to comply with certain policies, such as public peace and civic order. In more drastic circumstances, such as natural disasters or serious violence, governments may use public law enforcement agents to take control of private enterprises or restrict individual freedom. This final option is normally seen as a tool of last resort and is used for only a short time in democratic societies. One notable example occurred during the FLQ Crisis in Quebec in 1970.

Next along the continuum is public ownership of certain enterprises, which is generally used when a product or service is considered essential for the public good. Thus utilities such as hydro, water, and telephone service are often publicly owned, although we are seeing a trend toward privatization. At the far end of the continuum is a police state, which is a state in which democratic rights are taken away or do not exist. Such a state is usually run by a dictator or the army, or is imposed in a time of crisis. Canada witnessed such a measure during the FLQ Crisis, when hundreds of Quebeckers were arrested and detained without being told why and without any evidence that they supported the radical separatists.

Except during crises, it seems logical that policy makers usually choose the policy instrument that achieves the intended purpose for the least amount of resources, but they must also consider public perceptions. It may be cheaper to simply post speed limits on roads, but hiring police to enforce these limits is much more effective and is a choice of policy instrument that the public generally accepts. However, some experts contend that politicians make these decisions based on expected voter response.[10] Regardless, it should be clear that these choices have tangible consequences for you, both as a citizen and as a professional in the field of law enforcement. This is because there is considerable flexibility within each policy instrument.

This flexibility allows governments to signal the importance of a particular policy in the overall context of their administration. They are restricted in this exercise by legal traditions, social norms, and current public attitudes on the subject. For example, lawmakers may implement a "get tough" policy on speeding by increasing fines for offending motorists. On the other hand, punishing these individuals by sentencing them to life imprisonment would be seen as excessive and could be characterized as cruel and unusual punishment. Remember, too, the added costs to policing, the courts, and the prison system that this decision would have. As conscientious police officers, how might you and your colleagues react if life imprisonment was the penalty? Would you be less vigilant in apprehending speeders? This illustrates the necessity of common sense and prudence on the part of policy makers in order to secure willing compliance.

Get Real!

PUBLIC POLICY AND THE COST OF JUSTICE

We began this chapter with an example of a broken election promise: Dalton McGuinty assuring voters that, as premier, he would not create any new taxes. And, as we saw, he did just that in his inaugural budget, creating a new health care premium and increasing taxes on alcohol and tobacco. The McGuinty tax tale provides an example of how difficult it can be to make policy decisions that satisfy everyone involved. The fact of the matter is that government services cost money; this money, in large part, comes from taxpayers; and it can be a sometimes impossible balancing act to maintain and improve those services without resorting to unpopular ways to increase revenue. We want better health care; it costs money. We want improved education; it, too, costs. And when the McGuinty government, only a few months into its mandate, was faced with a scathing review of an overcrowded justice system, it was forced to make some tough policy decisions in order to address the crisis in its courts.

In December 2003, two months after the provincial election (and the promised tax break), the auditor general released a report that warned that a "massive" backlog in Ontario's courts could result in tens of thousand of cases being thrown out.[11] The reason: Under the *Charter of Rights and Freedoms*, Canadians have the right "to be tried within a reasonable period of time," a right that had been affirmed by the Supreme Court of Canada with the 1990 *Askov* decision.[12] With too few officials available to process too many cases, the system was on overload, and accused persons were waiting months, even years, for a court date. The McGuinty government responded with the Justice Delay Reduction Initiative, a suite of new hiring and training programs that included the appointment of 15 new judges and the hiring of 116 full-time court staff. "Blitz courts" were created to handle smaller cases, new Crown attorneys were hired, and retired justices of the peace were called back into duty.[13] In 2007, the Office of the Attorney General announced an additional 22 justices to aid municipalities in pushing through their caseloads.[14] Experts say hundreds more officials are needed—a pricey proposition when you consider that, in 2006, most Ontario Court judges earned in excess of $218,000 and some justices of the peace earned as much as $116,594.14.[15]

Imagine that you are an elected official responsible for addressing the above problem: What policy solutions would you propose? Would you follow the same route as the McGuinty government—hire more officials and look to taxpayers to foot the bill? Or would you formulate another way to clear the backlog, one that doesn't involve a tax hike? Is there a way to keep most minor cases from even getting to court? How might you reduce the number of charges being laid? Now consider what might happen if certain stakeholders in this policy issue disagree with your decisions and threaten to derail its implementation. What if the polls show that taxpayers are not happy with having to support your initiatives and are ready to show their displeasure at the ballot box? What if the unions representing court officials launch a publicity campaign saying your policy is not making any real change in courts, and that it is just window dressing for your upcoming election campaign? Finally, consider what you would do when it comes time for an evaluation of your policy, and you must ask taxpayers to foot the bill for a thorough audit.

While it may be true that what you are trying to do here is basically strike an acceptable balance between two entities—Charter rights versus the cost of justice—there are no easy answers. Making public policy is a complicated and difficult exercise, with many parties involved and countless potential repercussions for every decision made.

SUMMARY

Public policy refers to the action (and inaction) of government in a particular area of its operation. Public policy is characterized by an ongoing process of formulation, implementation, and evaluation that involves several actors both inside and outside formal government. Ultimately, however, it is the bureaucracy's job to implement the decisions resulting from these complex interactions.

Governments may choose from a variety of options when it comes to ensuring public compliance with particular policies. These can range from symbolic gestures, such as public information campaigns encouraging voluntary changes in behaviour, to rigid enforcement using police and the military. The policy instrument chosen depends on a number of factors, including the importance of the policy, current relevance, and necessity.

Many players other than politicians and bureaucrats influence public policy, and as such it is a reflection of democracy in our society. The example of the backlog in Ontario's court system illustrates the dilemma inherent in shaping and controlling public policy in a modern democracy such as Canada.

KEY TERMS

bureaucratic entrepreneur

classical technocrat

policy instrument

public policy

NOTES

1. Quoted in *Oxford Dictionary of Quotations*, 4th ed. (Oxford: Oxford University Press, 1992), 702:18.

2. Such measures included the elimination of 15,000 nursing positions in the province, large funding cuts to public education, and the forced amalgamation of municipal governments in Toronto.

3. For example, see definitions by Peter Aucoin, "Public-Policy Theory and Analysis," in G. Bruce Doern and Peter Aucoin, eds., *Public Policy in Canada* (Toronto: Macmillan, 1979), 2; and Malcolm Taylor, *Health Insurance and Canadian Public Policy: The Seven Decisions That Created the Canadian Health Insurance System and Their Outcomes* (Kingston, ON: McGill-Queen's University Press, 1987).

4. Thomas R. Dye, *Understanding Public Policy*, 5th ed. (Englewood Cliffs, NJ: Prentice-Hall, 1992), 1.

5. Robert Nakamura and Frank Smallwood propose five major types of relationship in *The Politics of Policy Implementation* (New York: St. Martin's Press, 1980), ch. 7.

6. The argument for the distinction put forth by some observers is that pressure groups represent a more powerful bloc of influence than do interest groups. See C. Richard Tindal, *A Citizen's Guide to Government*, 2nd ed. (Toronto: McGraw-Hill Ryerson, 2000), 59-62.

7. People for Education website: www.peopleforeducation.com.

8. On the role of lobbying as a positive force, see Robert L. Jackson and Doreen Jackson, *Canadian Government in Transition*, 3rd ed. (Toronto: Pearson Education, 2000), 240-241. For a darker summary of lobbying activity, see Tindal, supra note 6, at 58-62.

9. Reginald A. Whittaker, "Politicians and Bureaucrats in the Policy Process," in Michael S. Whittington and Glen Williams, eds., *Canadian Politics in the 1990s* (Toronto: Nelson, 1995), 429.

10. See, for example, Michael J. Trebilcock et al., *The Choice of Governing Instrument* (Ottawa: Economic Council of Canada, 1982), 27.

11. See "Criminal-Case Backlog 'Worst in a Decade'" (December 2, 2003), available online at www.cbc.ca.

12. The Askov case was a landmark decision for the Supreme Court of Canada. Four people—Askov, Hussey, Gugliotta, and Melo—were charged with conspiracy to commit extortion and related offences in November 1983, but the trial was delayed for two years. When it finally did go to court, the accused moved for a stay of proceedings on the ground of unreasonable delay. The judge granted it; the Crown appealed it; and the Ontario Court of Appeal sided with the Crown, setting the stay aside. The men then took their case to the Supreme Court of Canada, which ruled that their Charter right had indeed been violated. For the full text of the Supreme Court Decision, see *R v. Askov*, [1990] 2 SCR 1199, at www.canlii.org.

13. See Ministry of the Attorney General, Court Services Division, *Annual Report 2004/05*, available online at www.attorneygeneral.jus.gov.on.ca.

14. Ontario, Ministry of the Attorney General, "Attorney General Announces 22 Justice of the Peace Appointments" *Canada NewsWire* (February 11, 2007), available oneline at www.attorneygeneral.jus.gov.on.ca/english/news.

15. For a complete list of salaries for the Ontario public sector, see www.fin.gov.on.ca/english/publications/salarydisclosure/2007.

EXERCISES

Multiple Choice

1. In the classical technocratic approach to shaping public policy

   a. policy decisions originate with politicians

   b. politicians give bureaucrats clear direction on what should be done

   c. structure and communication are hierarchical

   d. instructions are commonly understood and accepted

   e. all of the above

2. Evaluating public policy involves

   a. ensuring that politicians and bureaucrats are acting responsibly

   b. accountability

   c. measuring the effectiveness of public sector activity

   d. demonstrating that goals are being achieved in an acceptable way

   e. all of the above

3. One challenge of evaluating public policy is

   a. the numerous criteria that can be used for measurement

   b. the tangible aspect of results

   c. conducting a simple cost–benefit analysis

   d. focusing on profit

   e. the often unquantifiable nature of outcomes

4. An example of voluntary compliance is

   a. the Canadian Institute of Chartered Accountants setting guidelines for the behaviour of its members

   b. offering a tax break to anyone who puts money in an RRSP

   c. police enforcement of highway speed limits

   d. requiring a licence to operate a business

   e. requiring citizens to file a tax return

5. Which of the following players influence(s) the policy-making process?

   a. politicians

   b. bureaucrats

   c. citizens

   d. the media

   e. all of the above

True or False?

_____ 1. The prime minister *not* abolishing the GST is an example of public policy.

_____ 2. The relative power of politicians and bureaucrats can have a significant effect on public policy.

_____ 3. At one extreme on the continuum of state coercion, individuals are encouraged to voluntarily comply with a government objective.

_____ 4. Public law enforcement comes into play at the point on the continuum of state coercion where a society becomes a police state.

Short Answer

1. What is public policy? Who are the key players in the process?

2. Briefly describe the process of public policy formulation, implementation, and evaluation.

3. What external factors can influence the nature of policy implementation? Give examples.

4. Relate the importance of policy evaluation to public accountability. How are the two connected?

5. What is a policy instrument? What factors influence a government's choice of instrument?

CHAPTER 9

The Bureaucratic Machinery: Government Operations

CHAPTER OBJECTIVES

After completing this chapter, you should be able to:

- Identify and explain the overall purpose of a government department and its role in the Canadian political system.
- Identify and compare a variety of other government bodies, including Crown corporations and regulatory agencies, and discuss their role in government operations.
- Analyze the nature and function of administrative law in relation to the activities of government.
- Discuss and debate the wisdom of government databases and the challenge of protecting and preserving citizen privacy in a post-9/11 world.

INTRODUCTION

Having surveyed the intricacies of the public policy process, the term "machinery of government" no doubt has greater meaning for you. Although this metaphor implies a somewhat negative image, it is useful if you imagine government as a series of organized components, each with a particular purpose, that are connected in some way to the greater whole. For example, the government of Canada is organized through the activity of departments, Crown corporations, and regulatory agencies, all of which make contributions to the public good. In this chapter, we will consider the nature and organization of each of these components to further demystify the process of public administration.

GOVERNMENT DEPARTMENTS AND WHAT THEY DO

When the Canadian government decides to undertake a new policy or launch a new program, it must decide what organizational form would best suit the task. One option is to create a **department** (or ministry at the provincial level). A government department is responsible for carrying out some aspect of government policy. For example, the Department of Health oversees public health; the Department of National Defence protects Canadians through the armed forces and fulfills many international responsibilities.

department
government division responsible for carrying out some aspect of government policy

All departments are statutory bodies—that is, they exist because a law to that effect has been passed in Parliament. At the federal level, the prime minister decides the number and types of departments that are required. There are no formal restrictions, but past practices and current needs guide decision making in this area. In 2007, there were 27 federal Cabinet members (including the prime minister), but under previous governments the number has reached as high as 40.[1] As we learned in the first half of this text, the prime minister and the ministers—the heads of the departments—form the Cabinet, where political power is centred and key policy decisions are made.

Most federal Cabinet ministers are chosen from the pool of MPs elected to the House of Commons. This is in deference to the democratic tenet that states that senior representatives of the public interest must be held accountable to the people they serve. In other words, they must be elected. Each minister is responsible for the official activities of his or her department and is answerable to the public for both good and bad actions taken by the department. This fundamental principle of parliamentary government is called **ministerial responsibility**. It may be easier to think of this concept in terms of a hockey team. When the team is doing poorly, it is not the players who accept ultimate responsibility, nor are they the ones who are fired. As head of the organization it is the coach who assumes responsibility, and hence it is he or she who suffers the consequences. Likewise, even if the minister is personally unaware of departmental wrongdoing, it is the minister who resigns as a symbolic gesture to preserve the public's faith in the political process.

ministerial responsibility
principle of parliamentary government that makes ministers responsible for the official activities of their departments

Traditionally, the principle of ministerial responsibility has carried much weight in Canadian parliamentary affairs. However, recent events have led to speculation that it is losing credibility, both symbolically and in practice. This is because the size and complexity of many government ministries make it virtually impossible for one person to keep track of everything that is happening. Additionally, elections and prime ministerial discretion mean that Cabinet ministers are shuffled in and out of **portfolios** (another term for departments) fairly frequently, in contrast to the private sector.

portfolio
department

A number of cases serve to illustrate this point. Consider for example the highly publicized sponsorship scandal in early 2004. It involved questionable payments during the years 1997–2002 to advertising and communications agencies in Quebec by the federal Public Works department, headed by Alfonso Gagliano. In January 2002, Gagliano was appointed Canada's ambassador to Denmark. When the scandal broke, the new Public Works minister Stephen Owen did not resign, but instead promised to investigate matters raised by the auditor general's report. Gagliano subsequently lost his job as ambassador.

Liberal Cabinet minister Jane Stewart found herself in a similar position in 1999. Formerly the minister of Indian Affairs and Northern Development, she assumed the Human Resources Development Canada (HRDC) portfolio in mid-1999 following a minor federal Cabinet shuffle. By November, stories had begun to surface about financial mismanagement of the Transitional Jobs Fund, an HRDC program that gives grants to promote job creation. Investigation revealed several serious problems, including political patronage, bureaucratic bungling, and lax regulation. Much of the damning information arose from an internal audit going back to 1997, during which Stewart's predecessor, Pierre Pettigrew, was minister.[2] As the scandal grew in early 2000, opposition party calls for Stewart to resign became a daily occurrence despite her brief time in the position until she was shuffled out of Cabinet in December 2003.

Strict adherence to the doctrine of ministerial responsibility dictated that Stewart resign, although most of the activity in question predated her appointment. As you can see, there is some justification for re-examining ministerial responsibility. But to simply abandon it would effectively sever the relationship linking the actions of bureaucrats to the democratic accountability of their political masters and produce a dangerous lack of accountability on the part of the people we elect to represent us. The temptation to abdicate responsibility or shift blame in politics must be kept in check if public faith in the political process is to be preserved.

Deputy Minister

The deputy minister's position marks the point at which political power becomes bureaucratic action. Reporting to the minister (the political head of the department), the deputy minister (DM) is the most senior bureaucrat within that department. While the minister directs the department, the DM ensures that directions are carried out. As such, the DM acts as the go-between for the minister and the civil servants, conveying departmental policy and voicing employee concerns. As we saw in chapter 8, communication is ongoing between the political and administrative components of government; thus, the role of deputy minister is crucial in the realms of policy advice, dispute resolution, and human relations (the "people management" part of the job).

Deputy ministers are appointed by the prime minister, but they report to and are responsible to the minister of their department. This may seem odd at first, but given the environment the justification for this is pretty straightforward. The relative transience of the Cabinet minister in any given portfolio puts departmental stability and continuity at risk (can you imagine having to switch course professors two or three times a semester?). Most DMs are career civil servants who have worked their way up through the ranks and have become experts in their particular area. (Recall Weber's model bureaucracy.) Their consistent presence in the world of political change promotes efficient departmental operation and a reliable source of information and advice for ministers who are new to the job.

As the administrative heads of their respective departments, deputy ministers wield considerable power, some of it in law and some of it in tradition. For example, the *Interpretation Act*, a federal statute relevant to this topic, states that

24(2) Words directing or empowering a minister of the Crown to do an act or thing, regardless of whether the act or thing is administrative, legislative or judicial, or otherwise applying to that minister as the holder of the office, include ...

(c) his or their deputy;[3]

In essence, this allows the minister to delegate a wide range of responsibilities to his or her deputy. DMs are also key players in the development of policy, advising the minister, recommending alternatives, and apprising the minister of expected public responses to and practical limitations of ministerial decisions.

MINISTER VERSUS DEPUTY MINISTER

While the minister–deputy minister relationship is characterized by mutual support, it is important to keep in mind the distinction. DMs cannot make regulations, answer to Parliament on behalf of the minister, or sign Cabinet memoranda. These restrictions aside, it is generally accepted that DMs will manage the day-to-day affairs of their departments, including supervising subordinates, tracking budgets, and performing other administrative activities. While ministers are free to intervene in departmental operations, these are usually left to the DMs. For one thing, Cabinet ministers are usually far too busy with other obligations to become overly involved with departmental affairs.[4] Thus, the degree to which ministers and their deputies venture into management and policy matters, respectively, varies according to their personality and preferences, and political necessity. This precarious balance can overwhelm deputy ministers, who often end up being overloaded with both managerial and policy responsibilities.

There are a couple of important aspects characterizing the position of deputy minister. First, it is non-partisan. This means that DMs remain neutral in their duties, favouring neither a particular party nor its ideological beliefs. Rather, they serve the broader public interest of good government. Of course, this is easier to say than it is to do because of the politicized nature of policy development and the partisan agenda dictated by individual political parties in power.

Second, the post of deputy minister is insulated from direct public scrutiny by virtue of its relative anonymity. This is appropriate, given that it is the minister—an elected representative—who ultimately must accept responsibility for policy decisions in his or her department. Related to this is the knowledge on the part of DMs that in return for their frank and honest advice they will be shielded from public attention. Thus, one rarely hears of a particular deputy minister or other senior bureaucrat in relation to government policy matters.[5]

Classification of Departments

Given the diversity of government departments at the provincial and federal levels, it is sometimes difficult to grasp how they interact with one another to coordinate and effectively carry out government policy. Political scientists use various categories to shed light on the inner workings and overall operation of the bureaucratic machinery.[6] Using these classification systems, we can develop a short series of questions to see where a department fits into the big picture.

FIGURE 9.1   Classifying Departments According to Service and User

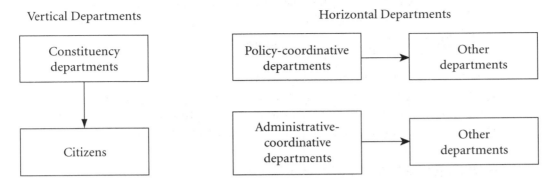

US OR THEM?

Who is the primary beneficiary of the service being provided? Departments exist either to help citizens directly or to assist other government departments. Those that provide services directly to citizens are called **constituency departments** and are considered "vertical" because they hand down services to citizens (see figure 9.1). These types of public services are the most visible and accessible to the public. For example, Public Safety Canada (the former federal Solicitor General) oversees five related programs: corrections, crime prevention, emergency management, national security, and law enforcement. Likewise, Human Resources and Social Development Canada has offices across Canada that provide job search assistance, access to employment insurance benefits, and career guidance. Because they are universal in scope (available to all residents), these departments employ many people and have large budgets.

constituency department
department that provides services directly to citizens

FOLLOW THEM OR LEAD THEM?

Departments that serve other departments are considered "horizontal" because they provide services within and through other departments. They can fall into one of two categories depending on whether they coordinate overall policy or facilitate it. Departments that coordinate policy across government are called **policy-coordinative departments** or central agencies. They set the broad regulation and policy framework under which all other departments operate. For example, the Department of Justice may advise other departments on legal issues, while the Department of Finance can express federal priorities by shrinking or expanding a department's capital and operating budgets. **Administrative-coordinative departments** facilitate the operation of government services. They are involved in the less glamorous but necessary tasks of administration. For example, the Department of Public Works and Government Services looks after common departmental needs such as printing, office space, and purchasing.

policy-coordinative department
department that coordinates policy across government

administrative-coordinative department
department that facilitates the operation of government services

OTHER GOVERNMENT BODIES

Departments represent one means by which public policy is developed, implemented, and enforced. Accordingly, circumstances may lead decision makers to choose other types of agencies to achieve these ends. We will examine some of the alternatives common to the practice of public administration in Canada: regulatory agencies and Crown corporations.

Regulatory Agencies

Regulatory agencies defy a simple definition because they can vary so widely in size, authority, and scope. Traditionally, they were used to regulate the private sector (marketing, competition, pricing, and so on), but more recently they have also become involved in areas of social regulation (workplace safety, culture, environmental protection).

In spite of their differences, regulatory agencies share some common characteristics in how and why they carry out their function. They can be viewed as extensions of a ministry in the sense that each is ultimately answerable to a minister. Unlike ministries, however, regulatory agencies are insulated from direct political interference and therefore demonstrate to the public that official decisions are fair and based on objective criteria. Thus, these agencies are a means through which governments can influence a particular sector without undermining public confidence.

delegated legislation
legislation handed down from a parent department that grants a regulatory agency political powers

The legislation that creates regulatory agencies sets out the general rules by which they must operate. Some agencies are granted powers of **delegated legislation**, which means they have the ability to set and enforce regulations. In effect, political powers are handed down from the parent department, allowing an agency to make specific decisions that have the force of law.

Some agencies are empowered to grant licences or investigate incidents within their jurisdiction. For example, in Canada, communication-related industries are subject to rules enforced by the Canadian Radio-television and Telecommunications Commission (CRTC). The commission has the power to grant, review, and revoke broadcast licences as well as set fees for some telephone services. Given the influence of broadcast media on public opinion, it is easy to see why this power should not remain under the direct control of the governing political party.

deregulation
reducing or eliminating bureaucratic processes that may hinder private enterprise and limit economic growth

As discussed in chapter 7, neoconservative ideology favours a limited role for government. This includes eliminating bureaucratic red tape in the form of government regulation of the private sector. The idea is to do away with bureaucratic processes that may hinder private enterprise and limit economic growth. Commonly referred to as **deregulation**, the approach seems logical and has struck a chord with many people who view government regulation as overbearing and excessive. However, critics argue that in the rush to deregulate, short-term economic gains may be far outweighed by long-term costs. For example, there is evidence to show that Britain's deregulation of the cattle industry in the 1980s led to the outbreak of "mad cow" disease in the late 1990s because beef producers were no longer subject to strict health standards.[7] Closer to home, a five-year-long 40 percent budget reduction at the Ontario Ministry of the Environment, coupled with deregulation and downloading of water quality inspection, were cited as factors contributing to the outbreak of E. coli bacteria in the town of Walkerton's water supply in 2000.[8]

Similarly, moves to deregulate and privatize the generation and provision of electricity in Ontario during the Progressive Conservative governments of Mike Harris and Ernie Eves caused uncertainty in the sector, fluctuations in prices, and an uncoordinated response to the major blackout of August 2003. Hoping to avoid these problems, the Liberal government led by Dalton McGuinty announced in June 2004 that it will create an arm's-length regulatory agency to oversee provincial power needs in the future.[9]

While incidents such as these are relatively rare, they demonstrate what can happen when the long-term consequences of deregulation are negated or ignored. As citizens, we need to ensure that our politicians do not compromise public health and safety for the sake of short-term fiscal savings.

Crown Corporations

Crown corporations are publicly owned businesses operating in the private sector and serving a public purpose. Like regulatory agencies, they are overseen by a ministry and are ultimately responsible to Parliament. Their distinctness arises from their corporate form and function. Crown corporations operate like any large private sector business, but because of their public accountability and legislated mandate, profit is often a secondary objective. Although the numbers vary from province to province, there are currently about 400 federal Crown corporations.[10]

Why choose a Crown corporation to facilitate government policy? There are two basic rationales: economic and nationalistic. As we learned in chapter 2, Canada was born out of several diverse regional interests. Reconciling and accommodating these interests with overarching national goals has become part and parcel of the Canadian political process. Crown corporations provide the federal government with a vehicle to redistribute national resources and encourage public infrastructure. There are also instances where provinces have used the Crown corporation models for similar purposes. For reasons of brevity and relevance, this discussion limits itself to the federal level. A Crown corporation can be created in an area of the economy where private business refuses to operate. By doing so, the new entity creates jobs and provides services or goods to an area that might otherwise go without. In addition, the corporation's presence in a community contributes to a sense of Canadian identity by connecting the area to a larger federal infrastructure.

A familiar illustration of the Crown corporation as "nation builder" can be found in the Canadian Broadcasting Corporation (CBC). When created in 1936, its aim was to foster communication among and through the various regions of Canada through a network of radio—and later television—stations. The CBC's nationwide access requires staff throughout Canada, including regions such as the Far North, where private broadcasting would be unprofitable. The CBC is also an example of how the Canadian government has used a Crown corporation to limit or prevent the encroachment of foreign (primarily American) influence in an aspect of Canadian culture or economy.

The Crown corporation may also be chosen to put it at "arm's length" from possible political meddling, as noted in the previous section; although, ironically, this may make it vulnerable to misuse by political officials. For example, the Crown corporations Canada Post and VIA Rail were both used to funnel federal sponsorship money to Quebec advertising firms, as part of the larger sponsorship scandal.[11]

By the same token, Crown corporations provide government with insight into the nature and current status of private sector actors engaged in similar activities. For example, Petro-Canada was created in 1975 to establish a Canadian presence in the overwhelmingly foreign-owned energy sector. In May 2004, the federal government announced it would sell off its interests in the company.

One of the major drawbacks of choosing a Crown corporation as a policy vehicle is that, unlike private business, the corporation is ultimately answerable to political masters who, in turn, must account for that corporation's management decisions. For example, when former CBC president Robert Rabinovich announced in the spring of 2000 his intention to eliminate local supper-hour newscasts, public outcry across Canada and the public admonition of several members of Parliament resulted in alterations to the original plan.[12]

The relatively recent trend toward limiting the role of government has prompted reconsideration of Crown corporations in their present form. Some right-wing critics have argued that they should be privatized (as were Air Canada and Petro-Canada) or eliminated entirely (as was the Cape Breton Development Corporation) because they compete unfairly in the private sector and are generally a waste of taxpayers' money. But this "slash-and-burn" approach not only ignores the historical context of the Canadian experience, but also assumes that private enterprise will assume the public interest for which Crown corporations were originally intended.

ADMINISTRATIVE LAW

So far this chapter has been dedicated to outlining the structure and form of political and bureaucratic institutions and their role within the machinery of government. This section briefly surveys the legal parameters governing public institutions, with reference to protection and fair treatment of citizens.

Imagine for a moment that you are a police officer on highway patrol. You clock a car going twice the speed limit. You pull over the vehicle, walk up to the driver's window, and ask for a driver's licence, registration, and insurance. The driver willingly complies, handing over all of the requested documents. Now consider the same scenario, except that this time your request for the three items is met with silence and suspicious gestures by the driver. Are your thoughts and responses different in this set of circumstances?

discretionary power
interpretive flexibility granted to some government employees to act within a given setting

The second scenario can help to illustrate the concept of **discretionary power**—that is, the interpretive flexibility granted to a police officer as a government employee (in this case, an agent of public law enforcement) to act within a given setting. In the second scenario, you might decide that the driver is mentally unstable, doesn't like the police, or is having a bad day. This, in turn, influences how you will deal with this citizen. There is a procedure police officers must follow in roadside situations such as this one, but it would be virtually impossible for lawmakers to write down all of the potential variations. Thus, government delegates authority and responsibility to civil servants, who then interpret and abide by the set of rules handed down to them. This delegation is limited or controlled by principles of **administrative law**. This body of legislation (usually drafted by bureaucratic experts in a particular field) details such things as safety standards, applications for immigration, licensing requirements, and the process for appeals. These are the

administrative law
body of legislation that details the rules civil servants must follow in doing their jobs

bureaucratic "rules of the game" to be followed by civil servants in their professional dealings with the public and with other government departments.

Although less visible than constitutional law, administrative law is bound by the same precepts and can be challenged in the court system. Laws can be ruled *ultra vires* (unconstitutional) if the Supreme Court of Canada finds that they in some way violate citizens' rights under the *Canadian Charter of Rights and Freedoms*.[13] For example, a directive from the provincial police instructing officers to stop all expensive sports cars and search drivers for drugs is a clear violation of the Charter rights of protection against unreasonable search and seizure and freedom from discrimination.

Principles of administrative law also preserve public faith in the rule of law by protecting citizens from unfair or arbitrary treatment by government agencies. In effect, administrative law acts to ensure that what politicians intend (as representatives of the people) ends up being implemented by bureaucrats in a just and equitable manner. The courts, through the process of judicial review, ensure this fairness. For example, a judge may rule that a regulatory agency has exceeded its authority by creating and enforcing rules that are outside its mandate or that go beyond the authority granted by its creators.

More directly, administrative law ensures that citizens affected by bureaucratic decisions have the right to due process and an appeal. This may include the right to represent themselves at relevant proceedings, the right to legal counsel and cross-examination, the right to be notified of hearing dates, and the disclosure of evidence held by the government body. In short, administrative law builds on the basic framework of constitutional law to ensure that governments and their delegates adhere to the rule of law in their day-to-day contact with the citizens they represent. When there is a dispute in this interaction, administrative law provides the protocol and forum necessary to resolve it.

Get Real!

DATA SECURITY IN THE ELECTRONIC BUREAUCRACY

Government, as we have seen, is a massive and complicated machine. There are many different levels of governance and administration, populated by thousands of officials and public servants, all trying to work together to formulate policy, provide services to Canadians, and take care of day-to-day business in their respective offices and agencies. Flowing through the maze of this government apparatus is an endless stream of information: paperwork, computer files, e-mail messages, census forms, tax returns, highly confidential documents, Cabinet memoranda, reams of miscellaneous personal data on Canadians, and more. The security of this information—and how to balance security concerns with an individual's right to privacy—has become a pressing issue in government in recent years, most especially since the terrorist attacks on the World Trade Center on September 11, 2001. As was pointed out in the preceding chapter, government employees must abide by certain bureaucratic "rules of the game" in their dealings with the public and other government departments. But what happens when the rules change?

Like businesses, governments must keep pace with rapid changes in technology. Today there are hundreds of government forms and services available online, from the Automated Earnings Reporting System (AERS), which lets employers submit payroll information, to electronic tax returns and passport applications. Information is stored, exchanged, and accessed through electronic channels, and this can present a serious challenge to maintaining the integrity and security of government data. The proliferation of electronic information can make accessing products and services more convenient, but it also increases our vulnerability to identity theft and other crimes. This is the new reality in the private sector (in stores and banks, for example) as well as in the public sector.

In the business realm, the parent company of Winners and HomeSense stores admitted in 2007 that data from 45.7 million credit and debit cards had been stolen by computer hackers.[14] The previous year, the BC provincial government revealed that a storage company responsible for 70,000 of its mainframe computer tapes, each containing sensitive data about British Columbians, could not account for the whereabouts of 31 tapes.[15] In Toronto, thieves broke into a doctor's car and stole a laptop containing the personal health information of almost 3,000 patients.[16] Mortgage fraud (stealing a homeowner's identity and selling the property without their knowledge) is one of the fastest-growing crimes in Canada. It increased over 400 percent between 1999 and 2001, costing Canadians $300 million that year.[17]

The government agency responsible for monitoring such issues is called the Office of the Privacy Commissioner (OPC). The OPC's mandate is (1) to ensure that government departments comply with the *Privacy Act* (which sets out the rules for handling Canadians' personal information within government) and (2) to ensure that the private sector does likewise, according to the *Personal Information Protection and Electronic Documents Act*, Canada's private sector privacy law. It is a huge responsibility, one that requires constant monitoring, analysis, investigation, reporting, and policy formulation. The terrorist attacks of 9/11 have only upped the ante. Since then, the federal government has come under increasing pressure, especially from the United States, to monitor the movement of citizens both inside and outside the country. This has, in turn, focused attention on the amount and type of data that governments collect, as well as the ways it can be used and who can access it. The regulation of this information flow becomes critical as the OPC strives to balance the Charter right to privacy with the need for increased national security.[18]

Further, while few would oppose measures designed to increase the security of citizens and thwart criminal activity, debate has arisen over whether government action in this area will, in fact, achieve these aims. Take, for example, the American government's implementation of a no-fly list containing about 70,000 names, intended to screen out passengers deemed to be a threat to air travel. Names on the list as common as "Robert Johnson" have caused countless headaches for innocent travellers. As well, US officials have admitted that the names of many suspected terrorists have been deliberately withheld, so as not to tip off these individuals, and because of concerns that the list may be acquired by terrorists. The Canadian government implemented a similar program in June 2007, but in light of the problems with the US program, one has to ask whether doing so constitutes good public policy and is a wise use of resources.[19]

How do you think the various levels of government in Canada are faring in protecting data on Canadian citizens, and in the private sector? Are you willing to sacrifice some of your privacy in the fight against terrorist activity? How vigilant are you in protecting your own personal information during everyday communication, banking, or shopping transactions?

SUMMARY

Government has been described as machinelike in its operation, and as citizens it sometimes feels like we are nothing more than numbers to the huge bureaucracy. The structure of bureaucracy in its various forms—departments, regulatory agencies, and Crown corporations—carries out government operations. A government department is responsible for carrying out some aspect of government policy, and the minister of a department is answerable to the public for all actions taken by the department, under the principle of ministerial responsibility. The deputy minister plays a critical role in any department, acting as the link between political and administrative power in the operations of government.

Departments are categorized according to whom they serve and their purpose in the bureaucratic hierarchy. Constituency departments deal directly with citizens, while policy-coordinative and administrative-coordinative departments carry out functions among other government departments and agencies. Regulatory agencies and Crown corporations serve different purposes, and they are two non-ministry bodies used by federal and provincial governments in certain circumstances to achieve policy goals.

Administrative law facilitates government activity. Part of its function is to ensure that government officials respect the rights of citizens and that disputes between the two groups are resolved in a just and equitable manner. Finally, government faces the challenge of both respecting and protecting citizens' rights to privacy while pursuing national security objectives.

KEY TERMS

administrative-coordinative
   department

administrative law

constituency department

delegated legislation

department

deregulation

discretionary power

ministerial responsibility

policy-coordinative department

portfolio

NOTES

1. This was during Brian Mulroney's first term in 1984. Organizational awkwardness necessitated the creation of an outer and inner Cabinet. For more information on the Mulroney approach to government, see Robert Bothwell, *Canada Since 1945: Power, Politics and Provincialism*, 2nd ed. (Toronto: University of Toronto Press, 1989), 433-444.

2. The audit, based on one-third of the total grant money handed out since 1997, found problems in 97 percent of the files examined. These included slipshod financial records and poor supervision of projects. See "Job Funds Fiasco Won't Fade Away Quickly," *Toronto Star* (February 9, 2000), A24.

3. *Interpretation Act*, RSC 1985, c. I-21, as amended.

4. Among the external duties of a typical Cabinet minister are collective Cabinet and party duties, constituency work, and attendance in the House of Commons, as well as representing Canadian interests abroad.

5. An exception to the principle of bureaucratic anonymity occurred when senior officials at Human Resources Development Canada responded publicly to then minister Jane Stewart's repeated attempts to blame "sloppy administration" for mismanagement of department funds. See Graham Fraser, "Canada's Chief Bureaucrat Comes Out of the Shadows," *Toronto Star* (February 26, 2000), K1; Allan Thompson, "Ottawa 'Sloppy' Over $1 Billion for Jobs," *Toronto Star* (January 29, 2000), A1.

6. For specific approaches, see J.E. Hodgetts, *The Canadian Public Service: A Physiology of Government* (Toronto: University of Toronto Press, 1973), ch. 5; G. Bruce Doern, "Horizontal and Vertical Portfolios in Government," in G. Bruce Doern and V. Seymour Wilson, eds., *Issues in Canadian Public Policy* (Toronto: Macmillan, 1974), 310-329.

7. The chain of events is explained in *Consequences: The Private Side of Britain* (Toronto: Indignant Eye Productions, 1998), a video documentary exploring the consequences of privatization under former British Prime Minister Margaret Thatcher.

8. The budget cuts resulted in one-third of ministry staff—many of whom were inspectors—being let go. The resulting lack of expertise and provincial testing have been cited as two of the potential causes of the tragedy. See Tanya Talaga et al., "Police Probe E. Coli Crisis," *Toronto Star* (May 26, 2000), A1; Royson James, "When the People You Know Don't Tell You About the Water," *Toronto Star* (May 26, 2000), A8.

9. John Spears and Richard Brennan, "New Agency Given Power to Ensure Power Supply," *Toronto Star* (June 16, 2004), E1.

10. Gregory J. Inwood, *Understanding Canadian Public Administration: An Introduction to Theory and Practice*, 2nd ed. (Toronto: Pearson Education, 2004), 149.

11. The transactions involved "highly irregular and questionable" payments to advertising firms by Public Works, through Canada Post and VIA Rail, for commissions and other suspect charges. For a summary of the auditor general's report, see Susan Delacourt et al., "Your Money, Their Friends," *Toronto Star* (February 11, 2004), A1.

12. The plan represented an attempt by the CBC to deal with over $400 million in budget cuts ordered by the Chrétien government. Some observers argued that the changes were made to avoid embarrassing Liberal MPs in the year of an anticipated federal election. See James Travers, "Risking the CBC Body to Save a Limb," *Toronto Star* (May 30, 2000), A25. For background, see Antonia Zerbisias, "CBC Local Newscasts Shrink—But Survive," *Toronto Star* (May 30, 2000), A1.

13. *Canadian Charter of Rights and Freedoms*, part I of the *Constitution Act, 1982*, RSC 1985, app. II, no. 44.

14. Mark Jewell, "TJX Filing Describes Hackers' Haul from 45.7 Million Cards," *Toronto Star* (March 30, 2007), F3.

15. Jeff Rud, "Telus Tightens Security After Tapes Vanish," *Victoria Times Colonist* (September 13, 2006), A8.

16. Allison Jones, "Stolen Laptop a Sign Canada Complacent About ID Theft: Ontario Privacy Czar" (March 8, 2007), available online at www.cbc.ca.

17. Dana Flavelle, "The Long Fight for Home, Sweet Home," *Toronto Star* (March 8, 2007), T3.

18. For information on the subject, see Office of the Privacy Commissioner of Canada, "Key Issues: Personal Data Breach" (July 4, 2006), available online at www.privcom.gc.ca/keyIssues/ki-qc/mc-ki-db_e.asp. For details on provisions of the *Personal Information Protection and Electronic Documents Act*, see Office of the Privacy Commissioner of Canada, "Privacy Legislation" (November 6, 2006), available online at www.privcom.gc.ca/legislation/02_06_01_e.asp.

19. Other concerns include how the list would be used, especially with respect to foreign governments, and its enforcement abroad and domestically. See CBC News, "Air Canada Fears No-Fly List Could Cause 'Unruly' Situations" (June 14, 2007), available online at www.cbc.ca.

EXERCISES

Multiple Choice

1. The number of federal government departments is set by

    a. legislation

    b. the prime minister

    c. the House of Commons

    d. custom and tradition

    e. the Senate

2. The principle of ministerial responsibility means that

    a. a department is responsible for its official activities

    b. the prime minister is responsible for the official activities of a department

    c. MPs are responsible for the official activities of a department

    d. Parliament is responsible for the official activities of a department

    e. the minister of a department is responsible for the official activities of that department

3. The deputy minister is

   a. the most senior bureaucrat in the department

   b. the head of the department

   c. appointed by the prime minister

   d. a and b

   e. a and c

4. A constituency department

   a. serves other departments

   b. coordinates overall policy

   c. facilitates the operation of government services

   d. provides services directly to citizens

   e. all of the above

5. Crown corporations are

   a. privately owned businesses operating in the private sector and serving a private purpose

   b. privately owned businesses operating in the public sector and serving a private purpose

   c. publicly owned businesses operating in the public sector and serving a public purpose

   d. publicly owned businesses operating in the private sector and serving a public purpose

   e. publicly owned businesses operating in the private sector and serving a private purpose

True or False?

_____ 1. A deputy minister is a politician.

_____ 2. Deputy ministers get their positions by belonging to the same political party as the government.

_____ 3. Administrative-coordinative departments provide services directly to Canadians.

_____ 4. Some government agencies have the authority to make specific decisions that have the force of law.

_____ 5. A police officer who stops a motorist for speeding and proceeds to search the car because the motorist is behaving suspiciously is using discretionary power.

Short Answer

1. Define and explain the purpose of a government department. What is its role in the Canadian political system?

2. Outline the roles and responsibilities of a minister and deputy minister. How do they interact with each other? Design an organizational chart showing the structure of a typical department.

3. What is a Crown corporation? How does it differ from a regulatory agency? Why do governments choose these forms rather than the departmental model?

4. What is administrative law? Explain its role in the bureaucratic process.

CHAPTER 10

Public Law Enforcement: Politics and Public Administration in Action

CHAPTER OBJECTIVES

After completing this chapter, you should be able to:

- Describe the functions of key government departments and their roles in the context of government and public law enforcement.

- Outline the general structure of a number of law enforcement agencies and how they are held publicly accountable.

- Examine possible consequences of conflicts among these agencies.

INTRODUCTION

Having established some of the fundamental principles of public administration and its relation to the political process in Canada, it is now time to see "where the rubber meets the road." In this chapter, we observe how government attempts to apply political and administrative ideals to the reality of public law enforcement. The situation is complicated by the inconsistent and arbitrary use of official names and titles to describe government bodies and the people who work in them.[1] Which departments do what, to whom, for whom, and with what consequences? As we will see, it is often a challenge to reconcile cherished democratic principles with the cut and thrust of everyday law enforcement.

FEDERAL AGENCIES[2]

Department of Justice Canada

The Department of Justice Canada has the primary responsibility for criminal justice policy at the federal level. It serves a dual purpose: to advise the federal government

attorney general function

the function of the federal Department of Justice to safeguard the legal interests of the federal government

on legal matters, and to watch over the administration of justice in areas of federal jurisdiction. The department's responsibility to the federal government is referred to as the **attorney general function**, which means that it safeguards the legal interests of the federal government in any situation where the government has jurisdiction. As we know from our discussion of federal and provincial powers in chapter 2, this restricts the department's ability to act in some areas. Further, the Department of Justice Canada provides legal advice to other federal government departments and agencies and may represent their legal position in matters of regulation and litigation. The Department of Justice Canada also prosecutes "violations of all federal legislation, other than the *Criminal Code*, in the provinces and for violations of all federal legislation, including the *Criminal Code*, in the territories."[3]

minister of justice function

the function of the federal Department of Justice to monitor federal legislation, directives, and regulations and to consider other justice-related issues

The second major responsibility of the Department of Justice Canada is carried out through the **minister of justice function**. This relates to the more familiar duties of a ministry, such as creating, implementing, and evaluating relevant policy, and overseeing the overall operation of the department. In the case of the Department of Justice Canada, this refers to monitoring federal legislation, directives, and regulations to ensure that they do not violate citizens' Charter rights, and in general to considering "issues related to a fair and equitable justice system."[4]

As part of its mandate, the Department of Justice Canada fulfills other responsibilities. It drafts and oversees the implementation of legislation in areas of criminal, family, and youth law, and it advises the federal government in such diverse policy areas as human rights, First Nations issues, and constitutional, administrative, and international law.

The Act that enables the Department of Justice Canada to carry out its dual mandate was created in 1868, but the process of remaining relevant and responsive to Canadians is an ongoing one. The review and reform of criminal law is a departmental priority, and the department has developed new policies to address such issues as high-technology crime, organized crime, human rights violations, and advances in investigative science and technology (for example, the implications of improved DNA testing). Increased international threats and concerns about domestic safety have also influenced departmental operations. Following the terrorist attacks on the World Trade Center on September 11, 2001, the department assumed new responsibilities, including shared operational oversight of several government agencies. For example, the department was instrumental in developing legislative reforms to the *Criminal Code* that enhance the power of justice officials to pursue and prosecute those suspected of engaging in terrorism, while preserving rights enshrined in the Charter (see "Get Real!" in chapter 3). The department's Anti-Terrorism Review Task Force is required to monitor and evaluate this new legislation, and to report annually to Parliament on its findings.[5]

Overall, the Department of Justice Canada is responsible for 45 statutes and areas of federal law. It employs more than 5,000 people, over half of whom are lawyers. Dozens of its lawyers work in regional offices throughout the country to ensure equitable representation for all Canadians.[6] The annual budget for the department in 2005–6 was just over $970 million.[7]

A justice minister performs a unique role in the federal Cabinet: he or she not only proffers political advice on legislative matters but also offers legal advice. The distinction is important because it is not unusual for one to be at odds with the other. For example, a justice minister may express the opinion that gun control legislation is an unwise political move because it is difficult to enforce and is un-popular in certain areas, but at the same time the minister may advise the Cabinet that such legislation is well within the federal government's right to act.[8]

Many people are frustrated when they hear government officials say that they refuse to give their views on a hot political issue because it is before the courts. This is not simply a convenient excuse to avoid controversy, although it is often perceived that way. The refusal to comment is based on the legal principle known as **subjudi-cial rule**, which strictly prohibits government officials from commenting on an issue that is before the courts. The rationale behind the principle is that, because govern-ment officials are closer to the process than other citizens, their opinions might be perceived as tainting the judicial process and thus may undermine public faith in that process. So the next time you are tempted to react cynically to "No comment," consider why the official has responded this way before judging his or her motives.

subjudicial rule
rule that prohibits government officials from commenting on an issue that is before the courts

COMMISSIONER FOR FEDERAL JUDICIAL AFFAIRS

In addition to the duties outlined above, the justice minister oversees the Office of the Commissioner for Federal Judicial Affairs. This body facilitates the operation of an independent judiciary—that is, it looks after judges' salaries, support, and train-ing. The Office of the Commissioner acts as a guarantor of judicial independence by distancing judges and their work from direct political interference by the minis-ter of justice. Its budget for 2006–7 was about $358 million.[9]

Law Commission of Canada

The Law Commission of Canada (LCC) monitors the quality and relevance of Canadian law and legal institutions. Although the commission is ultimately re-sponsible to Parliament through the justice minister, it can make recommenda-tions to Parliament on such matters as law reform and renewal. The commission operates at arm's length from the government to ensure that its decisions are not influenced by the political party in power.

Most of the work done by the LCC is informative in nature—that is, it consults with the Canadian legal community, holds conferences, and conducts research into issues of law and justice. For example, it may survey lawyers or conduct forums on an area of law that no longer meets the needs of Canadians. In this way, the LCC acts as a legal-administrative watchdog, keeping Canada's system of law current, ef-ficient, and effective. The LCC's budget for 2006–7 stood at just over $3 million.[10]

Public Safety Canada

Public Safety Canada (PSC) fulfills several functions in its mandate to manage the broad domains of justice and public safety in Canada. Formerly known as the Depart-ment of the Solicitor General and Corrections, and later as Public Safety and Emer-gency Preparedness Canada, this ministry saw its mandate significantly enhanced in December 2003. It now provides a coordinated government response in five major areas: emergency management, national security, law enforcement, corrections, and crime prevention.[11] In its entirety, PSC employs 52,000 people and has an annual budget of $6 billion.[12]

Overall coordination is performed by the department, which supports the minister and directs the work of five major agencies: Correctional Service Canada (CSC), the National Parole Board (NPB), the Canadian Security Intelligence Service (CSIS), the Royal Canadian Mounted Police (RCMP), and the Canada Border Services Agency (CBSA).

The department also includes a number of related organizations, including watchdog agencies that review and report on various aspects of public law enforcement and adherence to the rule of law. In this way, it seeks to demonstrate that the agencies under its jurisdiction are accountable not only to political authority but also to public scrutiny.

Public Safety Canada is composed of six branches.[13] The Emergency Management and National Security branch is responsible for emergency analysis and warning and response, as well as emergency management and national security policy. It also has responsibility for the Government Operations Centre, the Canadian Cyber Incident Response Centre, and the Canadian Emergency Management College. The Policing, Law Enforcement and Interoperability branch controls policy matters involving policing, law enforcement, and border security. It is also responsible for information-sharing among public safety agencies. The Community Safety and Partnerships section focuses on corrections and conditional release, crime prevention, and Aboriginal policing. Corporate Management handles department finances, information, accountability, and human resources. Public Safety Canada also includes a Strategic Policy office and the office of the CSIS Inspector General, who is responsible for reviewing the operation of Canada's intelligence service.

CORRECTIONAL SERVICE CANADA

CSC runs the federal prison system and is responsible for the custody and control of offenders sentenced to prison for two years or more. The 2005–6 budget for CSC was $1.6 billion: 50.6 percent of that went to salaries, 10.2 percent to the Employee Benefits Plan, 30.6 percent to the operating budget, and 8.6 percent to capital expenditures.[14] CSC's operations are divided geographically into five regions: Atlantic, Quebec, Ontario, Prairies, and Pacific.

The agency manages institutions across Canada that vary in security levels, and one of its prime goals is to rehabilitate offenders and prepare them for release into Canadian society. It also supervises offenders who have been conditionally released—on day parole, full parole, or statutory release—to serve the last third of their sentence in the community.[15]

NATIONAL PAROLE BOARD

The NPB exercises exclusive authority over the parole and conditional release of federal offenders (those imprisoned for two years or more). It also performs this function in all provinces except Quebec, Ontario, and British Columbia, which operate their own parole boards.

The NPB decides whether to release (or, in some cases, pardon) individuals who have applied for parole, basing its decisions on such factors as prisoner records and risk assessment. In doing so, the NPB works closely with CSC and the RCMP to share information and coordinate the supervision of successful applicants once they have re-entered Canadian society. The board may also decide whether to hold a prisoner in custody until he or she has served a full sentence. This is known as "detention during the period of statutory release." The NPB comprises 41 full-time and 45 part-time board members, and 225 employees. Its annual budget is $43.1 million.[16]

CANADIAN SECURITY INTELLIGENCE SERVICE

Created in 1984, CSIS monitors national security by collecting and analyzing information "on persons or groups whose activities may, on reasonable grounds, be suspected of constituting a threat to Canada's security."[17] The intelligence service was established after a government royal commission determined that this area—formerly within the jurisdiction of the RCMP—should come under a legislated framework of democratic control and be subject to more direct civilian accountability. The *CSIS Act* prevents the organization from either confirming or denying the existence of specific operations. However, it concerns itself with several key threats: "terrorism, the proliferation of weapons of mass destruction, espionage, foreign interference and cyber-tampering affecting critical infrastructure."[18] The agency's budget, which has increased greatly since 2001, totals approximately $346 million annually.[19]

The agency is also empowered to conduct security assessments of other government ministries, with the exception of the Department of National Defence and the RCMP, which do their own.

This mandate of CSIS is very broad and has caused some concern among civil rights advocates, who are afraid that its surveillance expertise may be used to investigate or intimidate political enemies of the federal government. In recognition of this concern, CSIS activities are subject to external review through a body known as the Security Intelligence Review Committee. This independent watchdog agency monitors CSIS actions and handles public complaints to ensure that the civil rights and liberties of Canadian citizens are being respected.

ROYAL CANADIAN MOUNTED POLICE

Since its creation in 1873 as the North-West Mounted Police, the RCMP has had a primary role in both federal and provincial law enforcement. Today the organization is involved in a wide range of activities, from battling organized crime to sharing expertise in and access to technology and information tools with other law enforcement agencies throughout Canada. As discussed in chapter 5, in addition to its national responsibilities, the RCMP performs provincial policing functions in all provinces except Ontario and Quebec.

The RCMP works with two external agencies to ensure public accountability and justice in its internal and external activities. First, the Commission for Public Complaints Against the RCMP handles public complaints about the conduct of members of the organization. The commission gives citizens an independent and impartial forum in which to present their concerns regarding RCMP officials' conduct.[20] Second, the RCMP External Review Committee provides members of the force itself with an independent forum for review in appeals of formal discipline, appeals of discharge or demotion, and other grievances forwarded to it.[21]

The RCMP also contracts to provide policing for 197 municipalities and over 190 Aboriginal communities across Canada. The service is organized geographically into four regions: Atlantic, Central, North West, and Pacific. As of September 10, 2007, the RCMP employed 25,417 people, over 10,900 of whom were constables.[22]

The RCMP is also involved in a number of other areas. Federal and International Operations "provides policing, law enforcement, investigative and preventative services to the federal government, its departments and agencies and to Canadians."[23] Protective Policing oversees personal security detail for dignitaries. The Criminal Intelligence Program focuses on intelligence gathering and research to combat organized crime (see National Police Services, below), while Technical Operations utilizes the latest advances in technology to assist policing activities.[24] The RCMP also participates in international peacekeeping operations as civilian police officers, to aid Canadian efforts in these areas.

National Police Services[25] coordinates activities that aid the RCMP and other law enforcement agencies in analyzing, sharing, and acting upon law enforcement information. Including Technical Operations, NPS comprises eight areas:

- Canada Firearms Centre—partners with other federal agencies in the administration of the *Firearms Act* and the Canadian Firearms Program.

- Forensic Laboratory Services—provides expertise in scientific analysis and research in collection and presentation of evidence.

- Information and Identification Services—coordinates a national justice information exchange system and collects, collates, and shares relevant information, such as criminal records and fingerprints, among Canadian and international justice organizations.

- Canadian Police College—offers senior-level advanced training and education in specialized areas such as organized crime, terrorism, intelligence, and high-technology crime.

- Criminal Intelligence Service Canada—coordinates gathering and storage of criminal intelligence, working in conjunction with nine similar provincial organizations (see also Criminal Intelligence Service Ontario [CISO], below, under the heading "Ministry of Community Safety and Correctional Services").

- Chief Information Officer Sector—manages the RCMP's IT systems and communication channels, including the National Radio Program, interagency information-sharing, and the fingerprint identification system.

- National Child Exploitation Coordination Centre—coordinates efforts to combat the online sexual exploitation of children.

- Technical Operations—provides technical support services, researches and develops investigative tools, and provides other related services.

CANADA BORDER SERVICES AGENCY[26]

The CBSA was created in December 2003, in response to concerns about national security and border integrity. It pulls together elements from a number of other government departments, "to manage the nation's borders by administering and enforcing approximately 90 domestic acts and regulations, as well as international agreements that govern trade and travel."[27] One of its main duties involves screening visitors and immigrants, and it has the power to investigate and detain individuals, conduct hearings, and carry out deportations, if necessary. The CBSA's other major area of concern is with ensuring safe and efficient international trade and commerce—that is, cross-border shipping and the transport of goods. In 2006, the agency operated from 1,200 domestic and 39 international locations and was responsible for about 266,000 travellers each day. It employs 12,000 people.

CANADA FIREARMS CENTRE

The Canada Firearms Centre (CFC), known popularly as the "gun registry," tracks the ownership, acquisition, and transfer of firearms in Canada. It was created in 1996 and became a stand-alone agency within Public Safety and Emergency Preparedness Canada in 2003. In 2006, it was transferred to the RCMP. The CFC conducts extensive background checks on licence applicants, to ensure that they are both capable and competent to own and store guns. Regulations contained in the *Firearms Act* are enforced by firearms officers, who report to the chief firearms officer for the province or territory. Although earlier legislation automatically designated police officers as firearms officers, this is no longer the case. However, police services have access to the agency's database, to aid investigations and help determine risk when called to incidents where firearms may be present. Firearms officers can conduct inspections at firearms businesses, businesses in a residence, or a residence. They have the power to inspect guns and weapons licences, and to ensure that all relevant material is in compliance with the *Firearms Act*. As discussed in chapter 2, the gun registry is a controversial topic and the Conservative government has been working for its elimination with the introduction of Bill C-21. However, as of September 2007, the bill had not moved past first reading and all three opposition parties continue to support the registry. An amnesty for long-term gun owners has been extended to May 2008.[28]

Department of National Defence

As the department responsible for civilian oversight of Canada's military, the Department of National Defence (DND) serves two major functions. First, it directs the activities of the Canadian Forces (including the army, navy, and air force), which protect Canada from outside military threats and provide assistance in times of natural disasters and other domestic crises. Second, the department works closely with the Department of External Affairs to fulfill Canada's international obligations in the areas of peacekeeping and disaster relief abroad, and as a member of NATO. The department's planned annual budget for 2006–7 is $15.9 billion.[29] The defence minister has ultimate authority over the armed forces even though it is not he or she who actually plans or executes military manoeuvres. Maintaining civilian over military authority represents another hallmark of democratic government, demonstrating to citizens that the coercive power of the state is accountable. Countries in which military power is no longer subject to civilian control are known as police states. Political regimes that use police or military power to violate democratic and human rights are also police states (discussed in chapter 8).

The Canadian Forces are managed by the chief of the defence staff, who works alongside a deputy minister. In this way, overall goals of the department are coordinated with those of the Canadian Forces. As with all departments, below these key players is a complex bureaucracy of individuals who coordinate and carry out the many aspects of DND policy, whether these involve marshalling equipment for duty in Afghanistan or assisting residents of eastern Ontario and Quebec during the ice storm of 1998.

As the federal government began to exercise fiscal restraint toward the closing decades of the 20th century, the DND suffered severe cuts to its budgets, making it increasingly difficult for the department to continue fulfilling its mandate. Public concern for safety, new international obligations, and criticism about Canada's military preparedness have sparked a renewed commitment to increase funding to the DND to correct years of underfunding (see table 10.1). In 2007 the minister announced new funding for the department: "Budget 2007 confirmed that the Department of National Defence and the Canadian Forces will receive a total of $3.1 billion over three years for the Canada First Defence Strategy announced in Budget 2006. This sum comprises $900 million to be spent in 2007-2008 (including an advance of $175 million made in 2006-2007 to accelerate implementation of the plan), $1.0 billion to be spent in 2008-2009, and $1.2 billion to be spent in 2009-2010."[30] This will bring the department's budget up to $19.4 billion.[31]

PROVINCIAL AGENCIES

The various provinces and territories have a variety of structural approaches, making it difficult to describe each one in detail in this chapter. There are many similarities among them, however, so in the interest of brevity the following sections describe the ministries, agencies, and boards that make up the law enforcement system in Ontario.[32]

Ministry of the Attorney General

In many respects, the attorney general can also be thought of as the provincial minister of justice.[33] He or she provides expert legal advice to the government and has

TABLE 10.1   Canada's Defence Budget: 1993–2007

Fiscal Year	Budget—National Defence ($B)	
	Main Estimates	Actual Expenditures
2006–7	14.80	15.70
2005–6	13.40	14.70
2004–5	13.30	13.90
2003–4	12.26	13.19
2002–3	11.83	12.42
2001–2	11.39	12.24
2000–1	11.20	11.47
1999–2000	10.30	11.52
1998–99	9.38	10.26
1997–98	9.92	10.19
1996–97	10.56	10.57
1995–96	11.08	11.37
1994–95	11.55	11.77
1993–94	11.97	12.00

Source: Department of National Defence, *Canada's Defence Budget: 1993-2007*, www.forces.gc.ca/site/reports/budget05/back05_e.asp. Reproduced with the permission of the Minister of Public Works and Government Services Canada, 2007.

overall responsibility for the administration of justice in the province. The statutory responsibilities of the attorney general are outlined in section 5 of the *Ministry of the Attorney General Act*[34] and can be classified into four broad areas: legal advice, civil litigation on behalf of the government, administration of the federal *Criminal Code*,[35] and administration of judicial affairs in the province.[36]

Like the Department of Justice Canada, provincial attorneys general advise their respective governments in a number of legal and legislative areas. They scrutinize proposed legislation from other government ministries to ensure that it is legal, constitutional, and in conformance with accepted principles of justice.[37] The ministry also represents the province in cases of civil litigation where government interests or public rights are at stake.

An attorney general also has the power to legislate in the area of administration of the *Criminal Code*. This means that provincial governments carry out the process of criminal justice, while the federal government retains the ultimate authority to determine the actual content of the Code. Another interesting part of this process is that it is not the attorney general who decides whether to prosecute criminal offences. These decisions are left to the many Crown attorneys, who, in turn, do not begin this consideration until police have laid charges. Once again, basic principles of justice underlie this process. "The attorney general's responsibility for individual criminal prosecutions must be undertaken—and seen to be undertaken—on strictly objective and legal criteria, free of any political considerations."[38] Reporting directly to the attorney general is the Office of Legislative Counsel. It ensures the legal integrity of government legislation and drafts private members' bills.

Finally, the Ministry of the Attorney General is responsible for the administration of a province's courts and its judicial affairs. The latter function is managed at arm's length by the Ontario Judicial Council, which operates in a manner similar to that of the Commissioner for Federal Judicial Affairs, described earlier.

As with the Department of Justice Canada, note the difference between policy advice and legal advice given by a minister in this portfolio. The first is a matter of opinion, while the second is a matter of law. The principle of subjudicial rule also applies in cases of criminal and civil law.

Other Affiliated Boards, Agencies, and Commissions of the Attorney General[39]

In keeping with its mandate to preside over all justice-related activity in the province, the ministry is also responsible for a number of boards, agencies, and commissions. Note how each contributes to the ministry's overall mandate.

SPECIAL INVESTIGATIONS UNIT (ONTARIO)

Since 1990, municipal, regional, and provincial police forces in Ontario have been subject to an independent watchdog agency known as the Special Investigations Unit (SIU). Created under provisions of part VII of the *Ontario Police Services Act*,[40] the SIU reports to the attorney general and looks into "circumstances involving police and civilians which have resulted in serious injury, including sexual assault, or death."[41]

Before the SIU's creation, investigations were done within the police force or by another police force. This led to public concerns about integrity and objectivity, which eventually led to the creation of the SIU.

The SIU met with resistance from many in the policing community, partly because it represented a new and, some would argue, unorthodox form of police oversight. Relations remained cool during most of the 1990s. However, following substantial funding increases and gradual implementation of recommendations outlined in a report released in 1997, trust in the process improved substantially. As the report's author, George Adams, noted, "Through the SIU, the province seeks to protect the fundamental human rights of all its citizens by ensuring that those charged with enforcing laws and advancing public safety remain accountable should they violate those rights."[42] The SIU's jurisdiction covers 65 police services across Ontario, representing 21,600 officers. Its annual budget for 2005–6 was approximately $5.4 million.

OTHER AGENCIES REPORTING TO THE ATTORNEY GENERAL

There are several other agencies that report to the attorney general:

- Law Reform Commission—studies and recommends changes to statute and common law, as well as judicial decisions. Also monitors the administration of justice and judicial procedures.[43]

- Office of the Public Guardian and Trustee—acts on behalf of mentally incapable people, oversees the public's interest in charities, searches for heirs of deceased persons whose estates it administers, invests perpetual care funds, and monitors issues arising from the dissolution of corporations.

- Office of the Children's Lawyer—acts for children under the age of 18 involved in certain aspects of the justice system, including disputes over custody, access, child protection proceedings, and inheritance.

- Office for Victims of Crime—provides policy advice and oversees principles set out in the *Victims' Bill of Rights*.

- Criminal Injuries Compensation Board—provides compensation to victims of violent crimes committed in Ontario that resulted in injury; people responsible for the care of a victim of crime who incurred losses or expenses as a result of the victim's injury or death; the dependants of victims of murder; and people injured while attempting to prevent a crime or assisting an officer in making an arrest.

- Human Rights Commission—protects human rights through enforcement of the Ontario *Human Rights Code*.

- Human Rights Tribunal—receives and adjudicates formal complaints made under the Ontario *Human Rights Code*.

- Legal Aid—provides access to legal expertise for low-income individuals involved in the justice system.

- Ontario Municipal Board—resolves complaints and appeals related to disputes over land use and community planning.

- Assessment Review Board—hears complaints regarding property assessments and/or classification.

- Board of Negotiation—negotiates compensation settlements in expropriation cases.

Ministry of Community Safety and Correctional Services (MCSCS)[44]

Like its federal counterpart, at one time this ministry's mandate was captured under the title of Solicitor General. However, in April 2002, the duties and title of its minister changed. Administratively, the ministry's responsibilities fall into three broad categories: policing services, correctional services, and public safety and security.

POLICING SERVICES

This branch of the MCSCS monitors the quality of public policing and the private security industry in Ontario. It sets out professional training standards and inspection requirements and advisory support to all police services, including the Ontario Provincial Police (OPP). It also operates Criminal Intelligence Service Ontario (CISO) and is involved in a number of community safety and crime prevention initiatives.

Ontario Provincial Police (OPP)[45]

The OPP provides a variety of policing services in contract, non-contract, and First Nations communities throughout the province. It is one of only two provincial police organizations, the other being in Quebec. As noted earlier, the RCMP is under contract with all other provinces to fulfill this function. The force divides its Field and Traffic Services operations into six geographic regions, each of which tailors its service to meet local community needs and priorities. Investigations/Organized Crime operates province-wide, providing specialized technical support to regions, in conjunction with other justice-related agencies. This division includes the Drug Enforcement Section, which manages joint forces operations with municipal police and the RCMP to "suppress illegal drug use, production, sale and distribution."[46] The First Nations and Contract Policing Bureau was created in 2005 and oversees contracts with municipalities, and with the 20 First Nations communities who currently do not exercise self-directed policing options available to them. (There are nine communities that operate police services.) It also supports the administrative affairs of the OPP. Of the OPP's workforce of more than 8,250, over 5,400 are uniform officers.[47]

Criminal Intelligence Service Ontario (CISO)

CISO oversees an independent Joint Forces Operation whose mission it is to coordinate the activities of local, provincial, and federal police engaged in fighting organized crime and other major criminal activity. The organization is one of nine provincial agencies that work within the framework of Criminal Intelligence Service Canada (see CISC at the federal level).

Ontario Civilian Commission on Police Services (OCCPS)[48]

OCCPS is an independent quasi-judicial agency that is responsible for monitoring the conduct and actions of all police services and police service boards in Ontario. It has the power to conduct hearings into the creation, amalgamation, reduction, or elimination of a police service, but most often adjudicates appeals of police disciplinary penalties and disputes between municipal councils and police service boards involving board members. In general, it ensures the adequacy and effectiveness of policing standards in the province.

Ontario Police Arbitration Commission (OPAC)

OPAC provides a formal administrative framework within which police associations and their employers negotiate collective agreements. It maintains a roster of arbitrators, sets fees for their services, and makes the necessary administrative arrangements for negotiations to occur. OPAC also sponsors research and is responsible for publishing information on agreements, decisions, and awards.

Other agencies reporting to Policing Services include:

- Ontario Police College—provides training for police and civilian members working in policing in Ontario.

- Private Investigators and Security Guards Branch—oversees licensing and standards.

- Policing Standards Section—ensures, monitors, and supports excellence in the standard of police professionalism and provides regulations and guidelines for use by the ministry, policing agencies, and municipalities.

- Police Quality Assurance Unit—ensures that policing services are being provided across Ontario. Monitors and coordinates police services and ensures compliance with rights guaranteed under the *Canadian Charter of Rights and Freedoms.*

- Program Development Section—oversees initiatives related to crime prevention and community safety. Liaises with police, community groups, and other levels of government on these issues.

- Ontario Sex Offender Registry—provides a non-public database available to police services in the investigation of sex-related crimes. Also used for tracking sex offenders in the community.

CORRECTIONAL SERVICES

Correctional Services manages the custody of adult offenders serving sentences of imprisonment or conditional sentences of less than two years and terms of probation up to three years. The agency also supervises those who have been granted parole by the Ontario Parole and Earned Release Board and handles individuals awaiting transfer to a federal correctional facility to serve sentences that exceed two years. As with its federal counterpart, provincial corrections manages a series of programs designed to help rehabilitate offenders and prepare them for reintegration into society.

Correctional Services currently maintains 40 facilities for adult offenders, including jails and detention centres, correctional centres and complexes, and probation and parole offices. Responsibility for Phase I (aged 12-15) and Phase II (aged 16-17) young offenders was transferred to Children and Youth Services in April 2004, where the Youth Justice Services Program manages over 25 Youth Intervention Centres (YICs). The YICs are designed to help young people in trouble with the law become contributing members of Canadian society through such programs as anger management, life skills, and employment readiness. In 2006, the McGuinty government announced the addition of 12 new YICs for the province at a cost of $3.9 million.[49] Correctional Services' estimated operating budget for 2006–7 was $663 million.[50]

In many respects, this provincial emphasis on intervention and rehabilitation is at odds with the approach touted by the federal government. Herein lies an example of public policy at odds with itself (see the discussion in chapter 2 regarding federal and provincial government jurisdiction). The federal Conservative government of Stephen Harper has indicated plans to introduce legislation that would see violent and repeat young offenders 14 years and older treated as adults, with automatic adult sentences.[51] It is part of the law-and-order agenda of the Harper government, one that critics say could create backlogs and overcrowding in an already stressed corrections system.

PUBLIC SAFETY AND SECURITY

Public safety and security in the province is covered by a variety of agencies. These include the Centre of Forensic Sciences, the Office of the Chief Coroner, the Office of the Fire Marshal, and Emergency Management Ontario (EMO).

Centre of Forensic Sciences (CFS)

Operating laboratories in Toronto and Sault Ste. Marie, the Centre of Forensic Sciences "conduct[s] scientific investigations in cases involving injury or death in unusual circumstances and in crimes against persons or property."[52] This includes biological, chemical, and toxicological analysis, firearms and toolmark assessment, and electronic enhancement such as document and photo analysis. The scientific examination and interpretation provided by the CFS provides independent expert testimony in courts, and is used by police, Crown and defence counsel, pathologists, and coroners in cases where scientific expertise is required.

The Office of the Chief Coroner

Drawing upon guidelines found in the *Coroners Act,* the chief coroner is responsible for overseeing the 350 coroners who work in the province, ensuring that all human deaths are reported and, if necessary, investigated. Individually, or through an inquest, coroners attempt to determine the identity of someone who has died and how, when, where, and by what means he or she died. With reference to law enforcement, inquests must be called when an individual has died while being "detained by or in the actual custody of a peace officer, or while an inmate on the premises of a correctional institution or lock-up."[53] Inquests are not intended to lay blame or assign responsibility in particular cases. However, jurors can make recommendations about how to prevent deaths from occurring under similar circumstances in the future.[54]

Office of the Fire Marshal (OFM)

The Office of the Fire Marshal is responsible for administering the *Ontario Fire Code* and the *Fire Protection and Prevention Act.* Although it is independent of municipal fire services, the OFM assists them by providing leadership in fire safety, prevention, and protection. As well, the OFM advises the government on proper standards and professional training. The OFM has investigative responsibilities for fires involving deaths and/or serious injury, suspicious fires, including those caused by explosions or arson, and fires resulting in losses in excess of $500,000. It also provides expert testimony in criminal prosecutions and coroners' inquests. Currently, there are 547 fire departments in Ontario, staffed by over 9,000 full-time and 17,000 volunteer firefighters.[55]

Emergency Management Ontario (EMO)

This body coordinates the development and maintenance of emergency management programs, based in large part on a network of local volunteers. It provides training to emergency management staff and, in the case of actual emergency, such as the flood that occurred in Peterborough in July 2004, provides advice and assistance to community officials by coordinating delivery of provincial and federal government assistance. EMO also plays a critical role in public education by providing information on how to prepare for and cope in emergency situations. Local activities are coordinated through Community Emergency Response Volunteers Ontario, which has teams across Ontario trained in basic principles of emergency management, disaster response, and light search and rescue techniques.

Get Real!

SPINOFFS, SHAKEUPS, AND TURF WARS

One of the challenges of writing a chapter like this one is that the roles and responsibilities of government departments and agencies can change in the proverbial blink of an eye. In the time between the previous and present editions of this textbook, for example, two federal elections and two Ontario provincial elections have occurred, the organizational structures of many ministries have been modified, budgets have been revised, mandates redefined, and responsibilities transferred between agencies. In fact, you may be aware of changes that have happened in the time between the book's publication and the start of this semester! It can be difficult to keep up—for an author as well as for a student of public administration. It can be difficult, too, for the departments and agencies themselves. When the structure of a government changes, the resulting bureaucratic scramble can be confusing, even disastrous.

Throughout this chapter, the stated mandates and aims of a variety of government agencies have

been outlined. No doubt, you've become aware that many of these goals can overlap, and, as is exemplified by the discussion regarding conflicting policy aims of the federal and Ontario governments over corrections, problems can result. This can lead to confusion over jurisdiction and sometimes even unhealthy competition among government organizations that hinders the greater goal of preserving justice. We can look at the case of the RCMP and CSIS as an example.

In 1984, following recommendations of the McKenzie (1969) and McDonald (1977) commissions, the Canadian Security and Intelligence Service was spun off as a separate agency from the Royal Canadian Mounted Police (RCMP). Prior to this decision, the RCMP held primary responsibility for intelligence services in Canada. However, the two commissions recognized that "the problem of balancing the need for accurate and effective security intelligence with the need to respect democratic rights and freedoms could not be adequately resolved as long as security intelligence responsibilities remained part of the Federal police force."[56] CSIS was born. The new service was staffed in large part by former RCMP officers, many of whom were eager to conduct intelligence gathering in ways different from those used by the RCMP. Having lost formal responsibility for intelligence, the RCMP attempted to reclaim many of its associated duties by creating a new in-house agency known as Criminal Intelligence Service Canada, a less formal network of security agencies across the country, mirroring jurisdictional areas given to CSIS. To add to the confusion, no formal protocols existed for communication between the agencies and the RCMP initially denied CSIS access to its criminal database; after all, it was (and is) not a police agency, but reported directly to the federal government. CSIS, in turn, proved reluctant to share information with the RCMP, since part of its mandate was to keep its intelligence secret and neither side was sure about what kind of information should be exchanged and when. Although this impasse was eventually resolved through the signing of memoranda of understanding, an underlying tension persisted in the relationship.[57]

The tension has increased post-9/11. Since the attacks on the World Trade Center and the Pentagon, and since the introduction of new anti-terrorism legislation into the *Criminal Code*, both CSIS and the RCMP have seen their mandates evolve to emphasize these new priorities of national security. In Canada, as in the United States, police and intelligence officers now have been given much broader powers of information gathering, and this has served to increase the need for clear and timely information-sharing. Given the history of the two entities and their turf war, this has some officials worried. In the fall of 2006, the minister responsible for both CSIS and the RCMP warned of the potential for serious mistakes if the agencies didn't keep pace with the new demand for seamless communication. "If it's not seamless, if people aren't sharing, if they're not listening to each other, you will miss something," cautioned the minister. "As we learned from 9/11, it can be a small thing that could have changed the course of history."[58] Many cite lack of information-sharing between the CIA and FBI as a key to the failure to stop the terrorist attacks in the United States.

The case of Ottawa software engineer Maher Arar underscores the necessity for good communication. On the basis of information provided by both agencies, Arar was deported by the United States to Syria, where he was imprisoned and tortured. (See chapter 3 for a discussion of the Arar case.) A subsequent review lambasted the RCMP for continuing to act in an "investigative silo," citing its failure to disclose key information to CSIS regarding Arar's alleged terrorist ties. The review outlined 23 strongly worded recommendations to the RCMP, chiding the force to stay within its policing mandate, and advising it to better implement its official policy of information-sharing.[59] Fallout from the inquiry eventually led to the resignation of RCMP Commissioner Giuliano Zaccardelli when it was revealed he contradicted himself about the Arar affair during his appearance before a Parliamentary committee.[60]

The Arar case makes it clear that agency rivalry can have real and tragic consequences for any Canadian. Thus, it is critical that all government organizations and employees, especially those involved in law enforcement and public safety, remain aware of the dangers of conflicts between government agencies. As one Ottawa journalist put it, "When security agencies don't exchange critical information … someone ends up tortured in a Syrian hellhole as a result."[61]

SUMMARY

This chapter has given you an opportunity to apply your knowledge of the structure and process of politics and public administration in relation to public law enforcement. Examining the respective powers of federal institutions such as the Department of Justice, Public Safety Canada, and the Department of National Defence demonstrates how each contributes to the overall system of justice and law enforcement at the federal level. The various watchdog agencies illustrate how these federal government institutions attempt to ensure fairness, accountability, and sensitivity to public concerns.

The federal bodies have their counterparts in provincial institutions such as the Ministry of the Attorney General, the Ministry of Community Safety and Correctional Services, and the many agencies and boards that have been put in place to monitor the activities of key actors within the government in general and the justice system in particular.

Even so, overlapping jurisdiction can sometimes lead to conflict among these agencies and cause problems that hinder the operation of our justice system.

KEY TERMS

attorney general function

minister of justice function

subjudicial rule

NOTES

1. For example, the words "ministry" and "department" may have the same meaning, while "commission" is used to describe agencies of varying size, function, and importance, making categorization by name alone virtually meaningless. Organizing agencies according to function is a better alternative.

2. In addition to the public agencies discussed, many professional, voluntary, and non-profit agencies exist that also contribute in various ways to the maintenance of justice in Canada. Because these organizations are not recognized as official government bodies, we will not deal with them in this section. The summaries of agency duties and responsibilities are drawn from the official ministry websites.

3. Mary Ferguson, ed., *Federal Guidebook: A Guide to the Canadian Federal Government and Its Decision-Makers, 1999–2000* (Perth, ON: J-K Carruthers, 1999), 43:1-43:2.

4. Ibid., at 43:2.

5. For more information of the department's anti-terrorism strategy, see Department of Justice Canada, "The Anti-terrorism Act" (February 7, 2007), available online at www.justice.gc.ca/en/anti_terr.

6. See Department of Justice Canada, "Canada's Department of Justice" (March 21, 2007), available online at www.justice.gc.ca.

7. From 2005–6 *Department Performance Report*, available online at www.justice.gc.ca/en/dept/pub/dpr/2005-2006/index.html.

8. Despite a constitutional challenge from a majority of the provinces, the Supreme Court ruled in favour of the federal government on this subject on June 15, 2000. See *Reference re Firearms Act (Can.)*, [2000] 1 SCR 783, available online at www.canlii.org.

9. Figure from Treasury Board estimates for 2006–7. See Office of the Commissioner for Federal Judicial Affairs, *Report on Plans and Priorities 2005-2006* (March 24, 2005), available online at www.fja.gc.ca/publications/rpp/rpp-index_e.html.

10. See Law Commission of Canada, *Report on Plans and Priorities 2006-2007 Estimates* (September 26, 2006), available online at www.tbs-sct.gc.ca/rpp/0607/LCC-CDC/LCC-CDC_e.asp.

11. For details on each area, see Public Safety Canada, "What We Do" (September 18, 2007), available online at http://publicsafety.gc.ca/abt/wwd/index-en.asp.

12. Public Safety Canada, "Who We Are" (September 18, 2007), available online at www.publicsafety.gc.ca.

13. The summary that follows is based on information from the new Public Safety Canada website, ibid.

14. Statistics from Correctional Service Canada, *2005-2006 Performance Report* (November 23, 2006), available online at www.tbs-sct.gc.ca/dpr-rmr/0506/CSC-SCC/CSC-SCC_e.asp.

15. For current spending estimates and personnel, see ibid. For more information on the organization and its programs, see the CSC website at www.csc-scc.gc.ca/text/home_e.shtml.

16. National Parole Board, "Overview," available online at www.npb-cnlc.gc.ca.

17. Ferguson, supra note 3, at 20:1.

18. See Canadian Security Intelligence Service, "Role of CSIS" (March 16, 2007), available online at www.csis-scrs.gc.ca/en/about_us/role_of_csis.asp.

19. CSIS annual public reports are available online at www.csis-scrs.gc.ca/en/publications/annual_report.asp.

20. Details on current investigations and other material are available on the Commission for Public Complaints Against the RCMP website at www.cpc-cpp.gc.ca.

21. See the RCMP External Review Committee website at www.erc-cee.gc.ca.

22. RCMP, "Organization of the RCMP" (September 10, 2007), available online at www.rcmp-grc.gc.ca/about/organi_e.htm.

23. Mandate quoted from the RCMP website at www.rcmp-grc.gc.ca/fio/fio_e.htm.

24. For details of programs, see RCMP, "Operations" (February 19, 2007), available online at www.rcmp-grc.gc.ca/prog_serv/operations_e.htm.

25. Summary provided here is based on information from RCMP, "National Police Services" (June 8, 2007), available online at www.rcmp-grc.gc.ca.

26. The following summary is based on information taken from CBSA, "About Us" (January 26, 2007), available online at www.cbsa-asfc.gc.ca/agency-agence/menu-eng.html.

27. These include "the Customs program from the Canada Customs and Revenue Agency, the Intelligence, Interdiction and Enforcement program from Citizenship and Immigration Canada, and the Import Inspection at Ports of Entry program from the Canadian Food Inspection Agency." See CBSA, "The Canada Border Services Agency" (August 29, 2005), available online at www.cbsa-asfc.gc.ca/media/release-communique/2004/1123ottawa_backg-eng.html.

28. For more on the gun registry, see Susan Delacourt, "Gun Registry Lives On," *Toronto Star* (June 11, 2007), A12.

29. Department of National Defence, *Report on Plans and Priorities 2007-2008* (March 29, 2007), available online at www.tbs-sct.gc.ca/rpp/0708/ND-DN/ND-DN_e.asp.

30. National Defence and the Canadian Forces, "Canada First Defence Newsletter" (April 2007), available online at www.forces.gc.ca/site/Minister/newsletter/2007-04/index_e.asp#2.

31. David Lea, "Why Are Our Soldiers in Afghanistan?" *Oakville Beaver* (November 17, 2007), available online at www.oakvillebeaver.com.

32. In addition to the public agencies discussed, many professional, voluntary, and non-profit agencies exist that also contribute in various ways to the maintenance of justice in Ontario. But because these organizations are not recognized as official government bodies, we will not deal with them in this section.

33. In fact, the federal minister of justice also holds the title of federal attorney general, although this term is rarely used.

34. *Ministry of the Attorney General Act*, RSO 1990, c. M.17.

35. *Criminal Code*, RSC 1985, c. C-46, as amended.

36. For a detailed analysis of these responsibilities, see Ministry of the Attorney General, "Roles and Responsibilities of the Attorney General" (October 23, 2003), available online at www.attorneygeneral.jus.gov.on.ca.

37. Because of the sensitive nature of this decision-making process, these considerations are delegated to the Office of Legislative Counsel to avoid allegations of political interference.

38. Ministry of the Attorney General, supra note 36.

39. The summary of agency duties and responsibilities is drawn from Ministry of the Attorney General, "What We Do" (February 28, 2007), available online at www.attorneygeneral.jus.gov.on.ca.

40. *Police Services Act*, RSO 1990, c. P.15, as amended.

41. Special Investigations Unit, "About the SIU," available online at www.siu.on.ca.

42. Known as the Adams report, the study sought to identify and remedy problems that had hindered relations between the SIU and police. Adams conducted a five-year follow-up report in 2003. See Special Investigations Unit, *Annual Report 2002–2003*, available online at www.sui.on.ca/siu_images/SIU%202003ReportENG.pdf.

43. See *Ontario Law Reform Commission Act*, RSO 1990, c. O.24, available online at www.canlii.org.

44. Information about all MCSCS agencies and operations is available on its website at www.mcscs.jus.gov.on.ca.

45. Summarized from the OPP website at www.opp.ca.

46. OPP, "Drug Enforcement Section" (2006), available online at www.opp.ca/Organization/InvestigationsOrganizedCrime/opp_000460.html.

47. See OPP, "2007 Provincial Business Plan," available online at www.opp.ca/Organization/index.htm. Click on the link "Business Plan."

48. Information summarized from the OCCPS website at www.occps.ca.

49. Information summarized from the Ministry of Children and Youth Services website at www.children.gov.on.ca.

50. Ministry of Finance, "Ministry of Community Safety and Correctional Services—The Estimates, 2007-08—Summary" (April 11, 2007), available online at www.fin.gov.on.ca.

51. Jance Tibbetts, "Youth Crime Bill Lets Judges Add to Jail Sentences," *The Ottawa Citizen* (February 5, 2007), A5.

52. Quoted from MCSCS, "About the Centre" (May 30, 2006), available online at www.mcscs.jus.gov.on.ca/english/pub_safety/centre_forensic/about/intro.html.

53. Quoted from Office of the Chief Coroner, "When Things Are Done" (May 30, 2006), available online at www.mcscs.jus.gov.on.ca/english/pub_safety/office_coroner/coroner_when.html.

54. Office of the Chief Coroner, "About the Office" (May 18, 2007), available online at www.mcscs.jus.gov.on.ca/english/pub_safety/office_coroner/about_coroner.html.

55. Summarized from Office of the Fire Marshal, "Who We Are—Structure, Organization, Responsibilities, Programs" (July 31, 2007), available online at www.ofm.gov.on.ca/english/about/whoweare.asp#structure.

56. CSIS, "Backgrounder No. 5: A Historical Perspective on CSIS" (January 2001), available online at www.csis.gc.ca.

57. Lynda Hurst, "Distrust, Rivalry Between Cops, Spooks," *Toronto Star* (June 21, 2003), H3.

58. James Gordon, "End of Innocence for Canada: Focus off of US; Work on Prevention, McLellan Urges," *The Gazette (Montreal)* (June 6, 2006), A4.

59. See CBC News, "The Arar Inquiry: Recommendations and Documents" (August 9, 2007), available online at www.cbc.ca.

60. "RCMP's Embattled Chief Quits over Arar Testimony" (December 6, 2006), available online at www.cbc.ca.

61. Dianne Rinehart, "Culture of Secrecy Surrounds Laws to Fight Terrorism," *The Gazette* (Nov 7, 2006), A27.

EXERCISES

Multiple Choice

1. The Department of Justice Canada
   a. monitors the quality and relevance of Canadian law and legal institutions
   b. watches over the administration of justice in areas of federal jurisdiction
   c. advises the federal government on legal matters
   d. a and b
   e. b and c

2. At the federal level, the minister of justice function involves
   a. considering issues of fairness in the justice system
   b. monitoring federal legislation
   c. commenting on issues that are before the courts
   d. a and b
   e. b and c

3. The rationale for the subjudicial rule is that

   a. some cases before the courts are hot political issues

   b. politicians need a convenient way to avoid controversy

   c. public faith in the justice system may be undermined by politicians' comments

   d. officials' opinions might be perceived as influencing the judicial process

   e. b and c

4. Civilian agencies monitor police activity

   a. to give objectivity to investigations of alleged police misconduct

   b. to ensure the integrity of policing

   c. to report to the solicitor general on the adequacy of police services

   d. to report to the solicitor general on the effectiveness of police services

   e. all of the above

5. The Ontario Ministry of Community Safety and Correctional Services is similar to its federal counterpart in all respects except:

   a. it operates prisons

   b. it is responsible for inmates serving sentences of two years or more

   c. it forms part of a larger ministry

   d. its mandate is provincial in scope

   e. none of the above

True or False?

_____ 1. The Department of Justice Canada performs both the attorney general and the minister of justice functions.

_____ 2. It is not unusual for justice ministers to find that their political advice contradicts their legal advice.

_____ 3. The attorney general is responsible for deciding whether to prosecute criminal offences.

_____ 4. Government attempts to influence the professional actions of judges contravene the principle of judicial independence.

_____ 5. The existence of the Office of the Commissioner for Federal Judicial Affairs is one way of guaranteeing judicial independence.

Short Answer

1. Outline the broad mandate of the Department of Justice Canada. How does it protect the federal justice system from political interference?

2. Compare and contrast the roles of the public safety minister and the justice minister at the federal level. Who is considered the chief law officer, and why?

3. What criterion determines whether an offender is sent to a federal correctional facility? What factors do you think should be considered when assessing an offender's application for parole?

4. Drawing upon fundamental principles of democracy discussed in chapter 1, explain why it is critical that justice agencies establish and maintain clear channels of communication while in pursuit of their respective mandates.

5. What is the justification for civilians overseeing the police? Do you agree with it? Explain.

6. Under what circumstances do you think governments are justified in actively influencing the justice system? What risks do they take in this regard?

7. Outline some of the ways that governments attempt to protect the independence of the judiciary. Why is this so important?

PART IV

Bringing It Home

CHAPTER 11

Don't Just Sit There—Do Something!

CHAPTER OBJECTIVES

After completing this chapter, you should be able to:

- Understand how a grasp of politics and public administration can enhance your personal and professional life.

- List some activities in which you can participate as a citizen in order to better understand and appreciate the political process.

- Assemble an intellectual "toolbox" to help you analyze and understand a variety of political issues.

INTRODUCTION

No one pretends that democracy is perfect or all-wise. Indeed, it has been said that democracy is the worst form of Government except all those other forms that have been tried from time to time.

—Winston Churchill[1]

With all of the negative news stories we are exposed to on a daily basis, it is tempting to dismiss politicians and the political process as irretrievably corrupt and hopelessly inefficient. One reason for this may be that so many of our political opinions are based on sensational media reports that tend to simplify complex political issues and emphasize particular types of stories, such as personal scandal and fiscal mismanagement. While the media no doubt play a critical role in keeping governments accountable to their constituents, it can be argued that the power they have to manipulate the political process presents an equal danger.[2] If we as citizens are to hold our elected representatives accountable for their actions, we need to familiarize ourselves with the process, procedures, and constraints under which they operate.

As a constituent, you may believe that your role in the political process is simply to vote when there's an election. In a democratic country such as Canada, voting is indeed one of the fundamental privileges of being a Canadian citizen. However, leaving it at that misses the point of this book, which is to acquaint you with politics and help you to make informed decisions about the people, parties, and processes that characterize the Canadian political system. Hopefully, having come this far, you feel more attuned to the world of politics. However, like many people, you may also feel powerless to do anything about what is going on in the world of government and politics. This chapter suggests some ways you can begin to make a difference while honing your political acumen.

COMMON EXCUSES FOR AVOIDING POLITICS

When first confronted with politics, many students admit that they are confused, intimidated, or disgusted by the subject, or a combination of the three. This is not surprising given popular stereotypes and the mass media's obsession with scandal. Hopefully, with the knowledge you have gained from this book and the course it represents, you will be able to critically analyze political events in a way that informs both your personal and professional life. Below are a few of the most common excuses given for avoiding politics, and some counterarguments.

Politicians Are Corrupt

This is a throw-away generalization that not only irks most politicians but also is unfair and untrue. The vast majority of politicians are honest, hardworking individuals who dedicate themselves to public life in order to benefit their constituents. It is to their credit that they continue to serve in spite of the negative stereotypes reinforced by the popular media. Politics turns the popular adage "No news is good news" into "Good news is no news at all," for we rarely learn from the media that politicians are doing a good job. This rebuttal is not intended to be an indictment of all media, for they too serve a purpose as watchdogs over public affairs. But the industry's tendency to simplify and shorten news stories may mask the complexity of some issues and thus misstate the issues. In any case, it's important not to approach the subject of politics from a cynical perspective. Keep an open mind and realize that, ultimately, politics is the art of compromise.

It Doesn't Affect Me

Nothing could be further from the truth. When it comes to politics, ignorance is *not* bliss. Law enforcement students sometimes believe that political issues not directly related to policing are of no concern to them. The reality is that it is virtually impossible to isolate the impact of political decisions. Government spending in one area may mean cutbacks in other areas or an increase in taxes to cover the extra cost. For example, spending more on health care may mean cutbacks to environmental programs such as water quality. The end result may be that contaminated water sources end up increasing health costs more than the amount of the cutbacks. These connections extend through municipal, provincial, and federal levels of government. Having a sound knowledge of the relationships among these many political actors allows you as a citizen to form opinions in a context that then informs the decision you ultimately make come election time. As well, this knowledge can help you understand the decisions made by others that affect your day-to-day work life.

Politicians Break Election Promises

Economist John Kenneth Galbraith once described politics as the art of "choosing between the disastrous and the unpalatable."[3] Admittedly, politicians as a group are not known for keeping promises, but they should not be blamed exclusively for this shortcoming. As you have learned in the second half of this text, pledging to do something and then actually accomplishing it poses significant challenges in the world of public policy. In addition, the contemporary game of politics requires that issues be simplified so that they appeal to as many voters as possible. This approach can backfire, however, when it comes to actually implementing the promised solution to a problem.

Let Someone Else Do It

Although this statement suggests laziness, it may also stem from the reality that even those of us who choose not to participate in the political realm reap the benefits it bestows upon Canadian society. For example, most of us assume that regardless of whether we are involved, fundamental services such as hospitals and schools will continue to be provided by our governments. Law enforcement will protect us and our property, and social problems, when they occur, will be dealt with accordingly. This may be true, but as the old saying goes, "The Devil is in the details." If you disagree with a government's policy direction, or want to have a say regarding an issue that affects you directly, you have to be knowledgeable about *how* the system responsible for the decision has arrived at that decision. Remember, bureaucracies run on formal rules and procedures; they are not equipped to respond to emotional outbursts and rants. Getting angry and calling the local news media may be a useful first step; however, it may only grant you a brief public audience. Knowing such things as who is responsible, the nature of the timeline for approval, and avenues of appeal empowers you to challenge and possibly change government decisions. At the very least, officials must respond to your concerns. Think about it—saying nothing means you won't have a voice at all.[4]

DAZED AND CONFUSED?

Politics is by no means an easy science to grasp. Changing events, players, and circumstances render useless any hard and fast rules and formulas. Understandably, this can intimidate some people. However, you can take some steps toward overcoming this feeling.

1. Keep up on political events. Warnings aside, tuning into ongoing media coverage of current events will help to familiarize you with the people,

policies, and priorities of the day. Reading one or two newspapers a day is a great way to do this.

2. Discuss current political issues with friends. Talking over coffee or while walking home tests your understanding of events and exposes you to perspectives that are different from your own.

3. Make it a point to inform yourself at election time. Attend all-candidates' meetings, ask questions on subjects that concern you, and base your vote on the information and impressions you have gathered. Yes, some effort is involved, but it will have been well worth it when you finally cast your ballot as an informed citizen.

Sometimes the most difficult part of becoming politically aware is the overwhelming feeling that there are just too many things to which you could turn your attention and effort. This, in turn, can easily slide into cynicism and cause you to retreat from the process. However a smarter way to approach this challenge is to select an area of interest and become involved, if not professionally as a career choice, then personally as a volunteer.

GETTING INVOLVED

By volunteering, you accomplish several purposes. First, you gain valuable experience that contributes to your resumé and hence future job prospects. Second, you learn how to work in cooperation with others to achieve a common goal. Finally, you open yourself to different viewpoints and career options through the contacts and experience you acquire. As a result, you will broaden your political horizons and develop a much better sense of your community and the many others who are a part of it.

Volunteer opportunities abound, and you should decide first what your interests are and then pursue opportunities in those areas. If you are not sure where to start, contact a community volunteer placement centre or consult the *Yellow Pages* under headings such as "Volunteer" and "Social Service Organizations." Many coaching positions are also available in local youth sports leagues. These are valuable references for anyone considering a career working with young offenders.

To be directly involved in politics you might consider becoming a candidate for municipal government, but many other avenues of participation are open to you if you are interested in formal politics. Survey the various political parties in your area to find out whether your political views tend to complement one particular party's platform (but be careful not to look for the "perfect" party—remember, politics is the art of compromise). You can join a party, help at the constituency office, or assist in party-sponsored events. Elections provide excellent opportunities to volunteer and make contacts in your community that may be of help to you later.

If you are concerned about a specific issue, you may wish to join a related interest group. There are many active groups in Canada supporting a huge variety of causes. Neighbourhood Watch, Road Watch, and local police auxiliary services are just a few examples of organizations interested in civil peace and respect for the law. There are a host of socially oriented causes in the areas of environmentalism, poverty, and social justice. The Council of Canadians, the National Anti-Poverty

Organization, and the Centre for Social Justice are just three examples. You can also attend local council meetings and forums that focus on particular issues of local concern. Again, elections provide many opportunities of this nature, including all-candidates' meetings and party rallies.

As you can see, the opportunities are out there to get involved at whatever level is comfortable for you. Make your choice according to the amount of time and energy you have available. Volunteering demands some commitment if you and the organization are to derive any benefit from it, but remember that the rewards to yourself and your community are directly related to the amount of time you invest.

AN INFORMED STUDENT'S INTELLECTUAL TOOLBOX

A recurring theme of this text has been the importance of your responsibility as a citizen in the political process. Below are some tips to help you enhance your own intellectual toolbox. You'll also find a Quick Reference Checklist at the end of this chapter.

Tune In, Turn On ... Talk Out

Earlier, you were cautioned to be wary of the popular media because of the way they package news items. Still, there are ways to overcome this obstacle. First, when sizing up an issue, consider a variety of media (print, radio, television, Internet). Within each medium, individual providers reflect specific areas of the political spectrum in their news coverage and general viewpoints. For example, newspapers such as *The Globe and Mail*, the *National Post*, and the *Toronto Sun* represent a spectrum of right-of-centre conservative positions, while the *Toronto Star* reflects a left-of-centre liberal approach to current events. Each also markets itself to a different target audience to attract a certain niche of advertisers. The *Toronto Sun*, for example, is aimed more at moderately educated working-class readers, while *The Globe and Mail* and the *National Post* are targeted at well-educated, wealthier, middle to upper class readers. These distinctions can be a little more subtle in other mainstream media, but by observing how and what each presents you should be able to figure out where they fit on the political spectrum and what audience they're trying to appeal to.

Assess a Source's Credibility

A good rule of thumb when listening to political messages is not to trust anyone who's over-wordy. Don't allow yourself to be snowballed by slick presentations or sources that play to your emotions alone. Mentally step back and examine the argument being presented and the evidence being given to support it. Is the source quoting specific, credible data or making sweeping general statements without backing them up? Thinking about research in this way will help you to base your own opinions on solid evidence rather than on emotion alone. You can add the latter to your viewpoint once you have made up your mind on an issue.

In this regard, Internet sources can pose a more daunting challenge, since they often contain little evidence of tested empirical data, and are often accompanied by graphics and other distracting media. Remember, too, that the Internet has become an attractive vehicle for selling virtually everything, including values and viewpoints. It is your responsibility to distinguish academically credible sources from those that simply "spout off" about a particular topic. In each case, ask yourself:[5]

- Is it "personal"? Web pages are cheap and relatively easy to design, and there is no parent organization or domain to vouch for what's there. Personal Web pages are not bad per se, but they necessitate further research into the credibility of the information being presented.

- What is the domain? That is, is it government (.gc.ca for federal, .gov.on.ca for Ontario), education (.edu), or non-profit (.org)? Is the content appropriate for the domain? This helps "weed out" irrelevant and superfluous material.

- Who is the "publisher"? This refers to the parent organization responsible for page content. Can you link directly with that organization? If unsure about content credibility, contact the parent from its website, to verify what has been stated.

Keep an Open Mind

Try to keep an open mind when considering political issues. You may initially favour one side over another, but don't let these prejudgments turn into prejudices. Allow yourself some time to gather the facts and determine whether they counter your initial reaction. Open-mindedness in politics is not about having any opinion; rather, it is about listening to opposing viewpoints, weighing and challenging their credibility, and then drawing conclusions. Employing this strategy helps you to avoid being pigeonholed into one or another position before you have had a chance to explore the details of an issue.

Get Real!

POLITICAL ACTIVISM: DEAD OR ALIVE?

As we wrap up our journey through the past, present, and future of politics in Canada, our focus has shifted from the politicians and the bureaucrats, from the hallowed halls of Parliament Hill and Queen's Park, to an equally important player in the political process: you! How can you become more informed and involved in government and public administration? This chapter has provided you with some good ideas (and some important warnings) on how to participate in the political life of your municipality, province, and country. Now let's consider some recent examples of social and political activism that might be familiar to you, and that raise some very important questions about the potential effectiveness of your political activities.

Over 20 years ago, a British musician named Bob Geldof ushered in a new era of social and political activism—the era of the benefit concert—when he organized the historic Live Aid shows in England and the United States. The concerts were designed to raise awareness and funds for famine relief in Ethiopia, and an estimated 1.5 billion people worldwide tuned in to watch.[6] It remains a matter of some controversy as to whether or not Live Aid produced any real relief for the famine victims (one conservative American journalist claims much of the money was diverted to support the military leadership in Ethiopia[7]), but the benefit concert concept continues to spawn imitators. You may be familiar with two recent examples: Live 8, held in 2005 and designed to help eradicate global poverty, and Live Earth, held in 2007 to inspire action on the climate crisis. Their respective websites claim that over 3 billion people watched the televised Live 8 event and over 10 million people watched the Live Earth concert online alone. Were you one of them? Did you feel more informed? Did you feel more empowered about changing the problems these events were intended to address? Maybe you were even one of those who bought a souvenir Live 8 DVD, or a Live Earth t-shirt featuring the slogan "Green is the new black."[8]

Benefit concerts and their merchandise have the potential to inform and motivate mass audiences—including millions of young people worldwide. But how effective are they? Of course, no one would argue that watching a TV entertainment show is an adequate substitute for reading one or two good newspapers daily or, more importantly, for casting a ballot come election time. And we would all readily admit that sporting a clever slogan on your shirt is not the same as writing a letter to your member of Parliament. However, considering how popular and pervasive such cultural happenings have become in recent years, we need to consider the impact of shows such as Live 8, Live Earth, and other such events that are sure to happen in the years to come. Could it be possible that tuning in to politically or socially themed TV shows actually has the opposite effect of what was intended? In other words, do "Live" concerts end up creating political apathy and passivity in young voters?

In the 1960s, sociologists Paul F. Lazarsfeld and Robert K. Merton identified a phenomenon they called narcotizing dysfunction. Mass media, they claimed, provides us with such a steady stream of information that we eventually become numb and passive, instead of inspired and active. In today's world of 24-hour cable news, the Internet, and marathon benefit concerts, it is possible that we are being lulled into a false sense of being informed and involved in social or political processes, when, in fact, we are gradually withdrawing from those processes. The television set or computer screen may come to surpass the ballot box or the soapbox as our new sites for political engagement, but is this engagement real?[9] (Take note here that each of these end-of-chapter exercises has encouraged you to "Get Real"—that is, to apply the theories and concepts you are learning to real-world problems and situations. The authors chose that title quite deliberately.) Scholar and critic Neil Postman sounded a related alarm in his 1986 book, *Amusing Ourselves to Death: Public Discourse in the Age of Show Business*. Postman contended that when serious issues (such as famine, poverty, and global warming) are treated as entertainment, we will eventually be content just to be entertained, and will lose our capacity to think and act independently. For Postman, this was a frightening prospect, one that had the potential to land us smack in the middle of the bleak future envisioned by Aldous Huxley in *Brave New World*, a future that was darker and more dangerous even than the one described by George Orwell in *1984*. Postman's foreword reads:

> What Orwell feared were those who would ban books. What Huxley feared was that there would be no reason to ban a book, for there would be no one who wanted to read one. Orwell feared those who would deprive us of information. Huxley feared those who would give us so much that we would be reduced to passivity and egoism. Orwell feared that the truth would be concealed from us. Huxley feared the truth would be drowned in a sea of irrelevance. Orwell feared we would become a captive culture. Huxley feared we would become a trivial culture.[10]

Postman says his book, then, "is about the possibility that Huxley, not Orwell, was right."[11] Consider the phenomenon of the benefit concert as political activism. Do you think Huxley's (and Postman's) predictions have come to pass? Is the "Live" event breathing new political life into apathetic voters? Or are we merely "amusing ourselves to death"?

Given what this textbook has stated about the critical importance of citizen involvement in the political process, how might you counter such pessimism and apathy?

SUMMARY

Many people are frustrated by or avoid politics, but constituents have an important role to play in the political process. Getting involved in politics means more than simply casting a vote in an election—it can mean doing volunteer work for a political party, becoming informed about political issues and party platforms by attending all-candidates' meetings, or simply keeping up on political events through the mass media. No matter what your level of involvement, a greater understanding of the political process and current issues can enhance your personal and professional life and can help you to make a more informed decision when it comes time to cast your ballot.

NOTES

1. *Oxford Dictionary of Quotations*, 4th ed. (Oxford: Oxford University Press, 1992), 202:23.

2. One of the most prominent scholars to explore this phenomenon is Noam Chomsky. See Edward S. Herman and Noam Chomsky, *Manufacturing Consent: The Political Economy of the Mass Media* (New York: Pantheon Books, 1988); and Noam Chomsky, *Necessary Illusions: Thought Control in Democratic Societies* (Toronto: Anansi, 1991). For related subject matter, see Chomsky's *Secrets, Lies and Democracy* (Tucson, AZ: Odonian Press, 1994).

3. John Kenneth Galbraith, quoted from a letter to American President John F. Kennedy, March 2, 1962. *Oxford Dictionary of Quotations*, 5th ed. (Oxford: Oxford University Press, 1999), 328:11.

4. As a group, college students may already have overcome one of the great barriers to participation, in that they are educated. Poverty also has a significant impact on political participation, particularly in pressure groups. "One of the great weaknesses of the poor in the political system is that they are generally disorganized and collectively inarticulate. They lack the skills to organize effectively as pressure groups, primarily because they are without the education, time and money to develop such skills." See Rand Dyck, *Canadian Politics: Concise Student Edition* (Toronto: Thomson Nelson, 2002), 37.

5. These questions are summarized from a list developed by the University of California at Berkeley on its library website. See "Evaluating Web Pages: Techniques to Apply & Questions to Ask" (2007), at www.lib.berkeley.edu/index.html.

6. For an overview of Live Aid, see Bob Geldof's website at www.bobgeldof.info/Charity/liveaid.html.

7. See Bill O'Reilly, "Giving Money to Poor Africans" (June 8, 2005), available online at www.foxnews.com/story/0,2933,158902,00.html.

8. See www.live8live.com and www.liveearth.org.

9. For a discussion of Lazarsfeld and Merton's essay, as well as other aspects of media theory, see Michael R. Real, "Media Theory: Contributions to an Understanding of American Mass Communications," *American Quarterly* vol. 32, no. 3 (1980), 238-258.

10. Neil Postman, "Foreword," *Amusing Ourselves to Death: Public Discourse in the Age of Show Business* (London: Penguin Books, 1986), vii.

11. Ibid.

EXERCISES

Multiple Choice

1. Media coverage of political issues can be coloured by
   a. a tendency to simplify and shorten news stories
   b. a focus on the negative while ignoring politicians who are doing a good job
   c. the commentator's position on the political spectrum
   d. a news source's attempt to appeal to a particular audience
   e. all of the above

2. Becoming better informed about politics and political issues can help you
   a. make better decisions as a voter
   b. understand how political decisions affect your personal life
   c. know more about your community
   d. understand how political decisions affect your professional life
   e. all of the above

3. Making an informed decision about any issue involves
   a. going along with whatever your friends say
   b. gathering information from credible sources
   c. sticking with your first reaction to the issue
   d. taking a cynical attitude toward anything you read or hear
   e. tuning out anything you don't agree with

True or False?

_____ 1. Politics necessitates compromise.

_____ 2. Politics has no effect on public law enforcement.

_____ 3. Carrying out election promises is a significant challenge in the world of public policy.

_____ 4. One way to prevent being confused by politics is to keep up on political events by reading newspapers regularly.

_____ 5. Casting your vote at election time is one of your basic democratic rights.

Short Answer

1. Make a short list of some possible volunteer activities that interest you. What types of questions would you want answers to before considering each of these opportunities?

2. Would you consider running as a candidate for public office? Why or why not?

3. When considering political issues, why should you consult a variety of news sources?

4. How have your views of politics and public administration changed since you began reading this text? Give at least three specific examples.

5. Fill out the chart on the following pages as a reference for future inquiries.

QUICK REFERENCE CHECKLIST

MEMBER OF PARLIAMENT (MP)

Name: _____   Political Party: _____

    Phone: _____ Fax: _____ Website: _____

    Mailing Address: _____

    _____

    Constituency Office Location: _____

MEMBER OF PROVINCIAL PARLIAMENT (MPP)

Name: _____   Political Party: _____

    Phone: _____ Fax: _____ Website: _____

    Mailing Address: _____

    _____

    Constituency Office Location: _____

Municipal Government

MAYOR/REEVE

Name: _____

    Phone: _____ Fax: _____ Website: _____

    Mailing Address: _____

    _____

    Municipality Office Location: _____

LOCAL COUNCILLOR

Name: _____

Phone: _____ Fax: _____ Website: _____

Mailing Address: _____

_____

Municipality Office Location: _____

DIRECTOR OF EDUCATION

Name: _____

Phone: _____ Fax: _____ Website: _____

Mailing Address: _____

_____

School Board Office Location: _____

LOCAL SCHOOL TRUSTEE

Name: _____ Ward: _____

Phone: _____ Fax: _____ Website: _____

Mailing Address: _____

_____

School Board Office Location: _____

APPENDIX

The Canadian Charter of Rights and Freedoms

PART I OF THE CONSTITUTION ACT, 1982

Whereas Canada is founded upon principles that recognize the supremacy of God and the rule of law:

Guarantee of Rights and Freedoms

Rights and freedoms in Canada

1. The *Canadian Charter of Rights and Freedoms* guarantees the rights and freedoms set out in it subject only to such reasonable limits prescribed by law as can be demonstrably justified in a free and democratic society.

Fundamental Freedoms

Fundamental freedoms

2. Everyone has the following fundamental freedoms:
   (a) freedom of conscience and religion;
   (b) freedom of thought, belief, opinion and expression, including freedom of the press and other media of communication;
   (c) freedom of peaceful assembly; and
   (d) freedom of association.

Democratic Rights

Democratic rights of citizens

3. Every citizen of Canada has the right to vote in an election of members of the House of Commons or of a legislative assembly and to be qualified for membership therein.

Maximum duration of legislative bodies

4. (1) No House of Commons and no legislative assembly shall continue for longer than five years from the date fixed for the return of the writs at a general election of its members.

Continuation in special circumstances

(2) In time of real or apprehended war, invasion or insurrection, a House of Commons may be continued by Parliament and a legislative assembly may be continued by the legislature beyond five years if such continuation is not opposed by the votes of more than one-third of the members of the House of Commons or the legislative assembly, as the case may be.

Annual sitting of legislative bodies

5. There shall be a sitting of Parliament and of each legislature at least once every twelve months.

Mobility Rights

Mobility of citizens

6. (1) Every citizen of Canada has the right to enter, remain in and leave Canada.

Rights to move and gain livelihood

(2) Every citizen of Canada and every person who has the status of a permanent resident of Canada has the right

    (a) to move to and take up residence in any province; and

    (b) to pursue the gaining of a livelihood in any province.

Limitation

(3) The rights specified in subsection (2) are subject to

    (a) any laws or practices of general application in force in a province other than those that discriminate among persons primarily on the basis of province of present or previous residence; and

    (b) any laws providing for reasonable residency requirements as a qualification for the receipt of publicly provided social services.

Affirmative action programs

(4) Subsections (2) and (3) do not preclude any law, program or activity that has as its object the amelioration in a province of conditions of individuals in that province who are socially or economically disadvantaged if the rate of employment in that province is below the rate of employment in Canada.

Legal Rights

Life, liberty and security of person

7. Everyone has the right to life, liberty and security of the person and the right not to be deprived thereof except in accordance with the principles of fundamental justice.

Search or seizure

8. Everyone has the right to be secure against unreasonable search or seizure.

Detention or imprisonment

9. Everyone has the right not to be arbitrarily detained or imprisoned.

Arrest or detention

10. Everyone has the right on arrest or detention

(a) to be informed promptly of the reasons therefor;

(b) to retain and instruct counsel without delay and to be informed of that right; and

(c) to have the validity of the detention determined by way of *habeas corpus* and to be released if the detention is not lawful.

Proceedings in criminal and penal matters

11. Any person charged with an offence has the right

(a) to be informed without unreasonable delay of the specific offence;

(b) to be tried within a reasonable time;

(c) not to be compelled to be a witness in proceedings against that person in respect of the offence;

(d) to be presumed innocent until proven guilty according to law in a fair and public hearing by an independent and impartial tribunal;

(e) not to be denied reasonable bail without just cause;

(f) except in the case of an offence under military law tried before a military tribunal, to the benefit of trial by jury where the maximum punishment for the offence is imprisonment for five years or a more severe punishment;

(g) not to be found guilty on account of any act or omission unless, at the time of the act or omission, it constituted an offence under Canadian or international law or was criminal according to the general principles of law recognized by the community of nations;

(h) if finally acquitted of the offence, not to be tried for it again and, if finally found guilty and punished for the offence, not to be tried or punished for it again; and

(i) if found guilty of the offence and if the punishment for the offence has been varied between the time of commission and the time of sentencing, to the benefit of the lesser punishment.

Treatment or punishment

12. Everyone has the right not to be subjected to any cruel and unusual treatment or punishment.

Self-crimination

13. A witness who testifies in any proceedings has the right not to have any incriminating evidence so given used to incriminate that witness in any other proceedings, except in a prosecution for perjury or for the giving of contradictory evidence.

Interpreter

14. A party or witness in any proceedings who does not understand or speak the language in which the proceedings are conducted or who is deaf has the right to the assistance of an interpreter.

Equality Rights

Equality before and under law and equal protection and benefit of law

15. (1) Every individual is equal before and under the law and has the right to the equal protection and equal benefit of the law without discrimination and, in particular, without discrimination based on race, national or ethnic origin, colour, religion, sex, age or mental or physical disability.

Affirmative action programs

(2) Subsection (1) does not preclude any law, program or activity that has as its object the amelioration of conditions of disadvantaged individuals or groups including those that are disadvantaged because of race, national or ethnic origin, colour, religion, sex, age or mental or physical disability.

Official Languages of Canada

Official languages of Canada

16. (1) English and French are the official languages of Canada and have equality of status and equal rights and privileges as to their use in all institutions of the Parliament and government of Canada.

Official languages of New Brunswick

(2) English and French are the official languages of New Brunswick and have equality of status and equal rights and privileges as to their use in all institutions of the legislature and government of New Brunswick.

Advancement of status and use

(3) Nothing in the Charter limits the authority of Parliament or a legislature to advance the equality of status or use of English and French.

English and French linguistic communities in New Brunswick

16.1. (1) The English linguistic community and the French linguistic community in New Brunswick have equality of status and equal rights and privileges, including the right to distinct educational institutions and such distinct cultural institutions as are necessary for the preservation and promotion of those communities.

Role of the legislature and government of New Brunswick

(2) The role of the legislature and government of New Brunswick to preserve and promote the status, rights and privileges referred to in subsection (1) is affirmed.

Proceedings of Parliament

17. (1) Everyone has the right to use English or French in any debates and other proceedings of Parliament.

Proceedings of New Brunswick legislature

(2) Everyone has the right to use English or French in any debates and other proceedings of the legislature of New Brunswick.

Parliamentary statutes and records

18. (1) The statutes, records and journals of Parliament shall be printed and published in English and French and both language versions are equally authoritative.

New Brunswick statutes and records

(2) The statutes, records and journals of the legislature of New Brunswick shall be printed and published in English and French and both language versions are equally authoritative.

Proceedings in courts established by Parliament

19. (1) Either English or French may be used by any person in, or in any pleading in or process issuing from, any court established by Parliament.

Proceedings in New Brunswick courts

(2) Either English or French may be used by any person in, or in any pleading in or process issuing from, any court of New Brunswick.

Communications by public with federal institutions

20. (1) Any member of the public in Canada has the right to communicate with, and to receive available services from, any head or central office of an institution of the Parliament or government of Canada in English or French, and has the same right with respect to any other office of any such institution where

(a) there is a significant demand for communications with and services from that office in such language; or

(b) due to the nature of the office, it is reasonable that communications with and services from that office be available in both English and French.

Communications by public with New Brunswick institutions

(2) Any member of the public in New Brunswick has the right to communicate with, and to receive available services from, any office of an institution of the legislature or government of New Brunswick in English or French.

Continuation of existing constitutional provisions

21. Nothing in sections 16 to 20 abrogates or derogates from any right, privilege or obligation with respect to the English and French languages, or either of them, that exists or is continued by virtue of any other provision of the Constitution of Canada.

Rights and privileges preserved

22. Nothing in sections 16 to 20 abrogates or derogates from any legal or customary right or privilege acquired or enjoyed either before or after the coming into force of this Charter with respect to any language that is not English or French.

Minority Language Educational Rights

Language of instruction

23. (1) Citizens of Canada

(a) whose first language learned and still understood is that of the English or French linguistic minority population of the province in which they reside, or

(b) who have received their primary school instruction in Canada in English or French and reside in a province where the language in which they received that instruction is the language of the English or French linguistic minority population of the province,

have the right to have their children receive primary and secondary school instruction in that language in that province.

Continuity of language instruction

(2) Citizens of Canada of whom any child has received or is receiving primary or secondary school instruction in English or French in Canada, have the right to have all their children receive primary and secondary school instruction in the same language.

Application where numbers warrant

(3) The right of citizens of Canada under subsections (1) and (2) to have their children receive primary and secondary school instruction in the language of the English or French linguistic minority population of a province

(a) applies wherever in the province the number of children of citizens who have such a right is sufficient to warrant the provision to them out of public funds of minority language instruction; and

(b) includes, where the number of those children so warrants, the right to have them receive that instruction in minority language educational facilities provided out of public funds.

Enforcement

Enforcement of guaranteed rights and freedoms

24. (1) Anyone whose rights or freedoms, as guaranteed by this Charter, have been infringed or denied may apply to a court of competent jurisdiction to obtain such remedy as the court considers appropriate and just in the circumstances.

Exclusion of evidence bringing administration of justice into disrepute

(2) Where, in proceedings under subsection (1), a court concludes that evidence was obtained in a manner that infringed or denied any rights or freedoms guaranteed by this Charter, the evidence shall be excluded if it is established that, having regard to all the circumstances, the admission of it in the proceedings would bring the administration of justice into disrepute.

General

Aboriginal rights and freedoms not affected by Charter

25. The guarantee in this Charter of certain rights and freedoms shall not be construed so as to abrogate or derogate from any aboriginal, treaty or other rights or freedoms that pertain to the aboriginal peoples of Canada including

(a) any rights or freedoms that have been recognized by the Royal Proclamation of October 7, 1763; and

(b) any rights or freedoms that may be acquired by the aboriginal peoples of Canada by way of land claims settlement.

Other rights and freedoms not affected by Charter

26. The guarantee in this Charter of certain rights and freedoms shall not be construed as denying the existence of any other rights or freedoms that exist in Canada.

Multicultural heritage

27. This Charter shall be interpreted in a manner consistent with the preservation and enhancement of the multicultural heritage of Canadians.

Rights guaranteed equally to both sexes

28. Notwithstanding anything in this Charter, the rights and freedoms referred to in it are guaranteed equally to male and female persons.

Rights respecting certain schools preserved

29. Nothing in this Charter abrogates or derogates from any rights or privileges guaranteed by or under the Constitution of Canada in respect of denominational, separate or dissentient schools.

Application to territories and territorial authorities

30. A reference in this Charter to a province or to the legislative assembly or legislature of a province shall be deemed to include a reference to the Yukon Territory and the Northwest Territories, or to the appropriate legislative authority thereof, as the case may be.

Legislative powers not extended

31. Nothing in this Charter extends the legislative powers of any body or authority.

Application of Charter

Application of Charter

32. (1) This Charter applies

(a) to the Parliament and government of Canada in respect of all matters within the authority of Parliament including all matters relating to the Yukon Territory and Northwest Territories; and

(b) to the legislature and government of each province in respect of all matters within the authority of the legislature of each province.

Exception

(2) Notwithstanding subsection (1), section 15 shall not have effect until three years after this section comes into force.

Exception where express declaration

33. (1) Parliament or the legislature of a province may expressly declare in an Act of Parliament or of the legislature, as the case may be, that the Act or a provision thereof shall operate notwithstanding a provision included in section 2 or sections 7 to 15 of this Charter.

Operation of exception

(2) An Act or a provision of an Act in respect of which a declaration made under this section is in effect shall have such operation as it would have but for the provision of this Charter referred to in the declaration.

Five year limitation

(3) A declaration made under subsection (1) shall cease to have effect five years after it comes into force or on such earlier date as may be specified in the declaration.

Re-enactment

(4) Parliament or a legislature of a province may re-enact a declaration made under subsection (1).

Five year limitation

(5) Subsection (3) applies in respect of a re-enactment made under subsection (4).

Citation

Citation

34. This Part may be cited as the *Canadian Charter of Rights and Freedoms.*

Glossary

Aboriginal self-government greater autonomy of First Nations to pursue their own political, social, cultural, and economic objectives with limited interference from the federal government

administrative-coordinative department department that facilitates the operation of government services

administrative law body of legislation that details the rules civil servants must follow in doing their jobs

amending formula a legal process for changing a constitution

attorney general function the function of the federal Department of Justice to safeguard the legal interests of the federal government

authority government's ability to make decisions that are binding on its citizens

bicameral legislature a government structure that consists of two Houses of Parliament; in Canada, the House of Commons and the Senate

bill a proposed law

bureaucracy the organizational structure through which government exercises its power

bureaucrat public servant

bureaucratic entrepreneur a model of public policy in which bureaucratic experts within government come up with policy ideas and then approach elected officials to obtain the resources and public legitimacy necessary to implement their programs

bylaw a local or municipal law

Cabinet the government body that consists of MPs appointed by the prime minister who oversee government departments and act as advisers in major policy areas

Cabinet solidarity the united front that Cabinet presents on given policy matters, although individual Cabinet ministers may privately be opposed

Canadian Charter of Rights and Freedoms part of the Canadian constitution that guarantees certain fundamental rights and freedoms to people in Canada

capitalism an economic system based on private ownership and competition in a free market

charismatic authority authority based on the unique talents and popular appeal of an individual

civil service people who are directly tied to the administrative function of a particular level of government

classical technocratic a model of public policy in which decisions originate with politicians, who then provide bureaucrats with clear direction as to what should be done

common law a body of law that has grown out of past court cases and is based on precedent or custom

community policing approach to policing based on the police and the community working together

Confederation the union of former British colonies that resulted in the formation of Canada on July 1, 1867

constituency department department that provides services directly to citizens

constitution a document that outlines the basic principles of government of a country and the fundamental rights and freedoms enjoyed by its citizens

continuity the long-term or ongoing nature of a bureaucracy; continuity means that the people working within an organization are full-time employees who can make a career out of what they do

cost sharing funding of provincial programs that combines federal contributions with provincial funding

delegated legislation legislation handed down from a parent department that grants a regulatory agency political powers

department government division responsible for carrying out some aspect of government policy

deregulation reducing or eliminating bureaucratic processes that may hinder private enterprise and limit economic growth

discretionary power   interpretive flexibility granted to some government employees to act within a given setting

division of powers   jurisdiction over major policy areas, as divided between the federal and the provincial governments

executive branch (federal)   the branch of government that includes the monarch's representative (governor general), the elected head of state (prime minister), and Cabinet

executive branch (provincial)   the branch of government that includes the monarch's representative (lieutenant governor), the elected head of state (premier), and the Cabinet

expertise   knowledge of or ability in a particular area or subject

federal spending power   the power of the federal government to raise the greatest share of tax revenues

federal system   Canada's government structure, which divides political power between the federal government and the provincial governments, with greater power resting in the federal government

government   a formal system within which political power is exercised

government bill   a bill proposed by a member of Cabinet

hierarchy   an organized system of labour characterized by a superior–subordinate relationship

human relations   management approach that recognizes and addresses the personal and social needs of individuals

impersonality   the objective nature of jobs and routines in a bureaucracy, based on written rules and records

isolationism   an economic remedy characterized by refusing to trade with other countries

judicial branch   the branch of government that consists of the court system

jurisdiction   sphere of influence or power

laissez-faire capitalism   free-market capitalism with minimal government interference (French for "let act")

left wing   a political attitude or philosophy that favours more government intervention to help achieve social equality

legal authority   authority based on the rule of law

legislative branch (federal)   the lawmaking branch of government (House of Commons and Senate)

legislative branch (provincial)   the lawmaking branch of government, called the National Assembly in Quebec and the Legislative Assembly in all other provinces

legislative union   a structure of government in which power is concentrated in a central Parliament

legitimacy   the moral obligation citizens feel to obey the laws and pronouncements issued by those in authority

majority government   a government that includes more than half of the total MPs in the House of Commons

member of Parliament   an elected representative in the House of Commons who represents a riding

minimalist state   approach to government in which state resources are used in the interest of the business, or capitalist, classes, to promote individual wealth and economic growth

minister of justice function   the function of the federal Department of Justice to monitor federal legislation, directives, and regulations and to consider other justice-related issues

ministerial responsibility   principle of parliamentary government that makes ministers responsible for the official activities of their departments

minority government   a government that has the greatest number of MPs in the House of Commons but not more than half of the total MPs

multiculturalism   cultural and racial diversity; in Canada, a constitutionally enshrined policy that recognizes the diversity of our population

municipal council   the governing body of a municipal government

neoconservatism   a conservative political philosophy that argues that government should revert to the limited role it played at the beginning of the 20th century, particularly in social and economic areas

new public management   an approach based on the belief that government has overextended itself by doing too much and becoming preoccupied with bureaucratic procedure

party loyalty   the requirement that all members of a political party vote according to the wishes of their leader

patriation   the process of removing the Canadian constitution from British control and bringing it under Canadian control

police services board   civilian board that oversees a local police service

policy-coordinative department   department that coordinates policy across government

policy instrument   method employed by governments to ensure compliance with public policy and to achieve their goals

political culture   the basic attitudes people have toward each other, the state, and authority

political spectrum   a model that shows political philosophy on a continuum from left wing to right wing

politics   the social system that decides who has power and how it is to be used in governing the society's affairs

politics–administrative dichotomy   theoretical framework that views politics as the decision-making apparatus of government and administration as performing the implementation function

portfolio   department

private bill   a bill proposed by a senator

private member's bill   a bill proposed by a non-Cabinet MP

protectionism   an economic remedy characterized by protecting domestic products with tariffs, import quotas, and other barriers to trade with other countries

public administration   the branch of the political structure, consisting of public employees, that turns the policy decisions of elected politicians into action

public good   the complex fabric of publicly funded goods and services that contribute to the collective well-being of a state

public policy   what government does or does not do

public service   the civil service

representative government   government that is based on members elected by citizens to represent their interests

responsible government   government that is responsible to the wishes of its citizens, as embodied in their elected representatives

right wing   a political attitude or philosophy that favours more individual freedom and less government intervention

rule of law   the concept that all citizens, regardless of social rank, are subject to the laws, courts, and other legal institutions of the nation

scientific management   management approach based on using resources in ways that maximize productivity and minimize waste

stagflation   a situation where an economy experiences high unemployment and high inflation at the same time

subjudicial rule   rule that prohibits government officials from commenting on an issue that is before the courts

theory of representativeness   theory that if the public service is to be responsive to the needs of all Canadians, it should represent a cross-section of Canadian society

traditional authority   authority based on heredity, religion, or divine right

triple E Senate   a Senate that is equal, elected, and effective

Answers to Multiple Choice and True or False Questions

CHAPTER 1

Multiple Choice

1. e
2. b
3. a
4. a
5. e

True or False?

1. True
2. True
3. False
4. True
5. False

CHAPTER 2

Multiple Choice

1. b
2. e
3. e
4. d
5. b

True or False?

1. True
2. False
3. False
4. False
5. True

CHAPTER 3

Multiple Choice

1. b
2. e
3. b
4. e
5. b

True or False?

1. False
2. True
3. True
4. False
5. False

CHAPTER 4

Multiple Choice

1. b
2. b
3. e
4. a
5. b

True or False?

1. False
2. True
3. False
4. True
5. True

CHAPTER 5

Multiple Choice

1. d
2. e
3. c
4. d
5. c

True or False?

1. True
2. True
3. False
4. False
5. False

CHAPTER 6

Multiple Choice

1. d
2. b
3. e
4. b
5. e

True or False?

1. False
2. True
3. False
4. False
5. True
6. True

CHAPTER 7

Multiple Choice

1. e
2. e
3. d
4. b
5. e

True or False?

1. False
2. True
3. False
4. True

CHAPTER 8

Multiple Choice

1. e
2. e
3. a
4. a
5. e

True or False?

1. True
2. True
3. True
4. False
5. True

CHAPTER 9

Multiple Choice

1. b
2. e
3. e
4. d
5. d

True or False?

1. False
2. False
3. False
4. True
5. True

CHAPTER 10

Multiple Choice

1. e
2. d
3. e
4. e
5. b

True or False?

1. True
2. True
3. False
4. True
5. True

CHAPTER 11

Multiple Choice

1. e
2. e
3. b

True or False?

1. False
2. False
3. True
4. True
5. True

Index